Ceremony & Celebration Family Edition
Ḥagim • Holidays

MAGGID

THE RABBI SACKS LEGACY

CEREMONY & CELEBRATION
Family Edition

ḤAGIM • HOLIDAYS

The Rabbi Sacks Legacy
Maggid Books

Ceremony & Celebration Family Edition
Ḥagim • Holidays

First Edition, 2023

Maggid Books
An imprint of Koren Publishers Jerusalem Ltd.

POB 8531, New Milford, CT 06776-8531, USA
& POB 4044, Jerusalem 9104001, Israel
www.korenpub.com

The publication of this book was made possible
through the generous support of The Jewish Book Trust.

ISBN 978-1-59264-615-9, *hardcover*

Printed and bound in Turkey

Contents

Introduction   ix

Rosh
HaShana   1

Yom
Kippur   13

Sukkot   27

Shemini Atzeret
Simḥat Torah   41

Hanukka   55

Tu
BiShvat   91

Purim   103

Pesaḥ   113

Yom
HaShoah   141

Yom
HaZikaron   147

Yom
HaAtzma'ut   151

The
Three Weeks   181

Yom
Yerushalayim   159

Bibliography   193

Shavuot   167

Image Credits   195

Introduction

The Israelites, slaves in Egypt for more than two hundred years, were about to go free…. On the brink of their release, Moshe, the leader of the Jews, gathered them together and prepared to address them. He might have spoken about freedom. He could have given a stirring address about the promised land to which they were travelling, the "land flowing with milk and honey." Or he might have prepared them for the journey that lay ahead, the long march across the wilderness.

*Instead, Moshe delivered a series of addresses that seemed to make no sense in the context of that particular moment. He presented a new idea, revolutionary in character, whose implications remain challenging even now. He spoke about children, and the distant future, and the duty to pass on memory to generations yet unborn…. **About to gain their freedom, the Israelites were told that they had to become a nation of educators.***

Freedom, Moshe suggested, is won, not on the battlefield, nor in the political arena, but in the human imagination and will. To defend a land, you need an army. But to defend freedom, you need education. You need families and schools to ensure that your ideals are passed on to the next generation, and never lost, or despaired of, or obscured. The citadels of liberty are houses of study. Its heroes are teachers, its passion is education and the life of the mind. Moshe realised that a people achieves immortality not by building temples or mausoleums, but by engraving their values on the hearts of their children, and they on theirs, and so on until the end of time.

*The Israelites built living monuments – monuments to life – and became a people dedicated to bringing new generations into being and handing on to them the heritage of the past. **Their great institutions were the family and education via the conversation between the generations.***[1]

A Nation of Educators

Early on in *A Letter in the Scroll*,[2] arguably the book in which Rabbi Sacks *zt"l* most clearly articulated his philosophy of Judaism, he wrote about the value of education in Judaism and Jewish civilisation. This theme permeated his work across the many mediums through which he impacted the world, from books to *parasha*

---

1 *A Letter in the Scroll*, 33–34.
2 Published in the United Kingdom under the title *Radical Then, Radical Now.*

commentary, from his frequent articles and broadcasts in the media to his speeches in the House of Lords. It was clear to him that "for Jews, education is not just what we know. It's *who we are*."[3]

But if you look closely, you will notice how he places this responsibility not solely on teachers and schools. He did not believe in the outsourcing of the responsibility for education to professionals. For Rabbi Sacks, the primary institution of education in the life of a Jewish child is the family, and the foremost educator with the deepest impact is the parent.

To launch the first annual *Communities in Conversation* initiative, marking Rabbi Sacks's *yahrzeit*, his daughter, Gila Sacks, said of her father:

> Perhaps the most defining feature of my father's life, one that I don't think I fully appreciated until after he died, was that he learned and learned, and continued to learn every single day, until his last. He learned from books, from text, from laws. He learned from history and from world events. But, mainly, he learned from people. He would seek out people to learn from, from every possible path of life. And he would seek out what he could learn from everyone he met. And he would do this through conversation, through talking and listening. So for him, conversation was a defining and spiritual act, a way of opening ourselves up to something beyond ourselves, of being challenged, the only way we could really become more than we were before. A training, perhaps, for opening ourselves up to God.

This captures the pedagogical vision behind the *Family Editions* – a resource for parents and families (as well as schools and teachers) to enhance the "conversation between the generations."

Overview

In 2007 Rabbi Sacks embarked on an ambitious new project – to write an essay on the weekly *parasha* every week, to be disseminated around the world. He called this *Covenant & Conversation*, and he continued the project through many more *parasha* cycles, until the end of his life. The brilliance of these essays was the way Rabbi Sacks found complex ideas of Jewish thought expressed in the week's Torah reading, articulated them and made them relevant to our lives today, enriching our understanding of them through contemporary wisdom (what he would later come to term *ḥokhma* – science, including the social sciences, as well as popular culture). In writing these essays in beautiful and elegant language which was nevertheless accessible to all (including non-Jews), he elevated style to the level of substance. As an educator and a parent, for many years I believed that these simple yet sophisticated essays could be adapted for a younger audience, and on several occasions I used them in my own classroom with middle and high school students.

In 2016 Rabbi Sacks and his team intensified their investment in resources to help Jewish educators in their work. I was privileged to be part of this initiative, and one of the projects we worked on together was two cycles of *Covenant & Conversation Family Edition*, and thereafter a cycle based on a similar approach focusing on the festivals, which we called *Ceremony & Celebration Family Edition*. Rabbi Sacks passed away between the release of the Sukkot and Ḥanukka editions, on the twentieth of Marḥeshvan 5781. We completed the cycle, and the team at The Rabbi Sacks Legacy has been dedicated to bringing the Torah of Rabbi Sacks to as wide an audience as possible ever since.

---

3   Letter 4: Jewish Education, in *Letters to the Next Generation*.

Educational Vision Behind the Family Editions

Just as *Covenant & Conversation Family Edition* is designed to make the ideas contained in the main parasha essay written by Rabbi Sacks accessible for younger audiences and families of various ages sitting around the Shabbat table, *Ceremony & Celebration Family Edition* does the same for the writings of Rabbi Sacks on the festivals. By taking sources from various areas of his writings and presenting them in manageable segments with questions for reflection and discussion, *Ceremony & Celebration Family Edition* gives families the opportunity to explore the core themes of the festivals as they are found in the writings of Rabbi Sacks. Each chapter contains several types of supporting resources and educational elements for various ages.

The following educational elements can be found in *Ceremony & Celebration Family Edition*:

 IN A NUTSHELL is a short summary of the core themes of the festival.

 WHAT THE ḤAG SAYS TO US presents a key thought extracted from the writings of Rabbi Sacks, focusing on the relevance of the festival in our times.

 DEEP DIVING INTO THE TEFILLA OF THE DAY presents a central liturgical text for that festival, a background to the prayer, and a deep analysis that explores the main themes and messages from the text.

 IT ONCE HAPPENED is a story that illustrates or complements the ideas found the themes of the festival as presented in the writings of Rabbi Sacks.

These sections are all followed by **REFLECTION QUESTIONS** and **POINTS TO PONDER**, which are designed to be used for reflection and conversation around the texts and the ideas found in them. Suggested answers to these questions are found in the **EDUCATIONAL COMPANION TO THE QUESTIONS** at the end of each chapter.

 TOP TEN FACTS and **FUN FACT!** provide fun and easy-to-understand facts on the festival.

 ḤIDON **ON THE ḤAG (A QUICK QUIZ)** is a fun festival quiz for the whole family. The answers to these questions can be found in the **EDUCATIONAL COMPANION TO THE QUESTIONS** at the end of each chapter.

 ḤANUKKA CHALLENGES and **PURIM CHALLENGES** are creative activities for children that connect to the festival. They include anagrams, riddles, scavenger hunts, spot the difference, wordsearches, and dingbats.

The chapter on Pesaḥ has a slightly different structure, and functions as an educational companion to the Seder night. It contains ideas and thoughts on ten of the core texts from the Haggada and how Rabbi Sacks understands them. These can be found in the **DEEP DIVE** and **FURTHER THOUGHTS** sections, which are accompanied by **REFLECTION QUESTIONS** and **QUESTIONS TO THINK ABOUT AND ASK AT YOUR SEDER**. This Seder night companion also includes activities, stories, and reflection questions designed to engage everyone around the Seder table, young and old alike.

 EXPERIENCING THE SEDER presents a central liturgical text for that festival, a background to the prayer, and a deep analysis that explores the main themes and messages from the text.

In the Words of Rabbi Sacks

When *Covenant & Conversation Family Edition* was launched for 5779 (in October 2018), and again when the *Ceremony & Celebration Family Edition* was launched for 5781 (September 2020), Rabbi Sacks made videos to explain the vision behind the projects. Here are excerpts from these transcripts:

I have called these essays Covenant & Conversation because this for me is the essence of what Torah learning is – throughout the ages and for us now. The text of the Torah is our covenant with God; the interpretation of this text has been the subject of an ongoing conversation that began at Sinai and has never ceased. Every age has added its commentaries, and so must ours. That is what I have tried to do each week through my Covenant & Conversation essays.

That is why I am so excited by the new Family Edition of Covenant & Conversation. The Family Edition is an accompanying resource which will take the core ideas from the main Covenant & Conversation essay for each parasha, and present them in a simpler fashion, as a way of engaging older children and teenagers.

We hope you'll find this a useful resource to deepen your understanding of the covenant of our Torah, but of equal importance to engage in a meaningful conversation about our Torah with our children and the next generation. Participating in that conversation, and encouraging your children to participate with you, is a major part of what it is to be a Jew, because we are the people who never stopped learning the Book of Life, our most precious gift from the God of Life. There is nothing more beautiful or life affirming than learning Torah with your children. Give them the space not only to be your students, but also to be your teachers, and they will grow tall. That's how we can truly secure the Jewish future.

A framework for engaging with these ideas and enhancing discussion around the Shabbat table. That is what the Shabbat table is really all about.

The Ceremony & Celebration Family Edition is a resource for families based around the ḥagim, which form such crucial aspects and key moments and educational opportunities throughout the year. This is a wonderful way of starting and sustaining a conversation with your children, and that is something through which you will grow and they will grow. Jewish education has always been based around three institutions: the school, the shul, and the home, and all three are important.

Acknowledgements

We are pleased to acknowledge and thank Lillian and Moshe Tabacinic for their critical support for this series of books. Lillian and Moshe are renowned for their support for Jewish education both in Florida and beyond and we are honoured that they have partnered with us on this exciting project. On behalf of all at Koren, and the families across the Jewish world that will learn from and enjoy these volumes, thank you.

Working for both Koren Jerusalem and The Rabbi Sacks Legacy has been a privilege and an honour and has given me the opportunity to collaborate with so many talented and creative people. Thanks to Joanna Benarroch, Dan Sacker, Debby Ifield, and Jonny Lipczer at The Rabbi Sacks Legacy, who, together with Rabbi Sacks, believed in the vision and possibilities for creating these educational resources, and gave me the opportunity of a lifetime to develop exciting projects such as this one. I would also like to thank the Sacks family for their belief in and support of this and all the educational projects I have been involved in on behalf of The Rabbi Sacks Legacy. Thank you for entrusting to us the holy work of continuing the legacy of Rabbi Sacks and bringing his ideas to a younger audience.

Thank you to our team at Koren whose professionalism, creativity, and expertise can be found on every page. These include Aryeh Grossman for being my educational soundboard, Tani Bayer for the creative design, Tomi Mager for typesetting what became a very complex project, and finally to Caryn Meltz who brings everything together in a way that defies description, as well as our proofreaders, Nechama Unterman and Tali Simon. Of course, thanks must always go to our boss, the publisher Matthew Miller, for his support, leadership, and vision.

Finally, to my family, for their love, support, and inspiration. Our Shabbat table was the first of many around the world to explore the ideas of Rabbi Sacks on the *parasha* as a family using this medium, and your input and inspiration can be found throughout these volumes.

The last word goes to my teacher and Rav, Rabbi Lord Jonathan Sacks *zt"l*. Not a day goes past without a sense of feeling bereft without you to lead and inspire us. Your commitment and passion to bring your ideas to young people and your belief in my ability to help you to do it gives me the strength to continue with this endeavour. The *Covenant & Conversation* essay that was sent around the world for the Shabbat that fell during the *shiva*, entitled *Beginning the Journey*, explored Avraham's faith in the covenant and the promises from God, despite only experiencing the very beginning of their fulfilment in his lifetime. The essay concludes with these words:

> *Leaders see the destination, begin the journey, and leave behind them those who will continue it. That is enough to endow a life with immortality.*[4]

It is my privilege to count myself among the many who are driven to continue your journey. It is my hope that these volumes will be a significant step in that journey.

Daniel Rose
Modiin
Elul 5783

---

4 *"Ḥayei Sara:* Beginning the Journey," in *Lessons in Leadership,* 23.

Rosh HaShana

ROSH HASHANA IN A NUTSHELL

The ten days that begin on Rosh HaShana and end with Yom Kippur are an intense period of preparation that leads us to the holy of holies of Jewish time, Yom Kippur. On the *Yamim Nora'im*, the Days of Awe, we can almost feel God's presence and sense His closeness. For although we know that God is always close to us, we do not always feel close to Him. He is always to be found, but we do not always seek Him out. The atmosphere in the synagogue is intense and serious (and for those who are unable to experience Rosh HaShana *shul* services, it is our challenge to find the spiritual energy to replicate this atmosphere in our own homes).

On Rosh HaShana, God judges the whole world and decides its fate for the coming year. It is as if the world has become a courtroom. God Himself is the Judge. The shofar announces that the court is in session, and we are on trial, giving an account of our lives. If taken seriously, this is a potentially life-changing experience. It forces us to ask the most fateful questions we will ever ask:

- Who am I?
- Why am I here?
- How shall I live?
- How have I lived until now?
- How have I used God's greatest gift: time?
- Whom have I wronged, and how can I put it right?
- Where have I failed, and how shall I overcome my failures?
- What is broken in my life and needs mending?
- What chapter will I write in the Book of Life?

These are days of reflection and introspection when we stand in the presence of God and acknowledge how short and vulnerable life really is, and how little time we have here on earth.

There is no time to waste to become the very best people we can be!

POINTS TO PONDER

1. *Aren't these questions we should ask ourselves every day? Why especially now on Rosh HaShana?*

2. *Does the recognition that life is short help or hinder the way you live your life?*

3. *Ask yourself these nine questions now. Do you have answers?*

WHAT ROSH HASHANA SAYS TO US

The genius of Judaism was to take eternal truths and translate them into time, into lived experiences. Other cultures have constructed philosophies and theologies, elaborate systems of abstract thought. Judaism prefers truth lived to truth merely thought. Ancient Greece produced the logical imagination. Judaism produced the chronological imagination, truth transposed into the calendar.

Rosh HaShana, the anniversary of the creation of humanity, invites us to live and feel the human condition in graphic ways.

Here are ten messages from Rosh HaShana that speak directly to our lives today.

1. Life is short

However much life expectancy has risen, we will not, in one lifetime, be able to achieve everything we might wish to achieve. This life is all we have. How shall we use it well? We know that we will not finish the task, but neither are we free to stand aside from it.

2. Life is a gift from God

Life itself, each day, every breath we take, is the gift of God. Life is not something we may take for granted. If we do, we will fail to celebrate it. God gives us one gift above all others, said Rambam (Maimonides): life itself, beside which everything else is secondary. Other religions have sought God in heaven, or in the afterlife, the distant past or the distant future. Here there is suffering, there reward; here chaos, there order; here pain, there balm; here poverty, there plenty. Judaism has relentlessly sought God in the here-and-now of life on earth. Yes, we believe in life after death, but it is in life before death that we truly find human greatness.

3. We are free

Judaism is the religion of the free human being freely responding to the God of freedom. We are not in the grip of sin. We are not determined by economic forces or psychological drives or genetically encoded impulses that we are powerless to resist. The very fact that we can do *teshuva*, that we can act differently tomorrow than we did yesterday, tells us we are free. Philosophers have found this idea difficult. So have scientists. But Judaism insists on it, and our ancestors proved it by defying every law of history, surviving against the odds, refusing to accept defeat.

REFLECT

What will you try to achieve today after reflecting on this?

REFLECT

How does understanding this change the way you are going to live?

REFLECT

Where do we find this concept reflected in the prayers of Rosh HaShana?

4. Life is meaningful

We are not mere accidents of matter, generated by a universe that came into being for no reason and will one day, for no reason, cease to be. We are here because a loving God brought the universe, and life, and us, into existence – a God who knows our fears, hears our prayers, believes in us more than we believe in ourselves, forgives us when we fail, lifts us when we fall, and gives us the strength to overcome despair. The historian Paul Johnson once wrote: "No people has ever insisted more firmly than the Jews that history has a purpose and humanity a destiny." He concluded: "The Jews, therefore, stand right at the centre of the perennial attempt to give human life the dignity of a purpose." This is one of the truths of Rosh HaShana.

REFLECT

Do you have a sense of the meaning of your life?

5. Life is not easy

Judaism does not see the world through rose-tinted lenses. The sufferings of our ancestors haunt our prayers. The world we live in is not the world as it ought to be. That is why, despite every temptation, Judaism has never been able to say the Messianic Age has come, even though we await it daily. But we are not bereft of hope because we are not alone. When Jews went into exile, the *Shekhina*, the Divine Presence, went with them. God is always there, "close to all who call on Him in truth" (Tehillim 145:18). He may hide His face, but He is there. He may be silent, but He is listening to us, hearing us and healing us in ways we may not understand at the time but which become clear in retrospect.

REFLECT

Does this message from Rosh HaShana resonate with you? Can you feel God's closeness in times of difficulty?

6. Life is still sweet

Life may be hard, but it can still be sweet, the way the challah and the apple are on Rosh HaShana when we dip them in honey. Jews have never needed wealth to be rich, or power to be strong. To be a Jew is to live for simple things: the love between husband and wife, the sacred bond between parents and children, the gift of community where we help others and others help us and where we learn that joy is doubled and grief halved by being shared. To be a Jew is to give, whether in the form of *tzedaka* or *gemilut ḥasadim* (acts of loving-kindness). It is to learn and never stop seeking, to pray and never stop thanking, to do *teshuva* and never stop growing. In this lies the secret of joy. Throughout history there have been hedonistic cultures that worship pleasure and ascetic cultures that deny it, but Judaism has a different approach altogether: to sanctify pleasure by making it part of the worship of God. Life is sweet when touched by the Divine.

REFLECT

Where is the sweetness in your life?

7. Our life is a work of art

Our life is the single greatest work of art we will ever make. Rabbi Joseph Soloveitchik, in one of his earliest works, spoke about *Ish HaHalakha*, the halakhic personality and its longing to create, to make something new, original. God, too, longs for us to create and thereby become His partner in the work of renewal. "The most fundamental principle of all is that man must create himself." That is what *teshuva* is, an act of making ourselves anew. On Rosh HaShana we step back from our life like an artist stepping back from their canvas, seeing what needs changing for the painting to be complete.

REFLECT

If you were going to create an expression of your life using any medium (e.g., visual art, poetry, prose, music, etc.), how would you do it?

8. We are what we are because of those who came before us

Our lives are not disconnected particles. We are each a letter in God's Book of Life. But single letters, though they are the vehicles of meaning, have no meaning when they stand alone. To have meaning they must be joined to other letters to make words, sentences, paragraphs, a story, and to be a Jew is to be part of the strangest, oldest, most unexpected and counter-intuitive story there has ever been: the story of a tiny people, never large and often homeless, who nonetheless outlived the greatest empires the world has ever known – the Egyptians, Assyrians, Babylonians, Greeks, and Romans, the medieval empires of Christianity and Islam, all the way to the Third Reich and the Soviet Union. Each in turn thought itself immortal. Each has gone. The Jewish people still lives. But we do not start with nothing. We have inherited wealth, not material but spiritual. We are heirs to our ancestors' greatness.

REFLECT

Think of all the ways your life has been enriched by your parents, grandparents, and great-grandparents (and beyond).

9. Judaism asks great things of us and by doing so makes us great

We walk as tall as the ideals for which we live, and those of the Torah are very high indeed. We are, said Moshe, God's children (Devarim 14:1). We are called on, said the prophet Yeshayahu, to be His witnesses, His ambassadors on earth (Yeshayahu 43:10).

Time and again Jews did things thought impossible. They battled against might in the name of right. They fought against slavery. They showed that it was possible to be a nation without a land, to have influence without power, to be branded the world's pariahs yet not lose self-respect. They believed with unshakeable conviction that they would one day return to their land, and though the hope seemed absurd, it happened.

Judaism sets the bar high, and though we may keep falling short, Rosh HaShana and Yom Kippur allow us to begin anew, forgiven, cleansed, undaunted, ready for the next challenge, the next year.

REFLECT

What do you think Judaism is asking of you in your life?

10. We are dust of the earth but within us is the breath of God

And finally comes the sound of the shofar, piercing our defences, a wordless cry in a religion of words, a sound produced by breath as if to tell us that all life is a mere breath – yet breath is nothing less than the spirit of God within us: "Then the Lord God formed man from the dust of the ground and breathed into his nostrils the breath of life, and man became a living being" (Bereshit 2:7).

Whether the shofar is our cry to God or God's cry to us, somehow in that *tekia, shevarim, terua* – the call, the sob, the wail – is all the emotion of the Divine-human encounter as God asks us to take His gift, life itself, and make of it something holy by acting in a way that honours God and His image on earth, humankind.

For we defeat death, not by living forever but by living by values that live forever; by doing deeds and creating blessings that will live on after us; and by attaching ourselves in the midst of time to God who lives beyond time, "the King – the living, everlasting God."

REFLECT

Close your eyes and hear the shofar. What is it saying to you? What do you want it to say to God on your behalf?

Adapted from the introduction to The Koren Rosh HaShana Maḥzor *with commentary and translation by Rabbi Sacks.*

> "We walk as tall as the ideals for which we live."

DEEP DIVING INTO THE *TEFILLA* OF THE DAY: *UNETANEH TOKEF*

וּנְתַנֶּה תֹּקֶף קְדֻשַּׁת הַיּוֹם / כִּי הוּא נוֹרָא וְאָיֹם
וּבוֹ תִנָּשֵׂא מַלְכוּתֶךָ / וְיִכּוֹן בְּחֶסֶד כִּסְאֶךָ / וְתֵשֵׁב עָלָיו בֶּאֱמֶת.
אֱמֶת, כִּי אַתָּה הוּא דַיָּן וּמוֹכִיחַ, וְיוֹדֵעַ וָעֵד
וְכוֹתֵב וְחוֹתֵם וְסוֹפֵר וּמוֹנֶה
וְתִזְכֹּר כָּל הַנִּשְׁכָּחוֹת / וְתִפְתַּח אֶת סֵפֶר הַזִּכְרוֹנוֹת
וּמֵאֵלָיו יִקָּרֵא / וְחוֹתַם יַד כָּל אָדָם בּוֹ.

וּבְשׁוֹפָר גָּדוֹל יִתָּקַע / וְקוֹל דְּמָמָה דַקָּה יִשָּׁמַע
וּמַלְאָכִים יֵחָפֵזוּן / וְחִיל וּרְעָדָה יֹאחֵזוּן
וְיֹאמְרוּ, הִנֵּה יוֹם הַדִּין / לִפְקֹד עַל צְבָא מָרוֹם בַּדִּין
כִּי לֹא יִזְכּוּ בְעֵינֶיךָ בַּדִּין
וְכָל בָּאֵי עוֹלָם יַעַבְרוּן לְפָנֶיךָ כִּבְנֵי מָרוֹן.

כְּבַקָּרַת רוֹעֶה עֶדְרוֹ / מַעֲבִיר צֹאנוֹ תַּחַת שִׁבְטוֹ
כֵּן תַּעֲבִיר וְתִסְפֹּר וְתִמְנֶה / וְתִפְקֹד נֶפֶשׁ כָּל חָי
וְתַחְתֹּךְ קִצְבָה לְכָל בְּרִיָּה / וְתִכְתֹּב אֶת גְּזַר דִּינָם.

בְּרֹאשׁ הַשָּׁנָה יִכָּתֵבוּן / וּבְיוֹם צוֹם כִּפּוּר יֵחָתֵמוּן.
כַּמָּה יַעַבְרוּן וְכַמָּה יִבָּרֵאוּן
מִי יִחְיֶה וּמִי יָמוּת / מִי בְקִצּוֹ וּמִי לֹא בְקִצּוֹ
מִי בַמַּיִם וּמִי בָאֵשׁ / מִי בַחֶרֶב וּמִי בַחַיָּה / מִי בָרָעָב וּמִי בַצָּמָא
מִי בָרַעַשׁ וּמִי בַמַּגֵּפָה / מִי בַחֲנִיקָה וּמִי בַסְּקִילָה.
מִי יָנוּחַ וּמִי יָנוּעַ / מִי יִשָּׁקֵט וּמִי יִטָּרֵף
מִי יִשָּׁלֵו וּמִי יִתְיַסָּר / מִי יֵעָנִי וּמִי יֵעָשִׁיר / מִי יִשָּׁפֵל וּמִי יָרוּם.

וּנְתַנֶּה תֹּקֶף Let us voice the power of this day's sanctity –
it is awesome, terrible;
on this day Your kingship is raised, Your throne is founded upon love,
and You, with truth, sit upon it.
In truth, it is You: Judge and Accuser, Knowing One and Witness,
writing and sealing, counting, numbering,
remembering all forgotten things,
You open the book of memories –
it is read of itself, / and every man's name is signed there.

וּבְשׁוֹפָר גָּדוֹל A great shofar sounds,
and a still small voice is heard,
angels rush forward / and are held by trembling, shaking;
they say, "Here is the Day of Judgment
visiting all the heavenly host for judgment –"
for they are not cleared in Your eyes in judgment.
And all who have come into this world pass before You like sheep.

כְּבַקָּרַת רוֹעֶה As a shepherd's searching gaze meets his flock,
as he passes every sheep beneath his rod, so You too pass Yours,
count and number, and regard the soul of every living thing;
and You rule off the limit of each creation's life,
and write down the verdict for each.

בְּרֹאשׁ הַשָּׁנָה On Rosh HaShana it is written / and on Yom Kippur it is
sealed: / how many will pass away and how many will be born; / who
will live and who will die; / who in his due time and who before; /
who by water and who by fire; / who by sword and who by beast; /
who by hunger and who of thirst; / who by earthquake and who by
plague; / who by strangling and who by stoning; / who will rest and
who will wander; / who will be calm and who will be harassed; /
who will be at ease and who will suffer; / who will become poor and
who will grow rich; / who cast down and who raised high.

צום   קול   ממון

וּתְשׁוּבָה וּתְפִלָּה וּצְדָקָה / מַעֲבִירִין אֶת רֹעַ הַגְּזֵרָה.

FASTING   CRYING   GIVING

But REPENTANCE, PRAYER, and CHARITY
avert the evil of the decree.

כִּי כְּשִׁמְךָ כֵּן תְּהִלָּתֶךָ / קָשֶׁה לִכְעֹס וְנוֹחַ לִרְצוֹת
כִּי לֹא תַחְפֹּץ בְּמוֹת הַמֵּת / כִּי אִם בְּשׁוּבוֹ מִדַּרְכּוֹ, וְחָיָה
וְעַד יוֹם מוֹתוֹ תְּחַכֶּה לּוֹ / אִם יָשׁוּב, מִיַּד תְּקַבְּלוֹ.

אֱמֶת, כִּי אַתָּה הוּא יוֹצְרָם / וְיוֹדֵעַ יִצְרָם / כִּי הֵם בָּשָׂר וָדָם.

אָדָם יְסוֹדוֹ מֵעָפָר / וְסוֹפוֹ לֶעָפָר
בְּנַפְשׁוֹ יָבִיא לַחְמוֹ / מָשׁוּל כְּחֶרֶס הַנִּשְׁבָּר
כְּחָצִיר יָבֵשׁ, וּכְצִיץ נוֹבֵל / כְּצֵל עוֹבֵר, וּכְעָנָן כָּלָה
וּכְרוּחַ נוֹשָׁבֶת, וּכְאָבָק פּוֹרֵחַ, וְכַחֲלוֹם יָעוּף.

כִּי כְּשִׁמְךָ For as Your name is, so is Your renown:
hard to anger, and readily appeased.
For You do not desire the condemned man's death,
but that he may come back from his ways, and live.
To the very day he dies, You wait for him;
and if he comes back: You welcome him at once.

Truly, it was You who formed them,
You know the forces moving them: / they are but flesh and blood.

Man is founded in dust / and ends in dust.
He lays down his soul to bring home bread. / He is like a broken shard,
like grass dried up, like a faded flower,
like a fleeting shadow, like a passing cloud,
like a breath of wind, like whirling dust, like a dream that slips away.

AND YOU ARE KING –
THE LIVING, EVERLASTING GOD.

וְאַתָּה הוּא מֶלֶךְ, אֵל חַי וְקַיָּם.

Background to the *tefilla*

No prayer more powerfully defines the image of the Days of Awe than does *Unetaneh Tokef*. The language is simple, the imagery strong, the rhythms insistent, and the drama intense.

We do not know exactly who composed *Unetaneh Tokef* or when. A famous tradition dates it to the time when Jews in northern Europe were suffering brutal Christian persecution. It tells of Rabbi Amnon of Mainz, how he was pressured by the bishop, who was also mayor of the town, to convert. Eventually, after repeated prevarication, the bishop subjected him to cruel punishment, inflicting on him wounds from which he would die. On Rosh HaShana, sensing that he was on the verge of death, Rabbi Amnon asked to be carried to the synagogue. As he entered, he found the congregation about to say the *Kedusha*, and asked for permission to say a prayer as his dying words. He then said *Unetaneh Tokef*, and died.

The discovery of ancient manuscripts in the Cairo Geniza suggests, however, that the prayer may be older than this. This and other factors suggest that, in its original form, it was composed in Israel several centuries before.

Analysis

It is structured in four movements.

The first sets the scene. The heavenly court is assembled. God sits in the seat of judgement. The angels tremble. Before Him is the book of all our deeds. In it our lives are written, bearing our signature, and we await the verdict.

The second defines what is at stake: Who will live, who will die? Who will flourish, who will suffer, who will be at ease, who will be in torment? Between now and Yom Kippur our fate is being decided on high.

The third is the great outburst of faith that defines Judaism as a religion of hope. No fate is final. Repentance, prayer, and charity can avert the evil decree. Life is not a script written by Aeschylus or Sophocles in which tragedy is inexorable. God forgives; God pardons; God exercises clemency – if we truly repent and pray and give to others.

The fourth is a moving reflection on the fragility of human life and the eternity of God. We are no more than a fragment of pottery, a blade of grass, a flower that fades, a shadow, a cloud, a breath of wind. Dust we are and to dust we return. But God is life forever.

POINTS TO PONDER

1. *What are the core themes of Rosh HaShana found in the text of this tefilla?*

2. *Why is it* teshuva, tefilla, *and* tzedaka *that can avert God's evil decree?*

3. *Do you think this is primarily a prayer of hope or despair?*

> "No prayer more powerfully defines the image of the Days of Awe than does *Unetaneh Tokef.*"

Tefilla text and commentary taken from The Koren Rosh HaShana Maḥzor *with commentary and translation by Rabbi Sacks.*

TOP TEN ROSH HASHANA FACTS

1. Rosh HaShana is the anniversary of the creation of the world.

2. The name of the festival in the Torah is not Rosh HaShana, but rather *Yom Terua* (the Day of Blasting). The name Rosh HaShana comes from the Mishna.

3. There are actually four New Years mentioned in the Mishna: the new year for trees (fifteenth of Shvat); the new year for tithes (first of Elul); the new year for counting the reign of the king and for counting the months of the calendar (first of Nisan); and the new year for years (first of Tishrei).

4. Rosh HaShana is the only festival that is always two days long, even in Israel.

5. We blow the shofar one hundred times on each day of Rosh HaShana (unless it is Shabbat).

6. The shofar is generally a ram's horn (although it can be from other animals) to remind us of the ram that was caught in a bush that Avraham used as a sacrifice in place of his son Yitzhak.

7. There are various symbolic foods we eat on the evening of Rosh HaShana, called *simanim*, each one representing a blessing for the new year. The best-known example is dipping apples in honey for a sweet new year.

8. The traditional Rosh HaShana greeting is "*Leshana tova tikatev vetehatem*" (May you be inscribed and sealed for a good year).

9. Many people have the custom to do *Tashlikh* on the first afternoon of Rosh HaShana (unless it falls on Shabbat, in which case we move it to the second day). This involves saying a special prayer and symbolically casting away our sins at a body of fresh water. (Some people throw breadcrumbs into the water to represent the casting away of the sins.)

10. There is a custom not to sleep during the day of Rosh HaShana so that we start the year in the way that we mean to continue it – utilising every minute.

IT ONCE HAPPENED...

Once it happened in the days of Rav Avraham Yitzhak HaKohen Kook, the chief rabbi of pre-State Israel, that a group of workers, under pressure to complete a building in one of the neighbourhoods of Jerusalem, worked on Rosh HaShana.

People living in the area sent word to Rav Kook, expecting him to order them immediately to stop. Instead, he sent a representative to blow shofar for the workers.

They stopped working to listen. Some began to cry. When the blowing was completed, they decided of their own accord not to continue working on the holy day. Some ran home, changed their clothes, and joined Rav Kook at his yeshiva for the rest of Rosh HaShana.

POINTS TO PONDER

1. *Why do you think Rav Kook chose to approach these workers in this way rather than ordering them to stop working?*

2. *Why do you think the shofar had this impact on the workers?*

3. *What Rosh HaShana lessons can we learn from this story?*

> "Rav Kook sent a representative to blow shofar for the workers. They stopped working to listen. Some began to cry."

ḤIDON ON THE ḤAG
(A QUICK QUIZ)

1. What do the words "Rosh HaShana" mean?

2. What date is Rosh HaShana?

3. How many names does Rosh HaShana have?

4. What are the names of the three kinds of notes we blow on the shofar?

5. How many notes do we blow on the shofar on each day of Rosh HaShana?

6. Name five of the *simanim* (symbolic foods) we eat on Rosh HaShana evening.

7. Why do we eat pomegranates on Rosh HaShana?

8. What kind of water is necessary to do *Tashlikh* on Rosh HaShana?

9. What are the three sections of the Rosh HaShana Musaf *Amida*?

10. Why do we have the custom to eat a new fruit on the second night of Rosh HaShana?

EDUCATIONAL COMPANION TO THE QUESTIONS

ROSH HASHANA IN A NUTSHELL

1. Anyone who wishes to live a life with meaning will find themselves asking these or similar questions. A thinking and reflective person will address them more often than once a year. Rosh HaShana ensures that even someone for whom introspection does not come naturally will still address these questions, and consider the answers to them, every year on the day that encourages the process of ḥeshbon hanefesh (self-accounting/introspection), when we stand in the presence of God and consider our lives.

2. The fleeting nature of life can lead to depression and a sense of nihilism and emptiness, or conversely it can inspire a search for meaning, and an aspiration to make every minute and every day count. Rosh HaShana and Judaism in general encourage the second approach.

3. From a young child to an elderly person, these questions are the basic questions of a self-aware being who aspires to the betterment of their life. This is a natural wish even in young children. Having an adult to guide them in the asking and answering of these questions will be a good catalyst for the process.

DEEP DIVING INTO THE *TEFILLA* OF THE DAY

1. From the list of ten themes found above in "What Rosh HaShana Says to Us," the following are clearly expressed in this *tefilla*:

- Life is short; life is a gift from God.
- We are free to act.
- Life is not easy.
- We are dust of the earth but within us is the breath of God.

Further Rosh HaShana themes also found here are:

- The awesome nature of the day

- God as King; God as a Judge and Rosh HaShana as a Day of Judgement
- The power of the sound of the shofar
- Our future is in the balance and is decided on this day.
- We can still affect the decision through acts of *teshuva*, *tefilla*, and *tzedaka*.
- God is a forgiving God.

2. These three mitzvot represent the best actions we can take to repair the three paradigm relationships a person can have: with ourselves (*teshuva* – repentance); with God (*tefilla* – prayer); and with other humans (*tzedaka* – charity). To make a change we must focus on improving these areas in our life.

3. While there are aspects of despair found in this prayer (such as the vulnerability and fleeting nature of human life), at its core there is a profound statement of hope and positivity. It declares that our fate is ultimately within our control, that we have the secret to averting the evil decree, and that God is a forgiving God.

IT ONCE HAPPENED ON ROSH HASHANA...

1. Rav Kook was famous for his love of all Jews. Rather than showing disapproval for their decision to work on Rosh HaShana, which may have alienated them further from Judaism, he offered them the chance to hear the shofar at their workplace. He showed that he cared, and this approach ultimately brought them closer to Judaism.

2. The sound of the shofar is a powerful sound that reflects the emotions of the soul. Perhaps the workers connected to its spiritual dimension, and it touched their souls. Perhaps it was a familiar sound from their youth and it spoke to them once more and woke them from the haze of the pressures of adult life. Or perhaps it represented the love of Rav Kook for his fellow Jew and it was this that moved them.

3. Some of the lessons we can learn are: the power of the sound of the shofar, if we are only open to hearing it; the power of acts of love and kindness, more important even than *teshuva* and repairing our relationship with God; and that fixing our human relationships comes first.

ḤIDON ON THE ḤAG (A QUICK QUIZ)

1. Head of the Year (not New Year!).
2. First and second of Tishrei.
3. Five: Rosh HaShana; *Yom Terua* (Day of Blasting); *Yom HaDin* (Day of Judgement); *Yom HaZikaron* (Day of Remembrance); *HaYom Harat Olam* (the Day of the Creation of the World).
4. *Tekia; shevarim; terua.*
5. One hundred.
6. Apples and honey; dates; pomegranates; carrots; leeks; beets; squash/gourds; fish; and the head of a fish or sheep. Your family may have additional traditions.
7. Because the many seeds are meant to represent the 613 mitzvot in the Torah.
8. "Flowing water," preferably a stream with fish.
9. *Malkhuyot* (kingship); *Zikhronot* (remembrances); and *Shofarot* (shofar blasts).
10. Because there is a difference of opinion as to whether the second day of Rosh HaShana is a new festival or a continuation of the first day, we eat a fruit that we have not eaten for thirty days so that we can make a *Sheheḥeyanu* blessing to cover both the fruit and, if needed, the new festival of the second day.

Yom Kippur

YOM KIPPUR IN A NUTSHELL

Yom Kippur is the holy of holies of Jewish time, when we give an account of our lives. We reflect on what has happened to us and what we plan to do in the coming year. The single most important lesson of Yom Kippur is that it's never too late to change, start again, and live differently from the way we've lived in the past. God forgives every mistake we've made as long as we are honest in regretting it and doing our best to put it right. Even if there's nothing we regret, Yom Kippur makes us think about how to use the coming year in such a way as to bring blessings into the lives of others by way of thanking God for all He has given us.

In ancient times Yom Kippur was celebrated in the form of a massive public ceremony set in the Temple in Jerusalem. The holiest man in Israel, the high priest, entered the most sacred space, the Holy of Holies, confessed the sins of the nation using God's holiest name, and secured atonement for all of Israel. It was a moment of intense drama in the life of a people who believed that their fate depended on their relationship with God, who knew that there is no life, let alone a nation, without sin, and who knew from their history that sin could be punished with catastrophe.

After the destruction of the Second Temple, everything changed. There was no longer a high priest, no sacrifice, no divine fire, no Levites singing praises or crowds thronging the precincts of Jerusalem and filling the Temple Mount. Above all, there was no Yom Kippur ritual through which the people could find forgiveness.

POINTS TO PONDER

1. *How does Yom Kippur help us focus on the future and on making a change?*

2. *How did Yom Kippur change after the ḥurban (destruction of the Temple)? What are the advantages of each approach?*

3. *How did this transition "save Jewish faith"?*

It was then that a transformation took place that constitutes one of history's great creative responses to tragedy. Yom Kippur was transferred from the Temple in Jerusalem to every synagogue in the world. Instead of the high priest acting as a representative, God Himself would purify His people without the need for an intermediary. Even ordinary Jews could, as it were, come face to face with the *Shekhina*, the Divine Presence. They needed no one else to apologise for them. The drama that once took place in the Temple could now take place in the human heart. Yom Kippur was saved, and it is not too much to say that Jewish faith was also saved.

HOW YOM KIPPUR CHANGES US

To those who fully open themselves to it, Yom Kippur is a life-transforming experience.

It tells us that God, who created the universe in love and forgiveness, reaches out to us in love and forgiveness, asking us to love and forgive others. God never asked us not to make mistakes. All He asks is that we acknowledge our mistakes, learn from them, grow through them, and make amends where we can.

No religion has held such a high view of human possibility.

The God who created us in His image gave us freedom. We are not tainted by original sin, destined to fail, caught in the grip of an evil that only divine grace can defeat.

To the contrary, we have within us the power to choose life. Together we have the power to change the world.

The following five concepts, all central to Yom Kippur, contain core Jewish values and ideas that mould us as Jews and human beings.

1. Shame and guilt

Judaism is the world's greatest example of a guilt-and-repentance culture as opposed to the shame-and-honour culture of the ancient Greeks.

In a shame culture such as that of Greek tragedy, evil attaches to the person. It is a kind of indelible stain. There is no way back for one who has done a shameful deed. They become a pariah and the best they can hope for is to die in a noble cause. Conversely, in a guilt culture like that of Judaism, evil is an attribute of the act, not the agent. Even one who has done wrong has a sacred self that remains intact. They may have to undergo punishment. They certainly have to make amends. But there remains a core of worth that can never be lost. A guilt culture hates the sin, not the sinner. Repentance, rehabilitation, and return are always possible.

A guilt culture is a culture of responsibility. We do not blame anyone else for the wrong we do. It is always tempting to blame others – it wasn't me, it was my parents, my upbringing, my friends, my genes, my social class, the media, the system, "them." That was what the first two humans did in the Garden of Eden. When challenged by God for eating the forbidden fruit, the man blamed the woman. The woman blamed the serpent. The result was paradise lost.

Blaming others for our failings is as old as humanity, but it is disastrous. It means that we define ourselves as victims. A culture of victimhood wins the compassion of others but at too high a cost. It incubates feelings of resentment, humiliation, grievance, and grudge. It leads people to rage against the world instead of taking steps to mend it. Jews have suffered much, but Yom Kippur prevents us from ever defining ourselves as victims. As we confess our sins, we blame no one and take full responsibility for our actions. Knowing God will forgive us allows us to be completely honest with ourselves.

> ## "Yom Kippur is a life-transforming experience."

REFLECT

How do you want to change today to become a better you tomorrow?

2. The growth mindset

Yom Kippur also allows us to grow. We owe a debt to cognitive behavioural therapy for reminding us of a classic element of Jewish faith: that when we change the way we think, we change the way we feel. And when we feel differently, we live differently. What we believe shapes what we become.

At the heart of *teshuva* is the belief that we can change. We are not destined to be forever what we were. In the Torah we see Yehuda grow from an envious brother prepared to sell Yosef as a slave into a man with the conscience and courage to offer himself as a slave so that his brother Binyamin can go free.

We know that some people relish a challenge and take risks, while others, no less gifted, play it safe and ultimately underachieve. Psychologists tell us that the crucial difference lies in whether you think of your ability as fixed or as something developed through effort and experience. *Teshuva* is essentially about effort and experience. It assumes we can grow.

Teshuva means I can take risks, knowing that I may fail but knowing that failure is not final. It means that if I get things wrong and make mistakes, God does not lose faith in me even though I may lose faith in myself. God believes in us, even if we do not. That alone is a life-changing fact if we fully open ourselves to its implications.

Teshuva means that the past is not irredeemable. It means that from every mistake, I grow. There is no failure I experience that does not make me a deeper human being, and there is no challenge I accept, however much I fall short, that does not develop in me strengths I would not otherwise have had.

That is the first transformation of Yom Kippur: a renewed relationship with myself.

3. Our relationships with others

The second transformation is a renewed relationship with others. We know that Yom Kippur atones only for sins between us and God, but that does not mean that these are the only sins for which we need to seek atonement. To the contrary: many, even most, of the sins we confess on Yom Kippur are about our relationships with other people. Throughout the prophetic and rabbinic literature, it is assumed that as we act to others, so God acts to us. Those who forgive are forgiven. Those who condemn are condemned.

What failure in your life have you grown from?

The Ten Days of Repentance from Rosh HaShana to Yom Kippur are a time when we try to mend relationships that have broken. It takes one kind of moral courage to apologise and another to forgive, but both may be necessary.

Failure to heal relationships can split families, destroy marriages, ruin friendships, and divide communities. That is not where God wants us to be. We are taught that after Sara died, Avraham took back Hagar and Yishmael into his family, mending the rift that had occurred many years before. Aharon, according to tradition, was loved by all the people because he was able to mend fractured friendships.

Without a designated day, would we ever get around to mending our broken relationships? Often we do not tell people how they have hurt us because we do not want to look vulnerable and small-minded. In the opposite direction, sometimes we are reluctant to apologise because we feel so guilty that we do not want to expose our guilt.

REFLECT

Which relationships do you need to mend this year?

4. Coming home

The third transformation is a renewed relationship with God. On Yom Kippur, God is close. Jewish life is full of signals of transcendence, intimations of eternity. We encounter God in three ways: through creation, revelation, and redemption.

Through creation: the more we understand of cosmology, the more we realise how improbable the universe is. The universe is too finely tuned for the emergence of stars, planets, and life to have come into existence by chance. The more we understand of the sheer improbability of the existence of the universe, the emergence of life from inanimate matter, and the equally mysterious appearance of Homo sapiens – the only life form capable of asking the question "Why?" – the more the line from Tehillim rings true: "How numerous are Your works, Lord; You made them all in wisdom" (Tehillim 104:24).

Through revelation: the words of God as recorded in the Torah. There is nothing in history to compare to the fact that Jews spent a thousand years (from Moshe to the last of the prophets) compiling a commentary on the Torah in the form of the prophetic, historical, and wisdom books of Tanakh, then another thousand years (from Malakhi to the Talmud Bavli) compiling a commentary on the commentary in the form of the vast literature of the Oral Torah (Midrash, Mishna, and Gemara), then another thousand years (from the *Geonim* to the *Aḥaronim*, the later authorities) writing commentaries on the commentary on the commentary.

REFLECT

Where do you connect to God the most: creation (science and nature), revelation (the Torah), or redemption (history)?

> "On Yom Kippur, God is close."

And through history: many great thinkers, including Blaise Pascal and Leo Tolstoy, believed that Jewish history was the most compelling evidence of the existence of God. Sometimes God comes to us not as the conclusion of a line of reasoning but as a feeling, an intuition, a sensed presence, as we stand in the synagogue on this holy day – listening to our people's melodies, saying the words Jews have said from Barcelona to Bergen-Belsen to Bnei Brak, from Toledo to Treblinka to Tel Aviv – knowing that we are part of an immense story that has played itself out through the centuries and continents, the tempestuous yet ultimately hope-inspiring love story of a people in search of God, and God in search of a people.

There has never been a drama remotely like this in its ups and downs, triumphs and tragedies, its songs of praise and lamentation, and we are part of it. For most of us it is not something we chose but a fate we were born into.

5. What chapter will we write in the Book of Life?

On this day of days we are brutally candid: "Before I was formed I was unworthy, and now that I have been formed it is as if I had not been formed. I am dust while alive, how much more so when I am dead." Yet the same faith that inspired those words also declared that we should see ourselves and the world as if equally poised between merit and guilt, and that our next act could tilt the balance, for my life and for the world (Rambam, *Hilkhot Teshuva* 3:4). Judaism lives in this dialect between our smallness and our potential greatness. We may be dust, but within us are immortal longings.

Yom Kippur invites us to become better than we were, in the knowledge that we can be better than we are. That knowledge comes from God. If we are only self-made, we live within the prison of our own limitations. The truly great human beings are those who have opened themselves to the inspiration of something greater than themselves.

Yom Kippur is about the humility that leads to greatness: our ability to say, over and over again, "*Al ḥeit sheḥatanu*," "We have sinned," and yet know that this is not said in self-pity, but rather, the prelude to greater achievement in the future, the way a champion in any sport, a maestro in any field, reviews his or her past mistakes as part of the preparation for the next challenge, the next rung to climb.

The power of Yom Kippur is that it brings us face to face with these truths. Through its words, music, and devotions, through the way it focuses energies by depriving us of all the physical pleasures we normally associate with a Jewish festival, through the sheer driving passion of the liturgy with its hundred ways of saying sorry, it confronts us with the ultimate question: How will we live? Will we

> **REFLECT**
>
> *What have you achieved this past year with the help of God, and what would you like to achieve with His help next year?*

> "Yom Kippur is about the humility that leads to greatness."

live a life that fully explores the capacity of the human mind to reach out to that which lies beyond it? Will we grow emotionally? Will we learn the arts of loyalty and love? Will we train our inner ear to hear the cry of the lonely and the poor? Will we live a life that makes a difference, bringing the world-that-is a little closer to the world-that-ought-to-be? Will we open our hearts and minds to God?

The most demanding day of the Jewish year, a day without food and drink, a day of prayer and penitence, confession and pleading, in which we accuse ourselves of every conceivable sin, still calls to Jews, touching us at the deepest level of our being. It is a day in which we run towards the open arms of God, weeping because we may have disappointed Him, or because sometimes we feel He has disappointed us, yet knowing that we need one another, for though God can create a universe, He cannot live within the human heart unless we let Him in.

It is a day not just of confession and forgiveness but of a profound liberation. Atonement means that we can begin again. We are not held captive by the past or by our failures. The Book of Life is open and God invites us – His hand guiding us the way a scribe guides the hand of those who write a letter in a Torah scroll – to write a new chapter in the story of our people, a chapter uniquely our own yet one that we cannot write on our own without being open to something vaster than we will ever fully understand. It is a day on which God invites us to greatness.

Adapted from the introduction to The Koren Yom Kippur Maḥzor *with commentary and translation by Rabbi Sacks.*

DEEP DIVING INTO THE *TEFILLA* OF THE DAY: *VIDUY* (CONFESSION)

אָשַׁמְנוּ,
בָּגַדְנוּ, גָּזַלְנוּ, דִּבַּרְנוּ דֹפִי
הֶעֱוִינוּ, וְהִרְשַׁעְנוּ, זַדְנוּ,
חָמַסְנוּ, טָפַלְנוּ שֶׁקֶר
יָעַצְנוּ רָע, כִּזַּבְנוּ, לַצְנוּ,
מָרַדְנוּ, נִאַצְנוּ, סָרַרְנוּ
עָוִינוּ, פָּשַׁעְנוּ, צָרַרְנוּ, קִשִּׁינוּ עֹרֶף
רָשַׁעְנוּ, שִׁחַתְנוּ, תִּעַבְנוּ, תָּעִינוּ, תִּעְתָּעְנוּ.

אָשַׁמְנוּ We have been guilty, we have acted treacherously,
we have robbed, we have spoken slander.
We have acted perversely, we have acted wickedly,
we have acted presumptuously, we have been violent, we have framed lies.
We have given bad advice, we have deceived, we have scorned,
we have rebelled, we have provoked, we have turned away,
we have committed iniquity, we have transgressed,
we have persecuted, we have been obstinate.
We have acted wickedly, we have corrupted,
we have acted abominably, we have strayed, we have led others astray.

Background to the *tefilla*

This is the first section of the *Viduy* (confession), said at every service
over the day, from Minḥa on Erev Yom Kippur until *Ne'ila* at the conclusion of Yom Kippur. Confession is the primary expression of repentance, the central theme of Yom Kippur. According to Rambam, it is
the biblical source of the command of *teshuva*: "Any man or woman
who wrongs another in any way and so is unfaithful to the Lord, is
guilty. They must confess the sin they have committed" (Bemidbar
5:6–7). It follows that "with regard to all the commandments of the
Torah, positive or negative, if a person transgressed any of them, wil-
fully or in error, and repents, turning away from his sin, he is under a
duty to confess before God" (Rambam, *Hilkhot Teshuva* 1:1). Although
repentance is a matter of thought and emotion, it must be given verbal
expression in the form of confession.

Confession is more than remorse, though this must also be part
of the process. Remorse is a state of mind. Confession is a formal act.
It is like the difference between feeling guilty at breaking the law and
pleading guilty in a court of law. The former is an emotion, the latter
a declaration. In the case of *teshuva*, it is a declaration to God. As well
as involving remorse, confession assumes there is a commitment not
to repeat the sin.

Analysis

Originally, the form of confession was simple: "Please, Lord, I have sinned, I have done wrong, I have rebelled before You." It then specified the particular act you were confessing. Over time, there developed the broader form of confession that we say ten times on Yom Kippur.

This is different from the original in three respects. First, it is said in the plural: not "I have sinned" but "We have sinned." This is because on Yom Kippur we stand before God not only as individuals but as members of a people, and because we hold that "*kol Yisrael arevim zeh bazeh*," "all Israel are responsible for one another." As R. Shimon bar Yoḥai put it: If a person drills a hole under his seat in a boat, when the water enters, not only he but everyone is in danger. We accept collective responsibility, especially for the wrongs we could have protested but did not.

The second difference is that we do not publicly specify particular sins. Instead, we read an alphabetical list. This is to avoid public humiliation and to make it easier to confess. It prompts us systematically to examine our conscience and reflect on whether we have done wrong, and if so, how and to whom. It is a way of saying that we have sinned with all the letters, as if the alphabet itself were testifying against us.

The third difference is that we now have two forms of confession, one brief (reproduced at the bottom of the previous page, "We have sinned, we have acted treacherously…"), the other longer ("For the sin we have sinned before You"). The former is closer to the original biblical form of confession and is more general: it articulates the general defects of character that lead us to do wrong. The latter goes deeper into specifics.

Confession is said standing, bowed in a gesture of humility. The custom is to beat one's breast lightly at each mentioned sin in the spirit of Yirmeyahu (31:18): "After I strayed, I repented; after I came to understand, I beat my breast."

Public confession, however, is not enough. As we recite the long checklist of sins, we must be asking ourselves: Did I commit a sin of this kind? Did I do something similar? If so, we must acknowledge that sin inwardly to God and resolve to put it right. Public confession is a mere prelude to the private admission which is the real act of *teshuva*, in which we examine our consciences, abandoning our usual defences in the knowledge that God forgives those who truly admit their wrongs, and that *teshuva* is the single greatest act of self-transformation any of us can undertake.

POINTS TO PONDER

1. *Why dwell on our sins? Why not just focus on being better in the future?*

2. *Why do you think the* Viduy *is written in alphabetical order (see the story below for a connected idea)?*

3. *If this public* Viduy *is more symbolic rather than an actual confession of our sins, when do we consider our actual sins and mistakes on Yom Kippur?*

"*Teshuva* is the single greatest act of self-transformation any of us can undertake."

Tefilla text and commentary taken from The Koren Sacks Yom Kippur Maḥzor *with commentary and translation by Rabbi Sacks.*

TOP TEN YOM KIPPUR FACTS

1. There is a mitzva to eat a festive meal before Yom Kippur starts.

2. There is a special custom to bless one's children on the eve of Yom Kippur before the fast begins.

3. Yom Kippur begins with one of the most famous Jewish prayers – *Kol Nidrei*. Except it isn't a prayer at all; rather it is a declaration to annul our vows.

4. Fasting is not the only prohibition on Yom Kippur. There are five prohibitions in total:

- eating and drinking
- washing/bathing
- anointing
- marital relations
- wearing leather shoes

5. If it is dangerous for a person to fast, then not only can they eat, but they must eat, to preserve their health (individuals must ask rabbinic and medical experts before making this decision).

6. Many have the custom to wear white on Yom Kippur. This reminds us of the shrouds we will one day be buried in, calling to mind the fragility of all human life, and it also reminds us that today we aspire to be pure like the angels.

7. Yom Kippur is the only day of the year when there are five prayer services:

- Maariv (evening service)
- Shaḥarit (morning service)
- Musaf (additional service)
- Minḥa (afternoon service)
- Ne'ila ("closing" service)

8. For the *haftara* of the Minḥa service, we read the story of the prophet Yona who eventually delivers God's warning to the people of Nineveh and convinces them to repent.

9. Yom Kippur ends with the blowing of the shofar to remind us of the departing of God's presence from Mount Sinai after the Giving of the Torah, which was also accompanied by the blowing of the shofar.

10. There is a widespread custom after the festive meal at the conclusion of Yom Kippur to immediately engage in the next mitzva to come – the building of the sukka.

IT ONCE HAPPENED...

One Yom Kippur, the Baal Shem Tov was praying together with his students, and he had a worrying sense that the prayers were not getting through, and that the harsh heavenly decree against the Jewish people was not being overturned. As *Ne'ila* approached, and with it the final opportunity for the Jewish people to avert this harsh judgement, he and his students increased their fervour and passion in their prayers, but to no avail.

As the ḥazan began the *Ne'ila* service, a simple shepherd boy wandered into *shul* to pray. He could barely read the letters of the *Alef-Beit*, let alone say all the words in the *maḥzor*. Feeling helpless, he opened the first page of his siddur and recited: *alef, beit, veit, gimel, dalet*. He said to God in his heart: "This is all I can do. God, You know how the prayers should be pronounced. Please, arrange the letters in the proper way."

Louder and louder, with more and more intensity he recited the letters. *Heh, vav, zayin, ḥet* …. The people around him began to mutter, complaining that he was disturbing their prayers. But the Baal Shem Tov immediately silenced them, and declared for everyone to hear that "because of this boy's prayers the gates to heaven are wedged open for the last few minutes of Yom Kippur, allowing our prayers in." So it was on that Yom Kippur that the simple, genuine prayers of a young shepherd boy who couldn't read resounded powerfully within the heavenly court and saved the Jewish people.

POINTS TO PONDER

1. *Is it important to know that the boy was a shepherd boy?*

2. *Why do you think the boy chose to say the* Alef-Beit *in the form of a prayer?*

3. *What message can you take from this story for your Yom Kippur?*

ḤIDON ON THE ḤAG
(A QUICK QUIZ)

1. What do the words "Yom Kippur" mean?

2. What date is Yom Kippur?

3. What happens on Yom Kippur to the Book of Life in which God wrote our fate on Rosh HaShana?

4. What happened on the first Yom Kippur after the Exodus?

5. What is added to *Minḥa* on Erev Yom Kippur and why?

6. What happened to the two goats in the special Yom Kippur service in the Temple?

7. What kinds of sins cannot be atoned for on Yom Kippur?

8. What story do we read at *Minḥa* of Yom Kippur and why?

9. What is the extra prayer service added at the conclusion of Yom Kippur?

10. What mitzva do we have the custom to begin immediately after Yom Kippur?

EDUCATIONAL COMPANION TO THE QUESTIONS

YOM KIPPUR IN A NUTSHELL

1. On Yom Kippur we stand before the King of kings in judgement in a court of law that He has convened, and we confess our shortcomings, while He decides what will happen to us in the next year. This focuses us on who we are and who we can become. As we plead with God for a good year and ask to be written in the Book of Life, we can't help but consider whether we truly deserve this, and how we can become more deserving of it in the future.

2. Before the Temple was destroyed, and the Temple service abolished, the sins of the entire nation were atoned for by the *kohen gadol* (high priest), through the performance of the rituals and service of the day. This happened on the holiest day of the year, in the holiest place in the world, on behalf of the nation as a whole. Once this ritual was lost, the Rabbis recreated Yom Kippur in a way that each Jew could engage in their own atonement process, through *tefilla*, together with their community in their *Mikdash me'at* (mini sanctuary – the synagogue). They no longer had to rely on a service that took place centrally on their behalf. Instead, they were each empowered to take responsibility for their own spiritual well-being.

3. Until this point in history, Jewish worship of God had been focused on the Temple service in Jerusalem. There was a danger that the destruction of the Temple, and the expulsion from Jerusalem, would spell the end for Judaism and the Jewish people. Yom Kippur's transformation represents Judaism's transition to a religion that could survive exile and dispersion. Every individual Jew from now on could worship God privately in synagogues that could be built anywhere in the world. It is no understatement to suggest that when the Rabbis created this pivot in Jewish worship, they saved Judaism as a religion and the Jewish people as a civilisation.

DEEP DIVING INTO THE *TEFILLA* OF THE DAY

1. It is important to face our mistakes so we can grow from them and ensure we don't repeat them in the future. If God can forgive our past sins then we can and must forgive them ourselves so that we can build a better future.

2. The *Viduy* represents a generality of sinful behaviour. The *Alef-Beit* as a poetic expression represents the entirety of sinful behaviour (from *alef* to *tav*), just as the boy in the story used the *Alef-Beit* to represent all possible words for his *tefilla*, pleading with God to arrange them in the correct order, promising that his intention was correct.

3. *Tefilla* is not the whole story of repentance on Yom Kippur. While the *tefillot*, including the *Viduy*, are there to help us repent, there is also plenty of opportunity during the day to reflect on our past mistakes in our hearts. This is the essence of repentance and we should find time for this introspection during Yom Kippur.

IT ONCE HAPPENED ON YOM KIPPUR...

1. Perhaps the boy understood responsibility and leadership from his work as a shepherd, in much the same way as Moshe and King David were fitting leaders because they were also shepherds.

2. He was illiterate. He could not read, but he knew the *Alef-Beit*. He said each letter over and over again with intense and pure *kavana* (intention) instead of saying the words of the *tefillot*, which he could not read. He was also asking God to rearrange the letters he was saying into the correct order so they would make up the words of the *tefilla*, and this could be considered as if he were saying the *tefillot* also.

3. Saying all the words of all the *tefillot* is not the most important thing on Yom Kippur (or any oth-

er day of the year). What is in your heart is more important, and we believe God sees that. This may mean that you can say the *tefillot* in a language you understand if your Hebrew is not fluent, or even use your own words to approach Hashem and pray. What is most important is that your intention is pure and you take the opportunity to stand before God and open your heart.

ḤIDON ON THE ḤAG (A QUICK QUIZ)

1. Day of Atonement (atonement means to make amends for a wrong).
2. Tenth of Tishrei.
3. Our fate is sealed.
4. Moshe came down from Mount Sinai with the second Tablets of stone (signifying God's forgiveness of the sin of the Golden Calf).
5. *Viduy* (confession) – in case one chokes at the special meal before Yom Kippur and does not have an opportunity to confess, we add *Viduy* to the Minḥa service.
6. Lots were drawn to choose between the goats. One was sacrificed on behalf of the people, and the other was sent into the wilderness, symbolically taking the sins of the people with it. (This is where the idea of a scapegoat comes from.)
7. Sins committed against other people – the sinner must ask for forgiveness directly, as God cannot forgive these sins.
8. The book of Yona, because the theme of repentance and forgiveness runs through the story. The repentance of the people of Nineveh serves as an inspiration to us to repent, and shows us that repentance can overturn a divine decree.
9. *Ne'ila*.
10. The mitzva to build a sukka.

Book of Life *by Shraga Weil*

Sukkot

SUKKOT IN A NUTSHELL

The Torah tells us: "Live in sukkot for seven days: All native-born Israelites are to live in sukkot so that your descendants will know that I had the Israelites live in sukkot when I brought them out of Egypt. I am the Lord your God" (Vayikra 23:42–43).

There are two opinions in the Mishna. R. Eliezer held that the sukka represents the Clouds of Glory that surrounded the Israelites during the wilderness years, protecting them from heat during the day and cold during the night, and bathing them with the radiance of the Divine Presence. R. Akiva on the other hand said, "*Sukkot mamash*," meaning a sukka is a sukka, no more and no less: it is a hut, a booth, a temporary dwelling. It has no symbolism. It is what it is.

If we follow R. Eliezer then it is obvious why we celebrate by making a sukka. It is there to remind us of a miracle. All three pilgrimage festivals are about miracles. Pesaḥ is about the miracle of the Exodus, Shavuot is about the miracle of the Revelation at Mount Sinai, and Sukkot is about God's tender care of His people during the journey across the desert. But according to R. Akiva, a sukka is merely a hut, so what was the miracle? There is nothing unusual about living in a hut if you are living a nomadic existence in the desert. Why should there be a festival dedicated to something ordinary, commonplace, and non-miraculous?

Rashbam (Rashi's grandson) says the sukka was there to remind the Israelites of their past so that at the very moment they were feeling the greatest satisfaction at living in Israel – at the time of the ingathering of the produce of the land – they should remember their lowly origins. They were once a group of refugees without a home, never knowing when they would have to move on. The festival of Sukkot, according to Rashbam, exists to remind us of our humble origins so that we never fall into the complacency of taking for granted our freedom, the land of Israel, and the blessings it yields.

However, there is another way of understanding R. Akiva. The sukka represents the courage the Israelites had to travel, to move, to leave security behind, and follow God's call, as did Avraham and Sara at the dawn of our history. According to R. Akiva the sukka is the temporary home of a temporarily homeless people. It symbolised the courage of a bride willing to follow her husband on a risk-laden journey to a place she had never seen before – a love that showed itself in the fact that she was willing to live in a hut, trusting her husband's promise that one day they would have a permanent home.

What is truly remarkable is that Sukkot is called, by tradition, "*zeman simḥateinu*," "our time of joy." That, to me, is the wonder at the heart of the Jewish experience: that Jews throughout the ages were able to experience risk and uncertainty at every level of their existence and yet they were still able to rejoice. That is spiritual courage of a high order. Faith is not certainty; faith is the courage to live with uncertainty. Faith is the ability to rejoice in the midst of instability and change, travelling through the wilderness of time towards an unknown destination.

POINTS TO PONDER

1. *Which of these three approaches to Sukkot speaks to you the most?*

2. *What is the link between the themes of Sukkot explained here and Rosh HaShana and Yom Kippur?*

3. *Can you think of examples from Jewish history when Jews lived through risk and uncertainty yet still managed to find joy in their lives?*

Succah *by Rochelle Blumenfeld*

SUKKOT FOR OUR TIME

Of all the festivals, Sukkot is surely the one that speaks most powerfully to our time. Kohelet (which we read on Sukkot) could almost have been written in the twenty-first century. Here is the ultimate success, the man who has it all – the houses, the cars, the clothes, the adoring women, the envy of all men – who has pursued everything this world can offer from pleasure to possessions to power to wisdom, and yet who, surveying the totality of his life, can only say, "Meaningless, meaningless, everything is meaningless."

Kohelet's failure to find meaning is directly related to his obsession with the "I" and the "Me": "I built for myself. I gathered for myself. I acquired for myself." The more he pursues his desires, the emptier his life becomes. There is no more powerful critique of the consumer society, whose idol is the self, whose icon is the "selfie," and whose moral code is "Whatever works for you." This is reflected in today's society that achieved unprecedented affluence, giving people more choices than they had ever known, and yet at the same time saw an unprecedented rise in alcohol and drug abuse, eating disorders, stress-related syndromes, depression, attempted suicide, and actual suicide. A society of tourists, not pilgrims, is not one that will yield the sense of a life worth living. Of all things people have chosen to worship, the self is the least fulfilling. A culture of narcissism quickly gives way to loneliness and despair.

By the end of the book, Kohelet finds meaning in simple things. "Sweet is the sleep of a labouring man. Enjoy life with the woman you love. Eat, drink, and enjoy the sun." That, ultimately, is the meaning of Sukkot as a whole. It is a festival of simple things. It is, Jewishly, the time we come closer to nature than any other, sitting in a hut with only leaves for a roof, and taking in our hands the unprocessed fruits and foliage of the palm branch, the citron, twigs of myrtle, and leaves of willow. It is a time when we briefly liberate ourselves from the sophisticated pleasures of the city and the processed artifacts of a technological age, and recapture some of the innocence we had when we were young, when the world still had the radiance of wonder.

REFLECT

Where do you find the most meaning in your life?

> "Kohelet's failure to find meaning is directly related to his obsession with the 'I' and the 'Me.'"

The power of Sukkot is that it takes us back to the most elemental roots of our being. You don't need to live in a palace to be surrounded by Clouds of Glory. You don't need to be rich to buy yourself the same leaves and fruit that a billionaire uses in worshipping God. Living in the sukka and inviting guests to your meal, you discover – such is the premise of *Ushpizin*, the mystical guests – that the people who have come to visit you are none other than Avraham, Yitzḥak, and Yaakov and their wives. What makes a hut more beautiful than a home is that when it comes to Sukkot, there is no difference between the richest of the rich and the poorest of the poor. We are all strangers on earth, temporary residents in God's almost eternal universe. And whether or not we are capable of pleasure, whether or not we have found happiness, we can all feel joy.

REFLECT

Where do you find the most joy in your life? Is your answer to this and the previous question the same?

Sukkot is the time we ask the most profound question of what makes a life worth living. Having prayed on Rosh HaShana and Yom Kippur to be written in the Book of Life, Sukkot and Kohelet force us to remember how brief life actually is, and how vulnerable. "Teach us rightly to number our days, that we may gain a heart of wisdom" (Tehillim 90:12). What matters is not how long we live, but how intensely we feel that life is a gift we repay by giving to others. Joy, the overwhelming theme of the festival, is what we feel when we know that it is a privilege simply to be alive, inhaling the intoxicating beauty of this moment amidst the profusion of nature, the teeming diversity of life, and the sense of communion with those many others with whom we share a history and a hope.

REFLECT

Take a moment to consider if you agree that it is a privilege to be alive, and how that understanding will impact the way you live your life.

Most majestically of all, Sukkot is the festival of insecurity. It is the candid acknowledgement that there is no life without risk, yet we can face the future without fear when we know we are not alone. God is with us, in the rain that brings blessings to the earth, in the love that brought the universe and us into being, and in the resilience of spirit that allowed a small and vulnerable people to outlive the greatest empires the world has ever known. Sukkot reminds us that God's glory was present in the small, portable *Mishkan* that Moshe and the Israelites built in the desert even more emphatically than in Shlomo HaMelekh's Temple with all its grandeur. A temple can be destroyed. But a sukka, broken, can be rebuilt tomorrow. Security is not something we can achieve physically but it is something we can

acquire mentally, psychologically, spiritually. All it needs is the courage and willingness to sit under the shadow of God's sheltering wings.

The sukka became in the course of time a symbol, not only of forty years in the wilderness, but of centuries of exile and dispersion. In the Middle Ages alone, Jews were expelled from England in 1290, from France several times (1182, 1322, 1394), from Vienna in 1421, Cologne in 1424, Bavaria in 1442, Milan in 1489, and most traumatically, from Spain in 1492. In the 1880s a wave of pogroms in Eastern Europe sent millions of Jews into flight to the West, and these migrations continue even today. Jewish history reads like a vast continuation of the stages of the Israelites' journey in the thirty-second chapter of the book of Bemidbar: "They travelled … and they encamped …. They travelled … and they encamped." Too often, home turned out to be no more than a temporary dwelling, a sukka. More than most, whether in the land of Israel or elsewhere, Jews have known the full force of insecurity.

Yet with its genius for the unexpected and its ability to rescue hope from tragedy, Judaism declared this festival of insecurity to be *zeman simḥateinu*, the season of our rejoicing. For the sukka, that quintessential symbol of vulnerability, turns out to be the embodiment of faith, the faith of a people who forty centuries ago set out on a risk-laden journey across a wilderness of space and time, with no more protection than the sheltering presence of the *Shekhina*. Sitting in the sukka under its canopy of leaves, I often think of my ancestors and their wanderings across Europe in search of safety, and I begin to understand how faith was their only home. It was fragile, chillingly exposed to the storms of prejudice and hate. But it proved stronger than superpowers and outlived them all.

Towards the end of his great book, *A History of the Jews*, Paul Johnson wrote:

> The Jews were not just innovators. They were also exemplars and epitomisers of the human condition. They seemed to present all the inescapable dilemmas of man in a heightened and clarified form …. The Jews were the emblem of homeless and vulnerable humanity. But is not the whole earth no more than a temporary transit camp?

Those words go to the heart of Sukkot. To know that life is full of risk and yet to affirm it, to sense the full insecurity of the human situation and yet to rejoice: this, for me, is the essence of faith. Judaism is no comforting illusion that all is well in this dark world. It is instead the courage to celebrate in the midst of uncertainty, and to rejoice even in the transitory shelter of the sukka, the Jewish symbol of home.

REFLECT

How can the message of Sukkot help us live through difficult times?

"The sukka, that quintessential symbol of vulnerability, turns out to be the embodiment of faith."

Adapted from the introduction to The Koren Sukkot Maḥzor *with commentary and translation by Rabbi Sacks.*

DEEP DIVING INTO THE *TEFILLA* OF THE DAY: BLESSING ON TAKING THE LULAV

סדר נטילת לולב

Some say the following:

יְהִי רָצוֹן מִלְּפָנֶיךָ ה׳ אֱלֹקַי וֵאלֹקֵי אֲבוֹתַי, בִּפְרִי עֵץ
הָדָר וְכַפֹּת תְּמָרִים וַעֲנַף עֵץ עָבֹת וְעַרְבֵי נַחַל, אוֹתִיּוֹת
שִׁמְךָ הַמְיֻחָד תִּקְרַב אֶחָד אֶל אֶחָד וְהָיוּ לַאֲחָדִים
בְּיָדִי, וְלֵידַע אֵיךְ שִׁמְךָ נִקְרָא עָלַי וְיִירְאוּ מִגֶּשֶׁת אֵלָי.
וּבְנַעְנוּעַי אוֹתָם תַּשְׁפִּיעַ שֶׁפַע בְּרָכוֹת מִדַּעַת עֶלְיוֹן
לְנֵוֵה אַפִּרְיוֹן לִמְכוֹן בֵּית אֱלֹקֵינוּ, וּתְהֵא חֲשׁוּבָה לְפָנֶיךָ
מִצְוַת אַרְבָּעָה מִינִים אֵלּוּ כְּאִלּוּ קִיַּמְתִּיהָ בְּכָל פְּרָטוֹתֶיהָ
וְשָׁרָשֶׁיהָ וְתַרְיַ״ג מִצְוֹת הַתְּלוּיוֹת בָּהּ, כִּי כַוָּנָתִי לְיַחֲדָא
שְׁמָא דְּקֻדְשָׁא בְּרִיךְ הוּא וּשְׁכִינְתֵּהּ בִּדְחִילוּ וּרְחִימוּ,
לְיַחֵד שֵׁם י״ה בו״ה בְּיִחוּדָא שְׁלִים בְּשֵׁם כָּל יִשְׂרָאֵל,
אָמֵן. בָּרוּךְ ה׳ לְעוֹלָם, אָמֵן וְאָמֵן:

The לולב is taken in the right hand, with the הדסים on the right, ערבות on the left. The אתרוג is taken in the left hand, with its pointed end towards the floor. Then say the following blessing:

בָּרוּךְ אַתָּה ה׳ אֱלֹקֵינוּ מֶלֶךְ הָעוֹלָם
אֲשֶׁר קִדְּשָׁנוּ בְּמִצְוֹתָיו וְצִוָּנוּ עַל נְטִילַת לוּלָב.

On the first day the לולב is taken, add:

בָּרוּךְ אַתָּה ה׳ אֱלֹקֵינוּ מֶלֶךְ הָעוֹלָם
שֶׁהֶחֱיָנוּ וְקִיְּמָנוּ וְהִגִּיעָנוּ לַזְּמַן הַזֶּה.

Invert the אתרוג, so that its pointed end is facing up, and wave the לולב and אתרוג in the following sequence, three times in each direction: ahead, right, back, left, up, down.

Blessing on Taking the Lulav

Some say the following:

יְהִי רָצוֹן May it be Your will, LORD my God and God of my fathers, that through the fruit of the citron tree, the palm frond, the myrtle branches, and willows of the brook, the letters of Your unique name draw close to one another and become united in my hand. Make it known I am called by Your name, so that [evil] will fear to come close to me. When I wave them, may a rich flow of blessings flow from the supreme Source of wisdom to the place of the Tabernacle and the site of the House of our God. May the command of these four species be considered by You as if I had fulfilled it in all its details and roots, as well as the 613 commandments dependent on it, for it is my intention to unify the name of the Holy One, blessed be He, and His Divine Presence, in reverence and love, to unify the name Yod-Heh with Vav-Heh, in perfect unity in the name of all Israel, Amen. Blessed is the LORD forever, Amen and Amen.

The lulav is taken in the right hand, with the myrtle leaves on the right, willow leaves on the left. The etrog is taken in the left hand, with its pointed end toward the floor. Then say the following blessing:

בָּרוּךְ Blessed are You, LORD our God, King of the Universe, who has made us holy through His commandments, and has commanded us about taking the lulav.

On the first day the lulav is taken, add:

בָּרוּךְ Blessed are You, LORD our God, King of the Universe, who has given us life, sustained us and brought us to this time.

Invert the etrog, so that its pointed end is facing up, and wave the lulav and etrog in the following sequence, three times in each direction: ahead, right, back, left, up, down.

Background to the *tefilla*

The *Arba Minim*, the "Four Species," is one of the central commands of the festival. The Torah specifies: "On the first day, you shall take for yourselves a fruit of the citron tree, palm fronds, myrtle branches, and willows of the brook, and be joyous in the presence of the Lord your God for seven days" (Vayikra 23:40).

What the Four Species have in common is that wherever you find them, there is water. They are the visible blessings of the rain that fell in the previous year. We bring them together now in thanks to God for the blessing of rain in the past year, and to pray for rain in the year to come.

The blessing we recite refers only to the lulav, since it is the tallest and most conspicuous of the four species. The lulav is waved in six directions: east, south, west, and north (i.e., straight ahead, right, rear, left), corresponding to the directions of the wind, then up and down. In each case it should be waved three times.

The Four Species represent four parts of the body. The lulav represents the spine, the myrtle the eyes, the willow the mouth, and the etrog the heart. As the etrog has both aroma and fruit, so there are those in the Jewish people who have knowledge of Torah and good deeds. As the palm tree has fruit but no aroma, so there are those in the Jewish people who have knowledge of the Torah but not good deeds. As the myrtle has aroma but no fruit, so there are those in the Jewish people who have good deeds but not knowledge of the Torah. And as the willow has neither aroma nor fruit, so there are those in the Jewish people who have neither Torah nor good deeds.

> "The Four Species are the visible blessings of the rain that fell in the previous year."

The Holy One, blessed be He, said: "To make it impossible for Israel to be destroyed, let all of them be bound together, and let each atone for the others" (*Pesikta DeRav Kahana* 27:9).

Analysis

The Four Species are a symbolic expression of our rejoicing that the Israelites left the wilderness, "a place with no grain or figs or vines or pomegranates; there was not even water to drink" (Bemidbar 20:25), and came to a country full of fruit trees and rivers. In order to remember this, we take the fruit which is the most pleasant of the land, branches that smell the best, the most beautiful leaves, and also the best of herbs, i.e., the willows of the brook. These four kinds have also these three purposes: First, they were plentiful in those days in the land of Israel so that everyone could easily get them. Secondly, they have a good appearance – they are green; some of them, namely the citron and the myrtle, are also excellent with regard to their smell, and the branches of the palm tree and the willow have neither good nor bad smell. Thirdly, they keep fresh and green for seven days, which is not the case with peaches, pomegranates, asparagus, nuts, and the like.

But is Israel really a land with plentiful water? Moshe described it to the people in a way that suggested it was not:

"The land you are entering to take over is not like the land of Egypt, from which you have come, where you planted your seed and irrigated it by foot as in a vegetable garden. But the land you are crossing the Jordan to take possession of is a land of mountains and valleys that drinks rain from heaven. It is a land the Lord your God cares for; the eyes of the Lord your God are continually on it from the beginning of the year to its end" (Devarim 11:10–12).

Israel would not have a regular, predictable water supply like the Tigris-Euphrates valley or the Nile Delta. It depends on rain, and in Israel rain is not something that can be taken for granted. Drought and famine led Avraham, Yitzḥak, and Yaakov into exile at some time in their lives.

The uncertainty of rain is another dimension of insecurity that frames Sukkot as a festival. The natural focus of attention for those who live in the land is to look up to heaven, rather than down to the naturally fertile earth. It meant the strongest possible connection between faith itself and the rainfall needed for the land to yield its produce, and for the nation to be able to celebrate a harvest of plenty. Israel is a land where the climate itself becomes a commentary on the faithfulness of the nation to God. Israel is the land of promise, but it will always depend on God's willingness to fulfil His promises.

The topography and climate of a country affects the culture and ethos of those who live there. In Mesopotamia and Egypt, the most powerful reality was the regularity of nature, the succession of the seasons which seemed to mirror the slow revolution of the stars. The cultures to which these cradles of civilisation gave rise were cosmological and their sense of time cyclical. The universe seemed to be ruled by the heavenly bodies whose hierarchy and order was replicated in the hierarchy and order of life on earth.

Israel, by contrast, was a land without regularities. There was no guarantee that next year the rain would fall, the earth would yield its crops, and the trees their fruit. So in Israel, a new sense of time was born – the time we call historical. Those who lived, or live, in Israel exist in a state of radical contingency. They can never take the future for granted. They depend on something other than nature. In Egypt, where the source of life was the Nile, you looked down. In Israel, where the source of life is rain, you had no choice but to look up.

When Moshe told the Israelites the full story about the land, he was telling them that it was a place where not just wheat and barley grow, but also the human spirit. It was the land where people are lifted beyond themselves because, time and again, they have to believe in a Being beyond themselves. Not accidentally but essentially, by its climate, topography, and location, Israel is the land where, merely to survive, the human eye must turn to heaven and the human ear to heaven's call.

Tefilla text and commentary taken from The Koren Sacks Sukkot Maḥzor *with commentary and translation by Rabbi Sacks.*

POINTS TO PONDER

1. *How do the Four Species connect us to the land of Israel, and how is this connected to the themes of Sukkot?*

2. *How does the land of Israel encourage the human spirit to grow?*

3. *Do you think that is still the case today?*

TOP TEN SUKKOT FACTS

1. Sukkot has three other names:
- *Ḥag HaAsif*, "The Festival of Gathering"
- *Ḥag*, "Festival"
- *Zeman Simḥateinu*, "The Time of Our Rejoicing"

2. Sukkot is a seven-day festival – the eighth day that follows it, Shemini Atzeret, is a separate festival.

3. Sukkot is one of the three annual *Shalosh Regalim* (the three pilgrimage festivals), when there was a special mitzva to travel to Jerusalem and participate in the Temple service (the other two pilgrimage festivals are Pesaḥ and Shavuot).

4. The main mitzva of Sukkot is to "live" in a sukka all eight days.

5. The *sekhakh* that forms the roof of the sukka must be made of organic material that has not been processed or made into something for another purpose.

6. The other unique mitzva of the festival of Sukkot is to take the *Arba Minim* – the Four Species.

The mitzva is fulfilled by waving them in six directions. The Four Species are:
- lulav (palm frond)
- etrog (citron)
- *hadassim* (myrtles)
- *aravot* (willows)

7. Each day of Sukkot (apart from Shabbat), we walk around the *bima* in *shul* while holding the Four Species and saying special prayers called *Hoshanot*.

8. The last day of the festival of Sukkot is called Hoshana Rabba (The Great Hoshana), when we circle the *bima* seven times with our lulav and etrog, saying *Hoshanot*.

9. During Temple times there were special joyous water-drawing celebrations called *Simḥat Beit HaSho'eva*, where water was poured over the altar.

10. Many people have the mystical custom to say *Ushpizin* in their sukka: seven biblical characters are welcomed to the sukka, a different one each night.

IT ONCE HAPPENED...

Rabbi Pinchas of Koretz was famous for his wisdom, and his house was always full of people seeking his advice. He found that this gave him no time to study or write the books he wished to write.

One year, he finally decided to refuse to see any more people, so that he could concentrate on study and prayer. As Sukkot approached, he invited a number of people to be his guests during the festival, but they were upset by his decision to shut himself away from the community, and they refused his invitation.

On the first night of Sukkot, as he sat alone in his sukka, he recited the *Ushpizin*, inviting Avraham to be his guest.

In a vision, he saw Avraham standing outside his sukka, refusing to enter. "Why will you not enter?" asked the rabbi. Avraham replied, "I will not enter a place where there are no other guests." Rabbi Pinchas, realising his mistake, once again opened his home to the whole community.

POINTS TO PONDER

1. *What lesson did Rabbi Pinchas learn in this story?*

2. *Why do you think it was Avraham who appeared to Rabbi Pinchas in the vision?*

3. *What is the connection between the mitzva of hospitality and the themes of Sukkot?*

ḤIDON ON THE ḤAG
(A QUICK QUIZ)

1. What are the other three names for the festival of Sukkot?

2. According to the Torah, why do we sit in the sukka on Sukkot?

3. How many walls must a sukka have?

4. What must the *sekhakh* for the sukka be made from?

5. What are the *Arba Minim*?

6. When do we have a mitzva to take the *Arba Minim*? When do we not?

7. What is *Ushpizin*?

8. Which *megilla* is read on Sukkot?

9. What is the *Simḥat Beit HaSho'eva*?

10. How many times do we walk around the *bima* on Hoshana Rabba?

EDUCATIONAL COMPANION TO THE QUESTIONS

SUKKOT IN A NUTSHELL

1. The three approaches are:

   i.   The sukka represents the Clouds of Glory that surrounded the Israelites during the wilderness years (R. Eliezer).

   ii. Sukkot exists to remind us of our humble origins so that we never fall into the complacency of taking for granted our freedom, the land of Israel, and the blessings it yields (R. Akiva according to Rashbam).

   iii. The sukka represents the courage the Israelites had to travel, to move, to leave security behind, and to follow God's call (R. Akiva according to Rabbi Sacks).

2. The underlying theme of Rosh HaShana and Yom Kippur is the fragility of life and how dependent we are on God for our well-being. We acknowledge this on these days and put our faith in God that He will do what is best for us. These themes are also found in the festival of Sukkot, as seen in the three approaches outlined in answer 1.

3. Examples can be found in every age of exile, when Jews often lived through persecution and uncertainty, yet kept their faith always and managed to hand on their love of Judaism to their children. Examples of these periods in Jewish history include the Crusades in the twelfth and thirteenth centuries, the expulsion from Spain in the fifteenth century, and the Holocaust in the twentieth century.

DEEP DIVING INTO THE *TEFILLA* OF THE DAY

1. The Four Species are all native to the land of Israel and can be found there in plentiful numbers. They represent the beauty and fertility of the land. But they are all species that require much water to grow. This connects us to Sukkot's themes of water and our dependence on God for water and all sustenance.

2. While other nations that have more reliable sources of water and therefore a more stable material life may live with an innate sense of security, the climate of the land of Israel causes its inhabitants to continuously look to God for rain and sustenance, thereby always encouraging spiritual growth as they examine their deeds and constantly strive to improve themselves so they are deserving of God's help.

3. While today we have technology that can help us live in an arid climate that has no reliable water source (such as the Middle East), we are still dependent on rain, and are not completely independent of the need for natural water sources. However, modern Jewish history has shown us that there are many other existential threats for the Jewish people who live in the land of Israel. Perhaps we can see these as a modern-day version of needing to continuously connect to God for protection and pray for our very survival.

IT ONCE HAPPENED ON SUKKOT...

1. There are various Jewish values that can sometimes compete with each other. In this case, the conflicting values were the study of Torah and the mitzva of hospitality and *ḥesed* (loving-kindness). The lesson he learned was that mitzvot concerning other people take priority over mitzvot that are more concerned with our own spiritual well-being and our personal connection with God.

2. Avraham is the first of the biblical guests we invite into our sukka during the custom of reciting *Ushpizin* (a different personality is invited in on each night of Sukkot). Avraham is also the most appropriate person from Jewish history to teach Rabbi Pinchas this message because he represented the core values of *ḥesed* and *hakhnasat orḥim* (hospitality), as shown in the story of the angels who came to visit him (Bereshit ch. 18).

3. One of the themes of Sukkot is God's protection and love for us in the desert as we travelled between

Egypt and the land of Israel. The mitzvot of hospitality and *ḥesed* in general are a way for us to be like God and behave in the same way towards our neighbours and friends.

ḤIDON ON THE ḤAG (A QUICK QUIZ)

1. *Ḥag HaAsif*, "The Festival of Gathering"; *Ḥag*, "Festival"; *Zeman Simḥateinu*, "The Time of Our Rejoicing."
2. To remember the way the Israelites lived in the wilderness after they left Egypt and journeyed to the land of Israel.
3. Two and a half (minimum).
4. Something natural that once grew, but is no longer growing, and that has not been manufactured into a utensil of some sort.
5. Lulav (palm frond), etrog (citron), *hadassim* (myrtles), *aravot* (willows).
6. On each of the seven days of Sukkot (except when it is also Shabbat). We do not have a mitzva to take the *Arba Minim* on Shemini Atzeret/Simḥat Torah.
7. *Ushpizin* is a mystical custom of inviting a different biblical character into the sukka each night of Sukkot.
8. Kohelet (Ecclesiastes).
9. Special joyous water-drawing celebrations of the Temple period during which water was poured over the altar.
10. Seven times.

Shemini Atzeret and Simḥat Torah

SHEMINI ATZERET AND SIMḤAT TORAH IN A NUTSHELL

Shemini Atzeret is a strange day in the Jewish calendar. It is described as the eighth day, and thus part of Sukkot, but it is also designated by a name of its own, Atzeret. Is it, or is it not, a separate festival in its own right? It seems to be both. How are we to understand this?

What guided the Sages was the detail that whereas on the seven days of Sukkot seventy young bulls were offered in the Temple, on Atzeret, the eighth day, there was only one. Connecting this to Zekharya's prophecy that in the Messianic time, all nations would celebrate Sukkot, they concluded that the seventy sacrifices of Sukkot represented the seventy nations of the world as described in chapter 10 of Bereshit. Even though Zekharya's vision had not yet been realised, it was as if all humanity were in some sense present in Jerusalem on the festival, and sacrifices were made on their behalf. On the eighth day, as they were leaving, God was inviting the Jewish people to a small private reception. The word "*atzeret*" itself was interpreted to mean, "Stop, stay a while." Shemini Atzeret was private time between God and His people. It was a day of particularity (between God and His people) after the universality of the seven days of Sukkot (a festival for all the nations, at least in Messianic times).

In February 1997, then-president of the State of Israel, Ezer Weizman, paid the first, and thus far the only, state visit to Britain as the guest of Her Majesty the Queen. The custom was that on the first night of such a visit, the queen hosted a state banquet at Buckingham

Palace. It was, for the Jews present, a unique and moving moment to hear *HaTikva* played in the banqueting hall of the palace, and to hear the queen propose a toast to the president with the word "*Leḥayim.*"

There is a protocol for such visits. Present are many representative figures, ambassadors, members of the government, and other members of the royal family. At the end of the evening, after most of the guests have taken their leave, there is a small and intimate gathering of just a few individuals – on that occasion, the queen, Prince Philip, the Queen Mother, the prime minister, and a few others – for a more relaxed and personal conversation with the guest of honour. It was this kind of occasion, with its royal protocol, that best illustrates how the Sages understood Shemini Atzeret.

Simḥat Torah (celebrated the day after Shemini Atzeret in the Diaspora, and combined into one day in Israel, as there is only one day of Yom Tov) is unique among festivals. It is not mentioned in the Torah, nor in the Talmud. Unlike Purim and Ḥanukka, it was not formalised by any decision on the part of the religious authorities, nor does it commemorate any historical deliverance. It grew from the grassroots, slowly developing over time.

It was born in Babylon, probably at the end of the period of the *Amora'im*, the Rabbis of the Talmud, in the fifth or sixth century. The Babylonian custom – now universal – was to divide the Torah into fifty-four portions to be read in the course of a year (in Israel there was a three- or three-and-a-half-year cycle). On the second day of Shemini Atzeret in Babylon (there was no second day in Israel), the custom was to read the last portion of the Torah, in which Moshe blessed the nation at the end of his life.

It had long been the custom to make a celebration on completing a section of study, a talmudic tractate, or an order of the Mishna (Shabbat 118b). Thus, the custom evolved to make a celebration at the completion of the Mosaic books, and it was considered a great honour to be called to the Torah for this last portion. The celebration became known as Simḥat Torah.

POINTS TO PONDER

1. *What themes of Sukkot are universal and relevant to all of humanity?*

2. *Does Shemini Atzeret mean that God loves the Jewish people more than His other creations?*

3. *Do you think that the source of Simḥat Torah (not the Torah or the Talmud, but the people) makes it less or more meaningful as a ḥag?*

WHAT SHEMINI ATZERET AND SIMḤAT TORAH TEACH US TODAY

SHEMINI ATZERET

Sukkot represents more clearly than any other festival the dualities of Judaism. The Four Species (lulav, etrog, *hadassim*, and *aravot*) are a symbol of the land of Israel, while the sukka reminds us of exile. The Four Species are a ritual of rain, while eating in the sukka depends on the absence of rain. Above all, though, there is the tension between the universality of nature and the particularity of history. There is an aspect of Sukkot – rainfall, harvest, climate – to which everyone can relate, but there is another – the long journey through the wilderness – that speaks to the unique experience of the Jewish people.

This tension between the universal and the particular is unique to Judaism. The God of Israel is the God of all humanity, but the religion of Israel is not the religion of all humanity. It is conspicuous that while the other two Abrahamic monotheisms, Christianity and Islam, borrowed much from Judaism, they did not borrow this. They became universalist faiths, believing that everyone ought to embrace the one true religion, their own, and that those who do not are denied the blessings of eternity.

Judaism disagrees. For this it was derided for many centuries, and to some degree it still is today. Why, if it represents religious truth, is it not to be shared with everyone? If there is only one God, why is there not only one way to salvation? There is no doubt that if Judaism had become an evangelising, conversion-driven religion – as it would have had to, had it believed in universalism – there would be many more Jews than there are today. A recent study (the Pew Report, undertaken in 2015) found that there are an estimated 2.3 billion Christians, 1.8 billion Muslims, and only 14 million Jews. The disparity is vast.

Judaism is the road less travelled, because it represents a complex truth that could not be expressed in any other way. The Torah tells a simple story. God gave humans the gift of freedom, which they then used not to enhance creation but to endanger it. Adam and Ḥava broke the first prohibition. Kayin, the first human child, became the first murderer. Within a remarkably short space of time, all flesh had corrupted its way on earth, the world was filled with violence, and only one man, Noaḥ, found favour in God's eyes. After the Flood, God made a covenant with Noaḥ, and through him with all humanity, but after the hubris of the builders of the Tower of Bavel, God chose another way. Having established a basic threshold in the form of the Noahide Laws, He then chose one man, one family, and eventually one nation, to become a living example of what it is to exist closely and continuously in the presence of God. There are, in the affairs of humankind, universal laws and specific examples. The Noahide covenant constitutes the universal laws. The way of life of Avraham and his descendants is the example.

REFLECT

If the national mission of the Jewish people is to model the universal values of the Torah, are we doing a good job?

What this means in Judaism is that the righteous of all the nations have a share in the World to Come (Sanhedrin 105a). In contemporary terms it means that our common humanity precedes our religious differences. It also means that by creating all humans in His image, God set us the challenge of seeing His image in one who is not in our image: whose colour, culture, class, and creed are different from our own. The ultimate spiritual challenge is to see the trace of God in the face of a stranger.

Zekharya, in the vision we read as the *haftara* for the first day of Sukkot, puts this precisely. He says that in the End of Days, "the Lord shall be king over all the earth; on that day the Lord shall be One and His name One" (Zekharya 14:9), meaning that all the nations will recognise the sovereignty of a single transcendent God. Yet at the same time, Zekharya envisages the nations participating only in Sukkot, the most universal of the festivals, and the one in which they have the greatest interest since they all need rain. He does not envisage them becoming Jews, accepting the "yoke of the commands," all 613 of them. He does not speak of their conversion. The practical outcome of this dual theology – the universality of God and the particularity of Torah – is that we are commanded to be true to our faith, and a blessing to others, regardless of their faith. That is the Jewish way.

REFLECT

What makes all of humanity the same? What makes Jews different?

Shemini Atzeret reminds us of the intimacy Jews have always felt in the presence of God. The cathedrals of Europe convey a sense of the vastness of God and the smallness of humankind. The small *shuls* of Tzefat, where the Arizal and Rabbi Yosef Karo prayed, convey a sense of the closeness of God and the greatness of humankind. Jews, except when they sought to imitate other nations, did not build cathedrals. Even the Temple reached its greatest architectural grandeur under Herod, a man better known for his political ruthlessness than his spiritual sensibilities.

So when all the universality of Judaism has been expressed, there remains something that cannot be universalised: that sense of intimacy with, and closeness to, God that we feel on Shemini Atzeret, when all the other guests have left. Shemini Atzeret is chamber music, not a symphony. It is quiet time with God. We are reluctant to leave, and we dare to think that He is reluctant to see us go. Justice is universal; love is particular. There are some things we share because we are human. But there are other things, constitutive of our identity, that are uniquely ours – most importantly our relationships to those who form our family. On Sukkot we are among strangers and friends. On Shemini Atzeret we are with family.

SIMḤAT TORAH

The emergence of Simḥat Torah signals something remarkable. You may have noticed that Sukkot and Shemini Atzeret are both described as *zeman simḥateinu*, the season of our joy. The nature of that joy was clear and signalled in different ways both by the sukka and by the Four Species. The sukka reminded the people how blessed they were to be living in Israel when they recalled how their ancestors had to live for forty years without a land or a permanent home. The lulav, etrog, *hadassim*, and *aravot* were a vivid demonstration of the fruitfulness of the land under the divine blessing of rain. The joy of Sukkot was the joy of living in the Promised Land.

But by the time Simḥat Torah had spread throughout the Jewish world, Jews had lost virtually everything: their land, their home, their freedom and independence, the Temple, the priesthood, the sacrificial order – all that had once been their source of joy. A single devastating sentence in one of the *piyutim* of Ne'ila (at the close of Yom Kippur) summed up their situation: *"Ein shiur rak haTorah hazot,"* "Nothing remains but this Torah." All that remained was a book.

Saadia Gaon, writing in the tenth century, asked a simple question. In virtue of what was the Jewish people still a nation? It had none of the normal preconditions of a nation. Jews were scattered throughout the world. They did not live in the same territory. They were not part of a single economic or political order. They did not share the same culture. They did not speak the same language. Rashi spoke French, Rambam Arabic. Yet they were, and were seen to be, one nation, bound by a bond of collective destiny and responsibility. Hence Saadia concluded: Our people is a people only in virtue of our Torah (*Beliefs and Opinions*, 3). In the lovely rabbinic phrase about the Ark, which contained the tablets: "It carried those who carried it" (Sota 35a). More than the Jewish people preserved the Torah, the Torah preserved the Jewish people.

It was, as we say in our prayers, "our life and the length of our days." It was the legacy of their past and the promise of their future. It was their marriage contract with God, the record of the covenant that bound them unbreakably together. They had lost their world but they still had God's word, and it was enough.

More than enough. On Simḥat Torah, without being commanded by any verse in the Torah or any decree of the Rabbis, Jews throughout

REFLECT

How could we find joy if we had lost everything as a people?

> "More than the Jewish people preserved the Torah, the Torah preserved the Jewish people."

the world sang and danced and recited poems in honour of the Torah, exactly as if they were dancing in the courtyard of the Temple at the *Simḥat Beit HaSho'eva*, or as if they were King David bringing the Ark to Jerusalem. They were determined to show God, and the world, that they could still be *akh same'aḥ*, as the Torah said about Sukkot: wholly, totally given over to joy. It would be hard to find a parallel in the entire history of the human spirit of a people capable of such joy at a time when they were being massacred in the name of the God of love and compassion.

A people that can walk through the valley of the shadow of death and still rejoice is a people that cannot be defeated by any force or any fear. Rambam writes (*Hilkhot Shofar* 8:15) that to experience joy in the fulfilment of a mitzva out of the love of God is to touch the spiritual heights. Whoever stands on their dignity and regards such things as beneath them is, he says, a sinner and a fool, and whoever abandons their dignity for the sake of joy is thereby elevated "because there is no greatness or honour higher than celebrating before God."

Simḥat Torah was born when the Jews had lost everything else, but they never lost their capacity to rejoice. Neḥemya was right when he said to the people weeping as they listened to the Torah, realising how far they had drifted from it: "Do not grieve, for the joy of the Lord is your strength" (Neḥemya 8:10). A people whose capacity for joy cannot be destroyed is itself indestructible.

REFLECT

How will you continue to find joy this Simḥat Torah despite the difficulties and challenges you have experienced over the past year?

Adapted from the introduction to The Koren Sukkot Maḥzor *with commentary and translation by Rabbi Sacks.*

Simchat Torah *by Sefira Lightstone*

DEEP DIVING INTO THE *TEFILLA* OF THE DAY: THE *HAKAFOT* OF SIMḤAT TORAH

סדר הקפות

אַתָּה הָרְאֵתָ לָדַעַת, כִּי ה' הוּא הָאֱלֹקִים, אֵין עוֹד מִלְבַדּוֹ:

לְעֹשֵׂה נִפְלָאוֹת גְּדֹלוֹת לְבַדּוֹ, כִּי לְעוֹלָם חַסְדּוֹ:

אֵין־כָּמוֹךָ בָאֱלֹקִים, ה', וְאֵין כְּמַעֲשֶׂיךָ:

יְהִי כְבוֹד ה' לְעוֹלָם, יִשְׂמַח ה' בְּמַעֲשָׂיו:

יְהִי שֵׁם ה' מְבֹרָךְ, מֵעַתָּה וְעַד־עוֹלָם:

יְהִי ה' אֱלֹקֵינוּ עִמָּנוּ, כַּאֲשֶׁר הָיָה עִם־אֲבֹתֵינוּ אַל־יַעַזְבֵנוּ וְאַל־יִטְּשֵׁנוּ:

וְאִמְרוּ, הוֹשִׁיעֵנוּ אֱלֹקֵי יִשְׁעֵנוּ, וְקַבְּצֵנוּ וְהַצִּילֵנוּ מִן־הַגּוֹיִם לְהֹדוֹת לְשֵׁם קָדְשֶׁךָ, לְהִשְׁתַּבֵּחַ בִּתְהִלָּתֶךָ:

ה' מֶלֶךְ, ה' מָלָךְ, ה' יִמְלֹךְ לְעוֹלָם וָעֶד.

ה' עֹז לְעַמּוֹ יִתֵּן, ה' יְבָרֵךְ אֶת־עַמּוֹ בַשָּׁלוֹם:

וְיִהְיוּ נָא אֲמָרֵינוּ לְרָצוֹן, לִפְנֵי אֲדוֹן כֹּל.

וַיְהִי בִּנְסֹעַ הָאָרֹן וַיֹּאמֶר מֹשֶׁה קוּמָה ה' וְיָפֻצוּ אֹיְבֶיךָ, וְיָנֻסוּ מְשַׂנְאֶיךָ מִפָּנֶיךָ:

קוּמָה ה' לִמְנוּחָתֶךָ, אַתָּה וַאֲרוֹן עֻזֶּךָ:

כֹּהֲנֶיךָ יִלְבְּשׁוּ־צֶדֶק, וַחֲסִידֶיךָ יְרַנֵּנוּ:

בַּעֲבוּר דָּוִד עַבְדֶּךָ, אַל־תָּשֵׁב פְּנֵי מְשִׁיחֶךָ:

וְאָמַר בַּיּוֹם הַהוּא, הִנֵּה אֱלֹקֵינוּ זֶה קִוִּינוּ לוֹ, וְיוֹשִׁיעֵנוּ זֶה ה' קִוִּינוּ לוֹ, נָגִילָה וְנִשְׂמְחָה בִּישׁוּעָתוֹ:

מַלְכוּתְךָ מַלְכוּת כָּל־עֹלָמִים, וּמֶמְשַׁלְתְּךָ בְּכָל־דּוֹר וָדֹר:

כִּי מִצִּיּוֹן תֵּצֵא תוֹרָה, וּדְבַר־ה' מִירוּשָׁלָיִם:

אַב הָרַחֲמִים, הֵיטִיבָה בִרְצוֹנְךָ אֶת־צִיּוֹן, תִּבְנֶה חוֹמוֹת יְרוּשָׁלָיִם:

כִּי בְךָ לְבַד בָּטַחְנוּ, מֶלֶךְ קֵל רָם וְנִשָּׂא, אֲדוֹן עוֹלָמִים.

HAKAFOT

אַתָּה הָרְאֵתָ You have been shown [these things]
so that you may know that the Lord is God;
besides Him there is no other.
To the One who alone does great wonders,
His loving-kindness is forever.
There is none like You among the heavenly powers, my Lord,
and there are no works like Yours.
May the Lord's glory be forever;
may the Lord rejoice in His works.
May the Lord's name be blessed from now and forever.
May the Lord our God be with us
as He was with our ancestors;
may He never leave us or forsake us.
Say, "Save us, God our Saviour;
gather and deliver us from the nations,
that we may give thanks to Your holy name,
that we may glory in Your praise."
The Lord is King, the Lord was King,
the Lord will be King for ever and all time.
The Lord will give strength to His people;
the Lord will bless His people with peace.
May our words find favour before the Lord of all.

Whenever the Ark set out, Moses would say,
"Arise, Lord, and may Your enemies be scattered;
may those who hate You flee before You."
Advance, Lord, to Your resting place,
You and Your mighty Ark.
Your priests are clothed in righteousness,
and Your devoted ones sing for joy.
For the sake of Your servant David,
do not reject Your anointed one.
In that day they will say,
"This is our God; we trusted in Him, and He saved us.
This is the Lord, we trusted in Him;
let us rejoice and be glad in His salvation."
Your kingdom is an eternal kingdom,
and Your dominion is for all generations.
For the Torah shall come forth from Zion
and the word of the Lord from Jerusalem.

Father of compassion, favour Zion with Your goodness;
rebuild the walls of Jerusalem.
For we trust in You alone, King, God, high and exalted,
Master of worlds.

Background to the *Tefilla*

Simḥat Torah as the name of the ninth day of Sukkot roughly dates back to Babylon in the eighth century. It began as the convergence of two distinct customs. The first was the Torah reading of the day, namely the passage at the end of the Torah in which Moshe blesses the tribes ("This is the blessing," Devarim 33:1). The other was the long-established custom of making a festivity at the conclusion of the study of a text – an order of the Mishna, for example, or the conclusion of a talmudic tractate (Shabbat 118b).

The day on which the Torah readings were completed was already known as Simḥat Torah by around the eighth century, and other customs rapidly followed. One was the practice of beginning the Torah anew immediately after the completion, so that the charge could never be levelled against the Jewish people that having reached the end of the Torah, they stopped, or even paused. Hence the reading of the beginning of Bereshit immediately after the conclusion of Devarim. The two honours of being called to read out the ending and the beginning were greatly prized, and soon became known by the name of ḥatan, bridegroom – ḥatan Torah for the former, ḥatan Bereshit for the latter. By the eleventh century the custom had already been established in many communities to call up every adult male to the Torah on that day. Shortly thereafter, we developed the custom of collectively calling up *kol hane'arim*, "all the children." The practice of *Hakafot*, walking around the *bima* seven times in procession holding the Torah scrolls, as was done with the Four Species on Hoshana Rabba, came later, originating in the mystical circle around Rabbi Yitzhak Luria in Tzefat in the late sixteenth century, at roughly the same time and in the same place that the service known as *Kabbalat Shabbat* was born.

Analysis

Simḥat Torah is one of the profoundest expressions of the Jewish spirit. The other festivals were either ordained by the Torah or, in the case of Purim and Ḥanukka, formally instituted to recall an event where the Jewish people were saved. Simḥat Torah, by contrast, emerged through a series of customs that rapidly spread throughout the Jewish world. It is what the mystics called *itaruta deletata*, an "awakening from below" – an initiative that emerged from the Jewish people itself. Through it, we recapture some of the joy and exuberance that marked the *Simḥat Beit HaSho'eva* celebrations in Jerusalem in Temple times. More than that: we turn the day into a wedding, in which the Jewish people is the groom, and the Torah the bride. As the Rabbis said, re-interpreting the verse "Moshe commanded us the Torah as the heritage of the congregation of Yaakov" – read not "heritage" (*morasha*) but "betrothed" (*me'orata*) (Devarim 33:4, Berakhot 57a). Never has a book been loved more.

The custom of reciting a long sequence of verses prior to taking out the Torah scrolls from the Ark (beginning with *Ata Hareta*/You have been shown) is first mentioned in the *Maḥzor Vitry*, a work emanating

---

POINTS TO PONDER

1. *Why is it important to celebrate the completion of a unit of study?*

2. *Why is it important to immediately begin the Torah cycle again?*

3. *Why do you think Simḥat Torah became so important for the people after the destruction of the Temple, during their exile from the land of Israel?*

> "Simḥat Torah is one of the profoundest expressions of the Jewish spirit."

from the school of Rashi in eleventh-century France. This *tefilla* includes not only the verses usually said on Shabbat or festivals on taking out the scrolls, but also others added in honour of the occasion.

Tefilla text and commentary taken from The Koren Sacks Sukkot Maḥzor *with commentary and translation by Rabbi Sacks.*

TOP TEN SHEMINI ATZERET AND SIMḤAT TORAH FACTS

1. Shemini Atzeret means "The Assembly of the Eighth Day."

2. There is a difference of opinion in the Talmud as to whether Shemini Atzeret is the eighth day of Sukkot or an independent festival of its own.

3. Some Jews in the Diaspora eat in the sukka on Shemini Atzeret, but do not make the *berakha* of "*Leishev BaSukka.*"

4. In Israel, Shemini Atzeret and Simḥat Torah are celebrated on the same day.

5. We begin praying for rain on Shemini Atzeret with the special *Tefillat Geshem* (Prayer for Rain) said during Musaf. This is reflected in the addition of the line "*Mashiv haruaḥ umorid hagashem*" ("He makes the wind blow and the rain fall") said in our private *Amida* on weekdays, from Shemini Atzeret until Pesaḥ.

6. The *ḥazan* who leads the *Geshem* prayer wears a white *kittel* just like on Rosh HaShana and Yom Kippur, because we pray for a favourable judgement for the world's rain in the coming year.

7. Some communities have the custom to read from the Torah on Simḥat Torah night. This is the only time in the year when the Torah is read publicly at night.

8. On Simḥat Torah we dance around the *shul bima* seven times, carrying the Torah scrolls as we go. These circuits are called *Hakafot*.

9. Many communities give every adult male an *aliya laTorah* (calling them to the reading of the Torah), which means the last part of the Torah is read many times over.

10. It is a special honour to be chosen to be the *ḥatan Torah* who completes the year's cycle, and to be chosen as the *ḥatan Bereshit*, the first person called for the new cycle.

IT ONCE HAPPENED...

Two brothers who were both famous hasidic rebbes, Reb Elimelekh of Lizhensk and Reb Zusha of Anipoli, were once arrested on false charges.

As the guard threw them into the cramped cell, already full of criminals and thugs, he pointed to a bucket in the corner and laughed as he told them this was their toilet.

Reb Zusha broke down and flung himself at the door of the cell, weeping.

Reb Elimelekh was taken aback. This was not like Zusha, who had pure faith that everything God did was for the good.

"Zusha, pull yourself together!" Elimelekh cried to his brother. "This is a *ḥillul Hashem* (a desecration of God's name); everyone thinks you have lost faith and hope!"

Reb Zusha turned to his brother and asked him tearfully, "How can you not cry? We are stuck here in this cell with this bucket, and because of it, the halakha is that we cannot study Torah or *daven*, or even think about Torah. What are we going to do? How can we live without any Torah, mitzvot, or prayers?"

Reb Elimelekh thought deeply about the situation and then he jumped up in joy. He explained excitedly to his brother that by not learning or *davening*, they were actually keeping the halakha to the letter of the law! So in fact all of their non-learning and non-*davening* was serving God in the most challenging way for them. "It's incredible," he said. "Every second that we are here, we do a mitzva by not studying Torah. When else will we ever have such a holy opportunity to serve God by not serving Him?"

Reb Zusha's face lit up, and he began to smile, and then laugh, and then dance. He picked up the bucket and began to dance with it, elevating it above his head as if it were a *sefer Torah* on Simḥat Torah! "How fortunate are we that we get a mitzva with this! How incredible is God that He gave us such a commandment!"

When their cellmates saw this bizarre behaviour, they thought the brothers had lost their minds. But one of them suggested that the Rabbis were praying to their God for a miracle to set them free, and before long they had all joined in, making circuits around the cell, dancing with the bucket.

When the guard heard all the commotion and saw what was going on, he soon put an end to it by confiscating the bucket. "From now on, anyone who needs to relieve himself will do so outside the cell!" he barked at them.

The cellmates collapsed in disappointment, but the brothers continued to dance, this time reciting at the top of their voices words from their holy Torah with pure joy, "*Shema Yisrael, Hashem Elokeinu, Hashem eḥad,*" for now they were permitted to learn the sweet words of their beloved holy Torah once again!

POINTS TO PONDER

1. *Why was the absence of learning Torah and praying something to celebrate?*

2. *What message can we take for our lives from the attitude and approach of the two brothers in the cell?*

3. *How can this story help us to appreciate the festival of Simḥat Torah?*

ḤIDON ON THE ḤAG
(A QUICK QUIZ)

1. What is the date of Shemini Atzeret?

2. What do the words "Shemini Atzeret" mean?

3. Is Shemini Atzeret part of the festival of Sukkot or a separate festival of its own?

4. Do we shake the *Arba Minim* on Shemini Atzeret?

5. How many *Hakafot* are there on Simḥat Torah?

6. Traditionally, who is asked to take the *sifrei Torah* out of the Ark for the first *Hakafa*?

7. Who gets called to the Torah for the *Kol Hane'arim aliya*?

8. After everyone has been called to the Torah on Simḥat Torah, how many *sifrei Torah* are removed again and read (and what is read from each of them)?

9. What is the title given to the last person called to the Torah before we complete the cycle of its reading, and what is the title of the first person called to the Torah for the new cycle?

10. What is the connection between sweets and Simḥat Torah?

EDUCATIONAL COMPANION TO THE QUESTIONS

SHEMINI ATZERET AND SIMḤAT TORAH IN A NUTSHELL

1. Sukkot has become known as the universal festival because the cumulative number of sacrifices brought on the seven days of Sukkot was seventy young bulls, and these could be said to represent the seventy nations of the world. Moreover, there are additional themes found in Sukkot that are universal and connected to all of humanity. These include the fragility of human life and our need for God's protection, the importance of water in our lives, and our general connection to nature. See the chapter on Sukkot, beginning on page 27, for more on this.

2. God's intimate relationship with the Jewish people (as embodied in the festival of Shemini Atzeret) does not mean He does not have intimate relationships with other nations. This is not the only interpretation of the term "chosen people" (which can just as easily be interpreted as a calling to a national mission). Judaism's approach to the particular relationship between God and the Jewish people is a model for all other national relationships with God (in a universal context).

3. It could be argued that as Simḥat Torah is not a biblical festival (such as Sukkot) and is not a rabbinically instituted festival commemorating a historical event (such as Ḥanukka or Purim), it therefore has less significance and meaning. However, it developed over time as an expression of the people's love of Torah and of the mitzva of learning Torah, and this gives the festival deep significance and importance.

DEEP DIVING INTO THE *TEFILLA* OF THE DAY

1. Completing a unit of study gives us a sense of accomplishment and encourages us to continue on to future achievements. Celebrating this completion expresses the value we find in what we have learned and the hope that we will return to it again in the future.

2. It is important to avoid "resting on our laurels" and taking a break from the important acts of study and spiritual growth. So we begin the new cycle immediately, continuing our journey of intellectual and spiritual development. This is also an important statement that we do not believe we have learned everything there is to learn, and instead we are eager to revisit the Torah with a new perspective in the hope of finding new insights.

3. After the destruction of the Temple and the exile and dispersion from the land of Israel, Judaism, which was previously a centralised Temple-focused system of worship, had to make a paradigm shift in order to survive and thrive in exile. Learning Torah itself, which could be taken with us wherever we found ourselves, and which united the dispersed and fractured Jewish people, became critical to Jewish survival and for the survival of Judaism. For this reason, Simḥat Torah, as a celebration of the Torah and the mitzva of learning Torah, became hugely important to the Jewish people.

IT ONCE HAPPENED...

1. For these two hasidic masters, the chance to serve God in any possible way was their first priority. In this case, they could serve God by refraining from learning Torah and praying, because the halakha forbids this in the presence of a toilet. They were happy that by abstaining from doing these mitzvot they were, in fact, following the halakha and therefore serving God.

2. Life rarely goes exactly according to plan. Throughout our lives there will be disappointments big and small, and things we cannot control. What we can control is how we react to these setbacks. The two rabbis reframed their experience in a radical way, and then found the opportunity for joy and service of God within the limitations of their situation. This is a powerful lesson for us, showing us that happiness and joy are intrinsic (dependent only on ourselves and our mindset) and not just based on external factors.

3. Despite their extreme restrictions, the brothers found a way to connect to the Torah from deep love, and this gave them joy. Similarly, when the Jewish people were exiled from their land, our rabbis were forced to pivot and refocus Judaism. One of the ways they did this was to allocate an annual celebration of Torah study – Simhat Torah. The Rabbis refused to despair when all seemed lost, but rather they refocused and reframed Jewish life, finding a new way, much like the Rabbis in our story. Sometimes we also find ourselves in times of restrictions and limitations, and when this happens, we too must find new and meaningful ways to connect to the mitzvot.

ḤIDON ON THE *ḤAG* (A QUICK QUIZ)

1. Twenty-second of Tishrei.
2. "Assembly of the Eighth Day."

3. Both. Both opinions are found in the Talmud.
4. No.
5. Seven.
6. The *kohanim*.
7. All the children of the community (and one adult, as an honour).
8. Three: one to complete the book of Devarim, one to start the book of Bereshit, and one to read the *maftir*.
9. *Ḥatan Torah* and *Ḥatan Bereshit*.
10. There is none! But because the day is one of fun and celebration, we make it as appealing to children as possible. Many communities therefore give out sweets to the children.

Ḥanukka

ḤANUKKA IN A NUTSHELL

Ḥanukka is the festival on which Jews celebrate their victory in the fight for religious freedom more than two thousand years ago. In 165 BCE Antiochus IV, ruler of the Syrian branch of the Alexandrian empire, began to impose Greek culture on the Jews of the land of Israel. He placed a statue of Zeus in Jerusalem and banned Jewish religious rituals such as circumcision and Shabbat. Those who continued to observe them were persecuted. This was an existential threat to Judaism as a religious civilisation.

A group of Jewish warriors rose in rebellion. Led by a priest, Mattityahu of Modi'in, and his son Yehuda the Maccabee, they began the fight for liberty. Outnumbered, they suffered heavy initial casualties, but within three years they had secured a momentous victory. Jerusalem was restored to Jewish hands and the *Beit HaMikdash* was rededicated. The Rabbis tell us there was only one cruse of pure oil found in the wreckage of the Temple, enough to light the Menora for one day. But the oil miraculously lasted for eight, enough time to make more. Ḥanukka (which means "rededication") is the eight-day festival established to celebrate the miracles of those days.

A ḤANUKKA MESSAGE FOR THE FIRST NIGHT

INSPIRED BY FAITH, WE CAN CHANGE THE WORLD

Twenty-two centuries ago, when Israel was under the rule of the empire of Alexander the Great, one particular leader, Antiochus IV, decided to force the pace of Hellenisation. He forbade Jews from practising their religion and even set up a statue of Zeus Olympus in the *Beit HaMikdash* in Jerusalem.

This was too much to bear, and a group of Jews, the Maccabees, fought for their religious freedom, winning a stunning victory against the most powerful army of the ancient world. After three years of conflict, they reconquered Jerusalem, rededicated the *Beit HaMikdash*, and relit the Menora with the one cruse of undefiled oil they found among the wreckage.

It was one of the most spectacular military achievements of the ancient world. It was, as we say in our prayers, a victory of the few over the many, the weak over the strong. It is summed up in a wonderful line from the prophet Zekharya: "'Not by might nor by strength but by My spirit,' says the Lord" (Zekharya 4:6).

The Maccabees had neither might nor strength, neither weapons nor numbers. But they had a double portion of the Jewish spirit that longs for freedom and is prepared to fight for it.

Never believe that a handful of dedicated people can't change the world. Inspired by faith, they can. The Maccabees did then. So can we today.

POINTS TO PONDER

1. *Why do you think the Greeks were against Jews keeping their religion?*

2. *What life lessons can you learn from the victory of the Maccabees over the ancient Greek army?*

3. *Can you give other examples from Jewish history of the "Jewish spirit"?*

FROM THE THOUGHT OF RABBI SACKS

Why did God choose this tiny people for so great a task, to be His witnesses in the world, the people who fought against the idols of the age in every age, the carriers of His message to humanity? Why are we so few?…Where did Jewish strength lie if not in numbers?

The Torah gives an answer of surpassing beauty. God tells Moshe: Do not count Jews. Ask them to give, and then count the contributions.

In terms of numbers we are small. But in terms of our contributions, we are vast. In almost every age, Jews have given something special to the world….

When it comes to making a contribution, numbers do not count. What matters is commitment, passion, dedication to a cause. Precisely because we are so small as a people, every one of us counts. We each make a difference to the fate of Judaism and the Jewish people.

Ten Paths to God – *Responsibility: The Jewish Future*, 3–4

POINTS TO PONDER

1. *Can you think of a reason why Hashem chose a small group of people for a great task?*

2. *What is the connection between this quote and "Inspired by Faith, We Can Change the World" (p. 56)?*

IT ONCE HAPPENED...

The Ḥanukka story as told in the Al HaNissim prayer in the siddur:

In the days of Mattityahu, son of Yoḥanan, the high priest, the Hasmonean, and his sons, the wicked Greek kingdom rose up against Your people Israel to make them forget Your Torah and to force them to transgress the laws of Your will. It was then that You in Your great compassion stood by them in the time of their distress. You championed their cause, judged their claim, and avenged their wrong. You delivered the strong into the hands of the weak, the many into the hands of the few, the impure into the hands of the pure, the wicked into the hands of the righteous, and the arrogant into the hands of those who were engaged in the study of Your Torah. You made for Yourself a great and holy reputation in Your world, and for Your people Israel You performed a great salvation and redemption as of this very day. Your children then entered the holiest part of Your House, cleansed Your Temple, purified Your Sanctuary, kindled lights in Your holy courts, and designated these eight days of Ḥanukka for giving thanks and praise to Your great name.

POINT TO PONDER

Which do you think is more impressive, the military victory or the miracle of the oil?

The Ḥanukka story continued, as told in the Talmud (Shabbat 21b):

When the Greeks entered the Sanctuary they ruined all the cruses of oil that were in the Sanctuary by touching them, which made them unfit. When the Hasmoneans overcame them and emerged victorious over them, they searched everywhere for oil to relight the Menora in the Temple, but could only find one cruse of oil that had the seal of the high priest unbroken, untouched by the Greeks. This cruse of oil was only enough to light the Menora for one day. A miracle occurred and the Menora was lit by this oil for eight days. The next year, the Sages instituted a festival to remember and celebrate those days, by singing Hallel and saying special prayers of thanksgiving.

ḤANUKKA CHALLENGE!

AMUSING ANAGRAMS

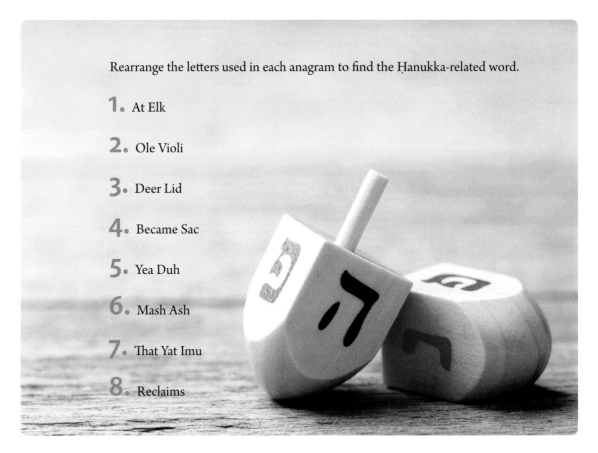

Rearrange the letters used in each anagram to find the Ḥanukka-related word.

1. At Elk

2. Ole Violi

3. Deer Lid

4. Became Sac

5. Yea Duh

6. Mash Ash

7. That Yat Imu

8. Reclaims

FUN FACT!

In Judaism, the number eight represents miracles. Why? Because it is beyond seven, which represents nature, as in the seven days of Creation.

EDUCATIONAL COMPANION TO THE QUESTIONS

INSPIRED BY FAITH, WE CAN CHANGE THE WORLD

1. Throughout their history, the Jewish people have faced both physical and spiritual threats. The Purim story represents a physical existential attack on the Jewish people, and the Ḥanukka story portrays a spiritual existential threat. These are two parallel paths to achieve the same goal: the destruction of Judaism and the Jewish people. We can never be sure about the motivation for these attacks, but we can speculate that there were those in Greek society who perceived the values of the Torah as a threat, as they were often diametrically opposed to the values of Greek culture.

2. Size and power are not what is important in life to achieve our goals. Might does not make right. Even a single individual can change the world. We have to put our faith in God that there is a plan for us as individuals and for the Jewish people.

3. Jewish history is brimming with examples of the Jewish spirit triumphing over adversity, inspired by faith in God. Examples include the survival of Jews and Judaism after the expulsion from Spain; the influx of millions of Russian and Eastern European Jews to the United States of America in the late nineteenth/early twentieth century, and how they established themselves there; and the significant contributions that Jews have made to wider society in areas such as science, culture, and economics. But perhaps the most powerful example is the return of Jewish sovereignty to the land of Israel just three years after the Holocaust, despite the devastating destruction of the majority of European Jewry.

FROM THE THOUGHT OF RABBI SACKS

1. Our very history as a people is a testament to the existence of God, who has protected us and ensured our survival against all the odds through thousands of years of persecution and wandering. The very existence and survival of the Jewish people transmits core Jewish messages to the world, among them: might does not make right, the dignity of difference, and faith in God.

2. The quote refers to the size of the Jewish people in relation to the importance of their task and national mission, and Ḥanukka is an example of a small people achieving great things, demonstrating core Jewish values and the Jewish destiny.

IT ONCE HAPPENED...

God can perform miracles through supernatural means, and through nature. The military victory represents a natural miracle, as the Maccabees fought hard, but they achieved an unlikely triumph that must have benefitted from God's help. This is no less impressive than the supernatural miracle of the oil that burned for eight days, when it should only have burned for one day. Both types of miracles come from God, but they are achieved by different means.

AMUSING ANAGRAMS

1. Latke
2. Olive oil
3. *Dreidel*
4. Maccabees
5. Yehuda
6. *Shamash*
7. Mattityahu
8. Miracles

A ḤANUKKA MESSAGE FOR THE SECOND NIGHT

THE LIGHT OF WAR AND THE LIGHT OF PEACE

There is a law about Ḥanukka I find moving and profound. Rambam writes that "the command of Ḥanukka lights is very precious. One who lacks the money to buy lights should sell something, or if necessary borrow money, so as to be able to fulfil the mitzva."

The question then arises: What if, on a Friday afternoon, you find yourself with only one candle? Should you light it as a Shabbat candle or a Ḥanukka one? It can't be both. Logic suggests that you should light it as a Ḥanukka candle. After all, there is no law that you have to sell or borrow to light the Shabbat lights. Yet the law is, surprisingly, that when faced with such a choice, you light your only candle as a Shabbat light. Why?

Listen to Rambam: "The Shabbat light takes priority because it symbolises *shalom bayit*, domestic peace. And great is peace because the entire Torah was given in order to make peace in the world."

Consider: Ḥanukka commemorates one of the greatest military victories in Jewish history. Yet Jewish law rules that if we can only light one candle, the Shabbat light takes precedence, because in Judaism the greatest military victory takes second place to peace in the home.

Why did Judaism, alone among the civilisations of the ancient world, survive? Because it valued the home more than the battlefield, marriage more than military grandeur, and children more than generals. Peace in the home mattered to our ancestors more than the greatest military victory.

So as we celebrate Ḥanukka, spare a thought for the real victory, which was not military but spiritual. Jews were the people who valued marriage, the home, and peace between husband and wife, above the highest glory on the battlefield. In Judaism, the light of peace takes precedence over the light of war.

POINTS TO PONDER

1. *Does Judaism think war is wrong (i.e., is Judaism a pacifist religion)?*

2. *How can* shalom bayit *(peace in the home) also help bring* shalom *(peace) into the wider world?*

3. *How will you contribute to* shalom bayit *in your home this Ḥanukka?*

> **"In Judaism, the light of peace takes precedence over the light of war."**

FROM THE THOUGHT OF RABBI SACKS

The family…is the best means we have yet discovered for nurturing future generations and enabling children to grow in a matrix of stability and love. It is where we learn the delicate choreography of relationship and how to handle the inevitable conflicts within any human group. It is where we first take the risk of giving and receiving love. It is where one generation passes on its values to the next, ensuring the continuity of a civilisation. For any society, the family is the crucible of its future, and for the sake of our children's future, we must be its defenders.

Morality, 74

> **"For any society, the family is the crucible of its future."**

POINTS TO PONDER

1. *Why is the family unit so important according to Rabbi Sacks?*

2. *What is the connection between this quote and the message from Rabbi Sacks in "The Light of War and the Light of Peace" (p. 60)?*

IT ONCE HAPPENED…

General Holofernes commanded a huge Syrian-Greek army. As part of his campaign to stamp out the Jewish revolt, his forces besieged the town of Bethulia, in the land of Judea. The people of the town soon found themselves in a desperate situation, critically lacking in food and water, and facing a far superior military force.

Living in the town was a widow named Yehudit, who was the sister of Mattityahu and the aunt of Yehuda the Maccabee. She courageously hatched and executed a plan to save her town. She sneaked out of the city and requested an audience with Holofernes, the enemy commander. She convinced him that she had intelligence that would help him conquer the town, in exchange for his guarantee to deal compassionately with the inhabitants. She brought food and wine to celebrate their arrangement, including very salty goat cheese and especially strong wine. The cheese made the general thirsty, and he drank so much wine that he became drunk and fell asleep. She seized her opportunity and killed him with his own sword.

When she brought news of his death back to the town, the Jews were inspired by the daring heroism of Yehudit, and they attacked the Greek forces. Without their commander, the Greeks retreated, and the town was freed. This proved to be a key turning point in the Jewish revolt against the Greeks.

POINT TO PONDER

How is Yehudit similar to her nephew Yehuda the Maccabee?

ḤANUKKA CHALLENGE!

RHYMING RIDDLES

1. I'm sweet and round, coming to a boil, in a pot of bubbling oil.

2. I'm a small town near Jerusalem. The Hasmoneans lived here – Mattityahu and his five sons, who fought the Greeks with no fear!

3. I have eight plus one, to remember the battle that we won.

4. I'm made from olives. I come out when they are pressed. You can burn me for light. Who am I? Have you guessed?

5. I get dizzy when you give me a spin. It's all about the Ḥanukka *gelt* you're trying to win.

6. I'm here to serve others. Eight friends get light from me. You'll see me every night of Ḥanukka. Can you guess who I might be?

7. I'm fried in oil and very yummy. With sour cream or applesauce, I'll fill your tummy.

8. Our brave soldiers fought without glamour. Our fearless leader was nicknamed "Hammer"!

FUN FACT!

The Maccabees were a group of Jewish Hasmonean warriors from Modi'in who rebelled against the Seleucid Greeks and defeated them, rededicating the Temple. The name "Maccabee" was the nickname of their leader, Yehuda, and means "Hammer" in Aramaic, in recognition of his strength as a warrior (although some say it was because he had a flat head like a hammer).

EDUCATIONAL COMPANION TO THE QUESTIONS

THE LIGHT OF WAR AND THE LIGHT OF PEACE

1. Judaism is not a pacifist religion. It believes firmly in the moral justification for war under certain circumstances, such as a war in spiritual or physical self-defence, or a war that has been commanded by God. However, peace is an ultimate value in Judaism, and whenever possible, the peaceful course should be taken.

2. When we are inevitably faced with challenging situations within the family structure, we learn skills such as negotiation, conflict resolution, and other interpersonal skills that help ensure *shalom bayit*. All these skills are also essential for ensuring *shalom* in the wider world when we will undoubtedly face similar situations of conflict.

3. Perhaps you can offer to help your parents with Ḥanukka preparations, or spend some time thinking about how you can show love to your siblings or other family members (e.g., buying or making presents, or preparing fun activities to do together).

FROM THE THOUGHT OF RABBI SACKS

1. The family unit is where we learn how to be good people and members of society and how to form relationships with others. It is where we learn to love and be loved. This gives us the skills to love and be loved by others outside of our families. It is where our values are received from the previous generation and transmitted to the next generation, and represents the future of our civilisation. The family unit is the foundation for a healthy society.

2. The family is a core value in Judaism, and this is seen in the halakha that Rabbi Sacks shared in the first message, where if one only has enough money for one candle, and is faced with the dilemma of using it either for Ḥanukka or as a Shabbat candle, one must light it as a Shabbat candle, because this brings *shalom bayit* to the family home.

IT ONCE HAPPENED…

They both demonstrated courage and self-sacrifice for their people. They put themselves in harm's way in order to triumph over the enemies of Israel. Yehudit is a particularly important character for us, as a strong female role model whose dedication to her people ranks alongside her nephew and the other heroic leaders of Israel.

RHYMING RIDDLES

1. *Sufganiyot* (doughnuts)
2. Modi'in
3. *Ḥanukkiya* (menora)
4. *Shemen zayit* (olive oil)
5. *Sevivon* (*dreidel*)
6. *Shamash*
7. Latkes
8. Maccabees

A ḤANUKKA MESSAGE FOR THE THIRD NIGHT

INSIDE/OUTSIDE

There is more than one command in Judaism to kindle lights. There are three. There are the Shabbat candles. There is the Havdala candle. And there are the Ḥanukka candles.

What is the difference between them? Shabbat candles represent *shalom bayit*, peace in the home. They are lit indoors. They can be thought of as Judaism's inner light, the light of the sanctity of marriage and the holiness of the home.

The Ḥanukka candles used to be lit outside – outside the front door. It was only fear of persecution that took the Ḥanukka candles back inside, and in recent times the Lubavitcher Rebbe introduced the custom of lighting giant *ḥanukkiyot* in public places to bring back the original spirit of the day.

Ḥanukka candles are the light Judaism brings to the world when we are unafraid to announce our identity in public, live by our principles, and fight, if necessary, for our freedom.

As for the Havdala candle, which is always made up of several wicks woven together, it represents the fusion of the two, the inner light of Shabbat, joined to the outer light we make during the six days of the week when we go out into the world and live our faith in public.

When we live as Jews in private, filling our homes with the light of the *Shekhina*, when we live as Jews in public, bringing the light of hope to others, and when we live both together, then we bring light to the world.

There always were two ways to live in a world that is often dark and full of tears. We can curse the darkness or we can light a light, and as the Hasidim say, a little light drives out much darkness. May we all help light up the world.

POINTS TO PONDER

1. *What parts of Judaism bring light into our homes, represented by the Shabbat candles?*

2. *What parts of Judaism bring light to the outside world?*

3. *How can we be Havdala candles, and fuse the two, bringing the Judaism from our homes into the outside world?*

> "Ḥanukka candles are the light Judaism brings to the world."

FROM THE THOUGHT OF RABBI SACKS

I admire other civilisations and traditions, and believe each has brought something special into the world, *"aval zeh shelanu,"* "but this is ours." This is my people, my heritage, my faith. In our uniqueness lies our universality. Through being what we alone are, we give to humanity what only we can give. This, then, is our story, our gift to the next generation. I received it from my parents, and they from theirs, across great expanses of space and time. There is nothing quite like it. It changed, and still challenges, the moral imagination of humankind.

A Letter in the Scroll, 229

POINTS TO PONDER

1. *What unique contribution can the Jewish people give to humanity?*

2. *What is the connection between this quote and the "Inside/Outside" message from Rabbi Sacks (p. 64)?*

IT ONCE HAPPENED...

It was a frigid Saturday night during Ḥanukka of 1974 when Rabbi Abraham Shemtov had the unusual idea of lighting a big *ḥanukkiya* right in front of Independence Hall in Philadelphia, which houses the Liberty Bell, the icon of American freedom.

The *ḥanukkiya* was crude and made of wood; he had fashioned it with the help of some visiting yeshiva students. Almost no one was there that night to witness the actual lighting, but that simple four-foot *ḥanukkiya* was the seed from which thousands of public *ḥanukkiyot* have sprouted up in public and private places throughout the United States and around the world.

Over the next few years, *ḥanukkiyot* began springing up in cities and towns all across America. The next major development was in 1979, when Shemtov collaborated with Stuart Eizenstat – President Jimmy Carter's chief domestic policy adviser and executive director of the White House domestic policy staff – to arrange for a *ḥanukkiya* to be placed on the White House lawn. Despite the fact that Carter was otherwise preoccupied during the opening weeks of the Iranian hostage crisis, he pointedly walked from the White House to the *ḥanukkiya*, where he lit the *shamash* – the helper candle from which the others are kindled – and shared greetings with the assembled crowd.

Throughout the following decades, the number of *ḥanukkiyot* and the scope of their reach has continued to blossom. It is estimated that as many as 15,000 Chabad-Lubavitch *ḥanukkiyot* are publicly lit worldwide.

One of the largest lightings is the one near the Eiffel Tower in central Paris, which has attracted as many as 20,000 French Jews. And in 1991, in the presence of approximately 6,000 Jews, longtime Chabad underground activist Avraham Genin kindled a giant *ḥanukkiya* inside the Kremlin Palace of Congresses.

In 2013, the tallest *ḥanukkiya* in Europe (more than thirty feet tall!) was constructed and lit on the first night of Ḥanukka at the Brandenburg Gate in Berlin, Germany, once a symbol of Nazi Party racism and hatred. Thousands of people attended the public ceremony, including local dignitaries. "Bringing light to places of darkness is the message of Ḥanukka," said Chabad-Lubavitch of Berlin's director, Rabbi Yehuda Teichtal. "There is no greater contrast than lighting a menora here – in the place that was once the epitome of darkness – and now flooding it with the essence of light."

POINT TO PONDER

Does the lighting of giant ḥanukkiyot *throughout the world make you uncomfortable or proud?*

Illustration by Naama Lahav

FUN FACT!

Every year the US president and first lady host an annual Ḥanukka party for hundreds of American Jewish politicians and leaders of the Jewish community, but this wasn't always the case. Ḥanukka was first celebrated at the White House after Prime Minister David Ben-Gurion gave Harry Truman a *ḥanukkiya* as a gift in 1951. George H. W. Bush attended a Ḥanukka party for staff in the Executive Office Building in 1991 and two years later, Bill Clinton hosted a candle-lighting ceremony in the White House for the first time with his staff. The first official White House Ḥanukka party was held on December 10, 2001. President George W. Bush borrowed a hundred-year-old *ḥanukkiya* from the Jewish Museum in New York for the event.

EDUCATIONAL COMPANION TO THE QUESTIONS

INSIDE/OUTSIDE

1. Mitzvot that regulate our relationships, especially relationships within families, such as a child's obligations to their parents and a parent's obligations to their child. The mitzvot of Shabbat, festivals, and learning and teaching Torah are all mitzvot that bring light into a Jewish home.

2. The mitzvot that regulate society, that contribute to *tikkun olam* (the redeeming of, or fixing, the world) bring light to the outside world. These are the civil laws, such as *tzedaka*, environmental laws, and the laws of returning of lost articles.

3. There is a core principle in Judaism called *"kiddush Hashem"* that expects a Jew to live their life so that it is a credit to God, and thus model the values of the Torah. We do this by keeping mitzvot for all to see, but also in all other areas of our lives, such as how we treat people. When Jews live their lives as ambassadors of God, they bring light to the outside world.

FROM THE THOUGHT OF RABBI SACKS

1. Judaism has a unique message for humanity that it transmits through modelling as a nation how to build communities and societies based on the moral and ethical values found in the Torah. This is the national mission of the Jewish people.

2. The Ḥanukka lights, which must face a window or be lit outside, illuminating the public square, represent the light that Judaism can and must shine on the outside world.

IT ONCE HAPPENED...

Rabbi Sacks often said that non-Jews respect Jews who respect their Judaism, and non-Jews are uncomfortable around Jews who are embarrassed by their Judaism. Ḥanukka is a time when we are proud to take our Judaism into the public space. We are not trying to impose our ideas on the non-Jewish world. We only hope to expose the world to the beauty of Judaism, so that everyone can benefit from its light.

A ḤANUKKA MESSAGE FOR THE FOURTH NIGHT

THE FIRST CLASH OF CIVILISATIONS

One of the key phrases of our time is "the clash of civilisations." And Ḥanukka is about one of the first great clashes of civilisation, between the Greeks and Jews of antiquity, Athens and Jerusalem.

The ancient Greeks produced one of the most remarkable civilisations of all time: philosophers like Plato and Aristotle, historians like Herodotus and Thucydides, dramatists like Sophocles and Aeschylus. They produced art and architecture of a beauty that has never been surpassed. Yet in the second century BCE they were defeated by the group of Jewish fighters known as the Maccabees, and from then on Greece as a world power went into rapid decline, while the tiny Jewish people survived every exile and persecution and are still alive and well today.

What was the key difference between the two groups? The Greeks, who did not believe in a single, loving God, gave the world the concept of tragedy: we strive, we struggle, at times we achieve greatness, but life has no ultimate purpose. The universe neither knows nor cares that we are here.

In stark contrast, ancient Israel gave the world the idea of hope. We are here because God created us in love, and through love we discover the meaning and purpose of life.

Tragic cultures eventually disintegrate and die. Lacking any sense of ultimate meaning, they lose the moral beliefs and habits on which continuity depends. They sacrifice happiness for pleasure. They sell the future for the present. They lose the passion and energy that brought them greatness in the first place. That's what happened to ancient Greece.

Judaism and its culture of hope survived, and the Ḥanukka lights are the ultimate symbol of that survival, of Judaism's refusal to abandon its values for the glamour and prestige of a secular culture, then or now.

A candle of hope may seem a small thing, but on it the very survival of a civilisation may depend.

POINTS TO PONDER

1. *What were the values of ancient Greek society, and how did they differ from the values of the Torah?*

2. *Where do we see that the Torah gave us the idea of hope?*

3. *How is this hope represented in the Ḥanukka candles?*

FROM THE THOUGHT OF RABBI SACKS

The military victory [of Ḥanukka] was short-lived. Within a century Israel was again under foreign rule, this time by the Romans. It was the spiritual victory that survived. Realising that the real battle was not against an empire but a culture, Jews set about constructing the world's first system of universal education. The effect was astonishing. Although they were later to suffer devastating defeats at the hands of the Romans, they had created an identity so strong that it was able to survive 2,000 years of exile and dispersion.

What history taught them was that to defend a country you need an army, but to defend a civilisation you need schools. In the short run, battles are won by weapons, but in the long run they are won by ideas and the way they are handed on from generation to generation. Oddly but appropriately, Ḥanukka comes from the same Hebrew root as the word "*ḥinnukh*," meaning "education."

Credo, The Times (**December 7, 2007**)

POINTS TO PONDER

1. *What was the real triumph of the Ḥanukka story?*

2. *What is the connection between this passage and the message from Rabbi Sacks in "The First Clash of Civilisations" (p. 69)?*

> **"To defend a country you need an army, but to defend a civilisation you need schools."**

IT ONCE HAPPENED...

When Rav Kook was a young man he studied in yeshiva in a small town called Lutzen. At the end of the year he returned home with a present for his parents – a bundle of poems. But this did not please his father, who was concerned his son was being influenced by the secular world of the *Haskala*. The following year, Rav Kook instead brought home a notebook full of original insights into complex halakhic topics. But the urge to read and write poetry was still strong in his heart. Later in his life, Rav Kook found a way to bring these two passions together, by writing a long poem that incorporated all the laws of Ḥanukka, utilising his mastery of the Hebrew language and halakha while also fulfilling his desire to express himself poetically.

POINT TO PONDER

Why was Rav Kook's father concerned about him being exposed to secular culture? How did Rav Kook respond to this?

ḤANUKKA CHALLENGE!

ḤIDON ON THE ḤAG (A QUICK QUIZ)

1. In total, how many candles are lit over the eight nights of Ḥanukka?

2. What does the word "Ḥanukka" mean?

3. What does the word "Maccabee" mean?

4. What is the name of the leader of the ancient Greeks who decreed laws against Judaism?

5. What is the name of the courageous Jewish woman who defied the Greeks and killed one of their generals?

6. What is another name for the festival of Ḥanukka?

7. What were the miracles of Ḥanukka?

8. What is the name of the town in Israel where the Maccabees lived?

FUN FACT!

Many have the custom to give children "Ḥanukka *gelt*" (Yiddish for "Ḥanukka money"). It is believed that this custom began in Poland in the seventeenth century, initially so that the children could then give coins to their teachers as a gift of gratitude. Later on, money was also given to the children to keep (this may be the source of the custom to give children Ḥanukka gifts). Ḥanukka *gelt* is also connected to the festival, as the Hasmoneans minted national coins to celebrate the victory of the Maccabees over the ancient Greeks. In the twentieth century, chocolate Ḥanukka *gelt* coins became a popular gift on Ḥanukka, with many families using them for playing *dreidel*.

EDUCATIONAL COMPANION TO THE QUESTIONS

THE FIRST CLASH OF CIVILISATIONS

1. The Greeks supremely valued the aesthetic – physical beauty and strength – rather than moral and spiritual beauty. They did not believe in a single, loving God, but rather in destiny, and they gave the world the concept of tragedy. They believed that it doesn't matter how hard we strive and work to achieve our own goals; destiny determines our end. Life has no ultimate purpose. The universe neither knows nor cares that we are here. In stark contrast, Judaism believes we are here because God created us in love, and He acts in history for our benefit, and through this love we discover the meaning and purpose of life.

2. Judaism tells us that the world can and will become better than it is today (and gives us the responsibility of partnering with God in making this a reality). The concept of *tikkun olam* (redeeming or fixing the world) and the anticipation of a Messianic time that has not yet arrived gives humanity hope in the future.

3. The Ḥanukka lights are the symbol of the survival of the Jewish people and Jewish culture. They represent hope and faith in the future, because even when the situation looked impossibly bleak, the Maccabees refused to give up hope for the future, and fought to triumph over the darkness (and continued to look for the cruses of oil despite the fact that the chances of finding any were very small).

FROM THE THOUGHT OF RABBI SACKS

1. While the military victory was also very impressive, the real victory was the spiritual triumph. This spiritual victory that we celebrate, how the Jews refused to give in to the seduction of Greek culture, which was the antithesis of the Torah's values, has had the longest-lasting impact on Jewish history. They fought to hold on to Torah values, and today, thousands of years later, while the ancient Greeks are long gone, the Jewish people continue to thrive.

2. Rabbi Sacks speaks of the clash of civilisations found in the Ḥanukka story. This passage demonstrates that the spiritual triumph of the Maccabees was everlasting. The Jewish people and Jewish civilisation have survived through the generations not by building armies, but by caring about the education of each generation.

IT ONCE HAPPENED...

Aspects of secular culture may have values that are antithetical to Jewish values contained in the Torah. Secular culture may also lead Jews astray from their own culture and the values of their religion. Rav Kook's response was to show how the good in secular culture can enrich Jewish culture and Jewish thought.

ḤANUKKA QUIZ

1. Forty-four.
2. "Dedication." (Bonus answer: "They rested on the twenty-fifth.")
3. Hammer. This was the nickname of Yehuda, the leader of the revolt against the Greeks.
4. Antiochus Epiphanes.
5. Yehudit.
6. *Ḥag Urim* (Festival of Lights).
7. The military miracle, that the small Maccabee forces defeated the mighty Greek army, and the miracle of the oil that burned for eight days.
8. Modi'in.

A ḤANUKKA MESSAGE FOR THE FIFTH NIGHT

ḤANUKKA FOR OUR TIME

Back in 1991, I lit Ḥanukka candles with Mikhail Gorbachev, who had, until earlier that year, been president of the Soviet Union.

For seventy years, the practice of Judaism had been effectively banned in Communist Russia. It was one of the two great assaults on our people and our faith in the twentieth century. The Germans sought to kill Jews; the Russians tried to kill Judaism.

Under Stalin the assault became brutal. In 1967, after Israel's victory in the Six-Day War, many Soviet Jews sought to leave Russia and go to Israel. Not only was permission refused, but often the Jews concerned lost their jobs and were imprisoned.

Around the world, Jews campaigned for the prisoners, called Refuseniks, to be released and permitted to leave the country.

Eventually Gorbachev realised that the whole Soviet system was unworkable. Communism had brought repression, a police state, and a new hierarchy of power, not freedom and equality. In the end it collapsed, and Jews regained the freedom to practise Judaism and go to Israel.

That day in 1991, after we had lit candles together, Gorbachev asked me, through his interpreter, what we had just done. I told him that twenty-two centuries ago in Israel, after the public practice of Judaism had been banned, Jews fought for and won their freedom, and these lights were the symbol of that victory. And I continued: "Seventy years ago, Jews suffered the same loss of freedom in Russia, and you have now helped them to regain it. So you have become part of the Ḥanukka story."

And as the interpreter translated those words into Russian, Mikhail Gorbachev blushed.

The Ḥanukka story still lives, still inspires, telling not just us but the world that though tyranny exists, freedom, with God's help, will always win the final battle.

POINTS TO PONDER

1. *What similarities are there between the Ḥanukka story and the story of Soviet Jewry under Communism?*

2. *How can we be sure that ultimately, we will always win the battle?*

3. *Rabbi Sacks applies the messages of the Ḥanukka story to contemporary times. What can we learn from Ḥanukka to help us in our generation?*

FROM THE THOUGHT OF RABBI SACKS

The symbol of Hanukka is the *chanukiah* we light for eight days in memory of the Temple Menora, purified and rededicated by the Maccabees all those centuries ago. Faith is like a flame. Properly tended, it gives light and warmth, but let loose, it can burn and destroy. We need, in the 21st century, a global Hanukka: a festival of freedom for all the world's faiths. For though my faith is not yours and your faith is not mine, if we are each free to light our own flame, together we can banish some of the darkness of the world.

"Why Hanukka Is the Perfect Festival for Religious Freedom," *The Washington Post* **(December 7, 2015)**

IT ONCE HAPPENED...

On Ḥanukka 1932, just one month before Hitler came to power, Rachel Posner, wife of Rabbi Dr. Akiva Posner, took this photo of the family *ḥanukkiya* from the window ledge of the family home looking out onto the building across the road decorated with Nazi flags.

On the back of the photograph, Rachel Posner wrote in German:

> Ḥanukka 5692 (1932)
> "Death to Judah"
> So the flag says
> "Judah will live forever"
> So the light answers

Rabbi Dr. Akiva Posner, doctor of philosophy from Halle-Wittenberg University, served from 1924 to 1933 as the last rabbi of the community of Kiel, Germany. After he wrote a protest letter in the local newspaper expressing indignation at the posters that had appeared in the city, "Entrance to Jews Forbidden," he was summoned by the chairman of the local branch of the Nazi party to participate in a public debate. The event took place under heavy police guard and was reported by the local press.

When the tension and violence in the city intensified, the rabbi, his wife Rachel, and their three children were forced to flee their home and make their way to *Eretz Yisrael*. Before their departure, Rabbi Posner was able to convince many of his congregants to leave as well and indeed most managed to leave for *Eretz Yisrael* or the United States. The Posner family left Germany in 1933 and arrived in *Eretz Yisrael* in 1934.

Some eighty years later, Akiva and Rachel Posner's descendants continue to light Ḥanukka candles using the same *ḥanukkiya* that was brought to Israel from Kiel. On Ḥanukka 5770 (2009), Akiva Mansbach, dressed in the uniform of the Israel Defense Forces, saluted and read out a poem he had written in Hebrew, inspired by the poem written by his great-grandmother Rachel Posner in 1932.

Translated it reads:

In 5692 the ḥanukkiya *is in exile, it stands in the window / It challenges the party flag that doesn't yet rule / "Judah die!" it says / And Grandma's rhyme responds / In its own tongue, without despair: So the flag says, but our candle answers and declares / "Judah will live forever."*

In 5770 the ḥanukkiya *stands in the window once again / Facing the flag of the ruling State / The descendant Akiva, named for his great-grandfather / Salutes through the window and lights the* ḥanukkiya */ Grandmother, give thanks above and say a prayer / That "the Redeemer will come to Zion" and not delay.*

YadVashem.org

POINT TO PONDER

Why do you think this photograph has brought so many people comfort?

ḤANUKKA CHALLENGE!

SPOT THE DIFFERENCE

FUN FACT!

In December of 1993, Space Shuttle Endeavour was sent into space to service the Hubble Space Telescope. One of the astronauts who bravely performed a spacewalk to repair the telescope was Jeffrey Hoffman. Knowing that he would be stuck in space over Ḥanukka, Hoffman made sure to bring along a *dreidel* and a travel-sized *ḥanukkiya* so that he'd be able to celebrate the *ḥag* (although, because of lack of gravity and safety concerns, there was no way to actually light candles). Via live satellite communication, he presented his Ḥanukka supplies, gave his *dreidel* a twirl in the air, and wished Jews everywhere a happy Ḥanukka.

EDUCATIONAL COMPANION TO THE QUESTIONS

ḤANUKKA FOR OUR TIME

1. The Soviet regime also tried to destroy Judaism as a religion. Under Communist rule, the Soviet Union tried to limit the influence of all religions, believing them to be opposed to the political and social ideologies of Communism. It was almost impossible to practise Judaism in Soviet Russia, and those Jews who expressed an interest in leaving Russia and making *aliya* risked everything. Yet there were thousands of Jews determined that they would not allow these restrictions to stop them from being Jewish. Ultimately this was another case in Jewish history of a tiny but brave minority taking on a mighty empire and triumphing against all the odds.

2. We are only sure because of the faith we have in God to guide history, and the faith we have in ourselves to make this happen.

3. In recent years we have found ourselves facing challenging times (including a global pandemic). The Ḥanukka story shows us that with hope in our hearts that the future will be better, we can have faith that we will get through this together.

FROM THE THOUGHT OF RABBI SACKS

1. On festivals such as Purim and Pesaḥ, we celebrate deliverance from a physical threat to the Jewish people and the delivery of physical freedom, but Ḥanukka is about celebrating our delivery from a force that wished to destroy Judaism itself. The message of Ḥanukka is that all people deserve to be able to practise their religion in peace.

2. Soviet Russia was not a place and time in history where there was religious freedom. Ḥanukka's message is that freedom will always triumph.

IT ONCE HAPPENED...

The photo (and the poem written on the back) is a reminder that no matter how dark times get, and how much it looks like our survival is at risk, the Jewish people will always survive and persevere. Taking it one step further, we can also note that the uniform of the Israel Defense Forces worn by the great-grandson of the original owners of this *ḥanukkiya* represents the modern-day Maccabees and a strengthened faith that the Jewish people will survive.

SPOT THE DIFFERENCE

1. The number of lit candles.
2. A Hebrew letter on a *dreidel* has changed.
3. A present has changed colour from yellow to green.
4. The drizzled icing on the doughnut is missing.
5. The number of presents the man is holding.
6. The t-shirt of the person lighting the candles.
7. An oil jug has disappeared.
8. The colour of the sprinkles on a doughnut.

A ḤANUKKA MESSAGE FOR THE SIXTH NIGHT

THE THIRD MIRACLE

We all know the miracles of Ḥanukka: the military victory of the Maccabees against the Greeks and the miracle of the oil that should have lasted one day but kept the Menora lights burning for eight. But there was a third miracle not many people know about. It took place several centuries later.

After the destruction of the Second *Beit HaMikdash*, many Rabbis were convinced that the festival of Ḥanukka should be abolished. After all, it celebrated the rededication of the *Beit HaMikdash*. And the *Beit HaMikdash* was no more. It had been destroyed by the Romans under Titus. Without a *Beit HaMikdash*, what was there left to celebrate?

The Talmud tells us that in at least one town, Lod, Ḥanukka was abolished. Yet eventually the other view prevailed, which is why we continue to celebrate Ḥanukka to this day.

Why? Because although the *Beit HaMikdash* was destroyed, Jewish hope was not destroyed. We may have lost the building but we still have the story, and the memory, and the light. And what had happened once in the days of the Maccabees could happen again. It was those words, "*Od lo avda tikvateinu*," "Our hope is not destroyed," words that became part of the song *HaTikva*, that inspired Jews to return to Israel and rebuild their ancient state.

So as you light the Ḥanukka candles remember this: The Jewish people kept hope alive, and hope kept the Jewish people alive. We are the voice of hope in the conversation of humankind.

POINTS TO PONDER

1. *Why do you think it is important to maintain festivals and remembrance days that commemorate historical events from generations ago?*

2. *How does Ḥanukka represent hope? Hope for what?*

3. *What connections are there between the Ḥanukka story and the modern State of Israel?*

FROM THE THOUGHT OF RABBI SACKS

Something in the human spirit survives even the worst of tragedies, allowing us to rebuild shattered lives, broken institutions, and injured nations.

That, to me, is the Jewish story. Jews survived all the defeats, expulsions, persecutions, and pogroms, even the Holocaust itself, because they never gave up the faith that one day they would be free to live as Jews without fear.

Whenever I visit a Jewish school today, I see on the smiling faces of the children the ever-renewed power of that faith whose symbol is Ḥanukka and its light of inextinguishable hope.

Credo, The Times **(December 8, 2012)**

POINTS TO PONDER

1. *What do Jewish school-children represent to Rabbi Sacks in this passage?*

2. *What is the connection between this passage and the message from Rabbi Sacks on "The Third Miracle" (p. 78)?*

IT ONCE HAPPENED...

In the days of the wicked kingdom of Greece, it was decreed upon the Jews that whoever had a bolt on his door must engrave upon it the words "I have no portion or heritage in the God of Israel."

Immediately, all Jews went and pulled out all the bolts from their doors and discarded them.

It was also decreed that whoever had an ox must write on its horn the words "I have no portion or heritage in the God of Israel."

Immediately, all the Jews went and sold all their oxen.

Midrash LeḤanukka, 5

POINT TO PONDER

How do these acts of defiance compare to the heroism of the Maccabees?

ḤANUKKA CHALLENGE!

THE ḤANUKKA STORY IN EMOJIS

From the days of Alexander the 💪 of ❄, 🇮🇱 was under the 🔃 of the Alexandrian Empire of 🏛. During the 2 nd century BCE, 🇮🇱 came ⬇ the 🔃 of the Seleucids who were based in 🇪🇬.

The Seleucid leader, Antiochus the 4 th, who modestly called himself Epiphanes, meaning "God made manifest," decided to 🏃 up the pace of Hellenisation on the ✡s of the land of 🇮🇱. He made it illegal to publicly practise ✡, erected a 🗿 of Zeus in the 🛕, and offered a 🐗 before it as a sacrifice.

An 👓 priest called Mattityahu, and his 👦👦👦👦👦 and their supporters known to history as the ⚒, ⚔ back. ⬆ the next 3 years, they scored a 💪 ✌ ⬆ the Seleucids, reconquering Jerusalem and bringing it 🔙 ⬇ ✡ sovereignty. They cleansed the 🛕 and rededicated it, 🔥 the 💪 🕎 that stood in the 🛕, for a celebration lasting 8 days.

FUN FACT!

There is a custom on Ḥanukka to play with special spinning tops called *dreidels* (in Yiddish) or *sevivonim* (in Hebrew). The Greeks forbade Jews to learn Torah and so Jews would meet in secret to learn, but if a Greek soldier walked past, they would pretend to be gambling with their *dreidels*. The words *dreidel* (Yiddish) and *sevivon* (Hebrew) both mean to turn or spin. The *dreidel* has four sides, each of which features a Hebrew letter. In Israel, the letters are *nun, gimel, heh*, and *peh*. Outside Israel, they're *nun, gimel, heh, shin*. The letters stand for the Hebrew phrase "*Nes gadol haya po/sham*," meaning, "A great miracle happened here/there" (here for those in Israel, there for those outside of Israel).

EDUCATIONAL COMPANION TO THE QUESTIONS

THE THIRD MIRACLE

1. The festivals that commemorate historical events are the way that we transmit our heritage and our history. They are the most effective way to build our values and our identity in future generations, creating a national DNA that is passed from one generation to the next. For Jews, these festivals do not represent just history, but national memory, and are the basis for national identity.

2. Hope is a recurring theme in the Ḥanukka story. The Maccabees had hope that despite overwhelming odds, they could defeat the mightiest and largest army in the world. They had hope that they could find oil to light the Menora. And despite the later destruction of the *Beit HaMikdash*, we still celebrate Ḥanukka because we have hope that one day it will be rebuilt.

3. The story of the establishment of the modern State of Israel is also a story of hope and miracles, and the overcoming of immense odds. Just three years after the Jewish people experienced the greatest tragedy in human history, they re-established Jewish sovereignty in their ancestral homeland, and thereafter had to fight several wars against numerous enemies, triumphing, despite the odds, again and again.

FROM THE THOUGHT OF RABBI SACKS

1. Children represent the future, and a society or community that invests in its children has hope for the future. Jewish children in Jewish schools prove that the Jewish people have overcome thousands of years of adversity and persecution, and today we continue to invest in our future, a hopeful future.

2. This message is the message of Ḥanukka, the story of inextinguishable hope.

IT ONCE HAPPENED...

Heroism comes in small and large acts. The Maccabees were brave military fighters, but these acts from the wider populace were equally heroic and courageous. They were acts of defiance in the face of persecution, making a clear statement that their will and spirit could not be broken.

THE ḤANUKKA STORY IN EMOJIS

From the days of Alexander the **Great** of **Macedonia**, **Israel** was under the **control** of the Alexandrian Empire of **Greece**. During the **second** century BCE, **Israel** came **under** the **control** of the Seleucids who were based in **Egypt**.

The Seleucid leader, Antiochus the **Fourth**, who modestly called himself Epiphanes, meaning "God made manifest," decided to **speed** up the pace of Hellenisation on the **Jews** of the land of **Israel**. He made it illegal to publicly practise **Judaism**, erected a **statue** of Zeus in the **Temple**, and offered a **pig** before it as a sacrifice.

An **elderly** priest called Mattityahu, and his **sons** and their supporters known to history as the **Hammers (Maccabees)**, **fought** back. **Over** the next **three** years, they scored a **great victory** over the Seleucids, reconquering Jerusalem and bringing it **back under Jewish** sovereignty. They cleansed the **Temple** and rededicated it, **lighting** the **great Menora** that stood in the **Temple**, for a celebration lasting **eight** days.

A ḤANUKKA MESSAGE FOR THE SEVENTH NIGHT

THE LIGHT OF THE SPIRIT NEVER DIES

There is an interesting question the commentators ask about Ḥanukka.

For eight days we kindle lights, and each night we make the blessing over miracles: *She'asa nissim laavoteinu*. But what was the miracle of the first night? The oil that should have lasted one day lasted eight. But that means there was something miraculous about days two to eight; nothing was miraculous about the first day.

Perhaps the miracle was this: that the Maccabees found one cruse of oil with its seal intact, undefiled. There was no reason to suppose that anything would have survived the systematic desecration the Greeks and their supporters did to the *Beit HaMikdash*. Yet the Maccabees searched and found that one cruse.

Why did they search? Because they had faith that from the worst tragedy, something would survive. The miracle of the first night was that of faith itself, the faith that something would remain with which to begin again.

So it has always been in Jewish history. There were times when any other people would have given up in despair: after the destruction of the *Beit HaMikdash*, or the massacres of the Crusades, or the Spanish Expulsion, or the pogroms, or the *Shoah*. But somehow, Jews did not merely sit and weep. They gathered what remained, rebuilt our people, and lit a light like no other in history, a light that tells us, and the world, of the power of the human spirit to overcome every tragedy and refuse to accept defeat.

From the days of Moshe and the bush that burned and was not consumed, to the days of the Maccabees and the single cruse of oil, Judaism has been humanity's *ner tamid*, the everlasting light that no power on earth can extinguish.

POINTS TO PONDER

1. *What did the Maccabees have faith in?*

2. *Why do you think Rabbi Sacks describes faith itself as a miracle?*

3. *Do you think having faith today is also a miracle?*

> "Judaism has been humanity's *ner tamid*, the everlasting light that no power on earth can extinguish."

FROM THE THOUGHT OF RABBI SACKS

When I stand today in Jerusalem, or in a Jewish school, or see a Jewish couple under the wedding canopy, or see parents at the Shabbat table blessing their children, there are times when I am overcome with tears, not in sadness nor in joy, but in awe at this people who came face to face with the Angel of Death and refused to give it a final victory.

The Jewish people lives, and still bears witness to the living God.

A Letter in the Scroll, 192

POINTS TO PONDER

1. *What is it about Jerusalem, a Jewish school, a Jewish wedding, or a Jewish family around their Shabbat table that caused Rabbi Sacks to feel awe?*

2. *How does this passage expand on the ideas found in "The Light of the Spirit Never Dies" (p. 82)?*

IT ONCE HAPPENED...

In the days when the Greeks had defiled the Holy Temple in Jerusalem, an elderly and respected *kohen* by the name of Mattityahu lived with his five sons in a town called Modi'in, near Jerusalem.

One day, the officers of Antiochus arrived in Modi'in and built an altar in the marketplace, demanding that Mattityahu offer sacrifices to the Greek gods.

Mattityahu replied to them, "I, my sons, and my brothers will always remain loyal to the covenant that our God made with our ancestors! We will not obey the king's orders or stray from our religion one inch!"

At this moment, a Hellenised Jew approached the altar to sacrifice to the Greek gods. Mattityahu was filled with righteous outrage, so he reached for his sword and killed him. Then, together with his sons, he also killed the king's officers and destroyed the altar that they had built.

Knowing that Antiochus would be furious when he heard about it, and knowing that he would send troops to kill them all, Mattityahu fled to the hills of Judaea, followed by his sons, calling out: "Whoever is for God and His Torah, follow me!" And so began the Hasmonean revolt against Antiochus and the Greeks.

POINT TO PONDER

Do you think Mattityahu's response was extreme? Is there a precedent for it in the Torah?

ḤANUKKA CHALLENGE!

WACKY WORDSEARCH

1. Latkes
2. Sevivon
3. Mattityahu
4. Yehudah
5. Modi'in
6. Maccabees
7. Oil
8. Antiochus

M	A	M	F	Y	S	U	W	M	N
A	R	O	P	E	E	U	B	A	Y
C	W	D	L	H	V	Y	S	T	Y
C	I	I	A	U	I	I	I	T	A
A	R	I	T	D	V	D	N	I	T
B	A	N	K	A	O	Z	J	T	L
E	R	R	E	F	N	S	O	Y	R
E	O	Q	S	Y	R	Q	H	A	U
S	Q	O	I	L	I	W	R	H	S
I	A	N	T	I	O	C	H	U	S

FUN FACTS!

We eat oily (and yummy!) food like potato latkes and *sufganiyot* (doughnuts) to remember the miracle of the cruse of oil that should have only lasted one night but burned for eight whole days and nights.

EDUCATIONAL COMPANION TO THE QUESTIONS

THE LIGHT OF THE SPIRIT NEVER DIES

1. The Maccabees had faith in God, and in the righteousness of their mission, and in their ability to achieve it (with the help of God). They had hope that they would be able to defeat the Greeks and re-institute the Temple service and sovereignty in Jerusalem. They demonstrated this by searching for the purified oil despite the improbability of finding any. The very act of searching for the oil amongst the destruction in the *Beit HaMikdash* demonstrated their faith in the future.

2. Despair is a natural response to tragedy and adversity. The Maccabees had every reason to despair. Their deep faith in themselves, in the future, and in God, was heroic and inspiring, and according to Rabbi Sacks it was miraculous because it was also so unlikely and took deep courage.

3. There are many reasons to despair in the face of the adversities before us today. Having faith in the future is always miraculous, but at the same time, it is something we can aspire to.

FROM THE THOUGHT OF RABBI SACKS

1. These things represent the courage of Jewish faith in the future. That we have returned to Jerusalem and it is now thriving, after thousands of years of exile and desolation, is reason to be in awe of the Jewish people. Jews investing in the future by getting married, raising families, and educating their children in their homes and schools left Rabbi Sacks feeling in awe of their courage and faith.

2. The faith in the future represented by these things is the same faith and courage seen in the Ḥanukka story, both when the Maccabees fought against a far superior army, against the odds, and when they searched for pure oil in Jerusalem. They, too, demonstrated courage and faith in the future.

IT ONCE HAPPENED...

When the core values of your very existence are threatened, extreme measures are called for. Mattityahu was a spiritual leader at this time, and he had to take a stand to save Judaism and the Jewish people. His role model in the Torah was Pinḥas, who took a similar stand in the face of immorality.

WACKY WORDSEARCH

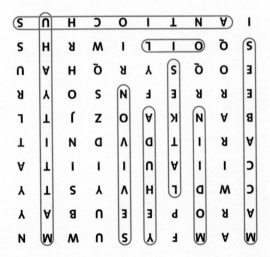

A ḤANUKKA MESSAGE FOR THE EIGHTH NIGHT

TO LIGHT ANOTHER LIGHT

There's a fascinating argument in the Talmud that debates the following question: Can you use one Ḥanukka light to light another? Usually, of course, we take an extra light, the *shamash*, and use it to light all the candles. But suppose we don't have one. Can we light the first candle and then use it to light the others?

Two great Sages of the third century, Rav and Shmuel, disagreed. Rav said no. Shmuel said yes. Normally we have a rule that when Rav and Shmuel disagree, the law follows Rav. There are only three exceptions, and this is one of them.

Why did Rav say that you may not use one Ḥanukka candle to light the others?

Because, says the Talmud, "*Mishum deka makhḥish mitzva*," "You will diminish the first candle." Inevitably, you will spill some of the wax or oil. And Rav says: Don't do anything that would diminish the light of the first candle.

But Shmuel disagrees, and the law follows Shmuel. Why?

The best way of answering this is to think of two Jews: both religious, both committed, both living Jewish lives. One says: "I must not get involved with Jews who are less religious than me, because if I do, my own standards will fall. I'll keep less. My light will be diminished." That's the view of Rav.

The other says: "No. When I use the flame of my faith to light a candle in someone else's life, my Jewishness is not diminished. It grows, because there is now more Jewish light in the world. When it comes to spiritual goods as opposed to material goods, the more I share, the more I have. If I share my knowledge, or faith, or love with others, I won't have less; I may even have more." That's the view of Shmuel, and that is how the law was eventually decided.

So share your Judaism with others. Take the flame of your faith and help set other souls on fire.

POINTS TO PONDER

1. *How is sharing material goods similar to the position of Rav?*

2. *How is sharing spiritual or moral goods similar to the position of Shmuel?*

3. *How will you be like Shmuel today?*

> "Take the flame of your faith and help set other souls on fire."

FROM THE THOUGHT OF RABBI SACKS

You can see religion as a battle, a holy war, in which you win a victory for your faith by force or fear. Or you can see it as a candle you light to drive away some of the darkness of the world.

The difference is that the first sees other religions as the enemy. The second sees them as other candles, not threatening mine, but adding to the light we share.

What Jews remembered from that victory over the Greeks twenty-two centuries ago was not a God of war but the God of light. And it's only the God of light who can defeat the darkness in the human soul.

From Optimism to Hope, 96

POINTS TO PONDER

1. *Does Judaism see religion as a battle or as a candle?*

2. *What is the connection between this passage and the message from Rabbi Sacks in "To Light Another Light" (p. 86)?*

IT ONCE HAPPENED...

The winter of 1777 was harsh, almost unbearable. The soldiers stationed in Valley Forge, Pennsylvania, had no inkling of why they were there. In their midst was a lone Jewish soldier and it was the first night of Ḥanukka. When all of the soldiers in the tent were fast asleep, he took out his *ḥanukkiya*. He lit the first candle, recited the blessings, and sat down to watch the small flame dancing merrily.

It fired his imagination and brought back a host of memories. The general appeared by his side. He looked at him and said gently, "Why are you weeping? Are you cold, my friend?" The soldier jumped to his feet and saluted.

Then he answered quietly, "I am weeping before my Father in heaven, sir. Everyone's fate lies in His hands; He controls the fate of millions, the world over. I was praying for your success, General Washington. I came to this country because I was fleeing the persecution of tyrants who have forever oppressed my family, my townspeople, and my nation. The despots will fall, sir, but you will be victorious!"

"Thank you, soldier!" the general replied heartily and sat himself on the ground before the *ḥanukkiya*. "And what have we here?" he asked, full of curiosity. "This is a candelabrum," answered the soldier. "Jews all over the world are lighting the first candle of our festival, Ḥanukka, tonight. This serves to commemorate a great miracle that occurred to our ancestors. They were only a handful compared to the massive armies of their enemies, but they held out, thanks to their faith in God, and were granted a miracle."

The bright flame ignited a flame of hope in the weary general's eyes and he cried out joyfully, "You are a Jew? Then you are descended from a people of prophets! And you say that we will win the war?" "Yes, sir!" he replied confidently. The general rose, his face glowing with renewed hope. They shook hands heartily. Washington asked the soldier for his name and address and disappeared into the night.

On the first night of Ḥanukka, in 1778, one year later, our Jewish veteran was sitting in his home on Broome Street in New York. The first Ḥanukka light was burning brightly on his windowsill. Suddenly, there was a knock on the door. His wife rose to open it wide. To her astonishment, there stood President Washington.

"There is that fabulous light, the Ḥanukka light," he cried out happily, spotting the candle by the window. "That flame, and your remarkable words, kindled a light in my heart on that dark and bitter night," he reminisced. "We were in a tight situation then, and your words encouraged me so! They spurred me on with new hope.

"You will soon be awarded a Medal of Honor from the United States of America for your bravery in Valley Forge, but tonight you will receive a personal memento from me." With these words he placed on the table a gold medal upon which was engraved a Ḥanukka menora with one light burning. Upon this medal was inscribed: "As a sign of thanks for the light of your candle. George Washington."

POINT TO PONDER

What did the Ḥanukka flames represent to Washington? What do they represent to you?

ḤANUKKA CHALLENGE!

DEVIOUS DINGBATS

1.   O  B̶ CH

2.    J̶ W

3.

4. D

5.   P̶ F  H̶

6.  J̶ M A

7.  AH

8.    H̶ P̶ CH

FUN FACT!

The Ḥanukka lights need to be lit at night, facing the outside world, at a time when people are around, so that they bring light and tell the world the story of the miracle.

EDUCATIONAL COMPANION TO THE QUESTIONS

TO LIGHT ANOTHER LIGHT

1. When material goods such as money, food, and clothes are shared, they are diminished for the giver. The giver now has less. This is called a zero-sum game. It is you or me. We cannot share the entirety of material goods equally.

2. Spiritual goods are increased when they are shared. Love, laughter, kindness, and knowledge are all spiritual goods, and when they are shared, they are not diminished for the giver. Rather, they are increased for the giver (for example, making someone laugh will make you laugh also, loving someone will increase love for you in turn, and teaching someone will increase your own knowledge).

3. Think about what spiritual goods you can share today, in the spirit of Shmuel's approach to Ḥanukka light.

FROM THE THOUGHT OF RABBI SACKS

1. According to Rabbi Sacks, Judaism does not see religion as a battle. Rather, Judaism sees itself as a candle, spreading light to the world, and through joining with other candles (other religions) it will increase light in the world. It wishes to shine its light on humanity, and makes space for receiving the light of other cultures and civilisations.

2. The sharing of light between Ḥanukka candles, as a metaphor for the sharing of Judaism's light with the world, is expressed in this quote about the God of light, and Judaism as a candle that brightens the world, not a religion of war that causes destruction.

IT ONCE HAPPENED...

Several possible answers are: Hope. Faith. Triumph over adversity. God's protection. History. Destiny. Freedom.

DEVIOUS DINGBATS

1. Antiochus
2. Candle wax
3. Kislev
4. *Dreidel*
5. *Sufganiyot*
6. Maccabees
7. *Ḥanukkiya*
8. *Ḥag same'aḥ*

Tu BiShvat

TU BISHVAT IN A NUTSHELL

Tu BiShvat (which means the fifteenth day of the Hebrew month of Shvat) marks the new year for the trees. The Mishna (Rosh HaShana 1:1) tells us there are four "New Years" or "Rosh HaShanas":

- The first of Nisan marks the new year for kings and festivals (i.e., this is the day when we begin counting the new year of a king's reign and the beginning of the festival calendar).
- The first of Elul marks the new year for the tithing of cattle (this is like the "tax year").
- The first of Tishrei (what we call Rosh HaShana) marks the new year for the counting of years (the calendar), *Shemitta* years, and the tithing of crops (and also the day on which all of humanity is judged by God).
- The fifteenth of Shvat (according to Beit Hillel) begins the new year for trees.

POINTS TO PONDER

1. *Do we have multiple "New Years" in our secular calendar?*

2. *Why do you think the meaning behind the festival of Tu BiShvat has evolved over time?*

3. *Do you think Tu BiShvat still has relevance for us today?*

Tu BiShvat became the date for calculating the beginning of the agricultural cycle for the purpose of biblical tithes, and it also marks the beginning of the season in which the earliest-blooming trees in Israel (namely the almond trees) begin to bloom, signifying a new fruit-bearing cycle.

In the Middle Ages the custom developed to celebrate Tu BiShvat with a feast of fruits, and in the sixteenth century the kabbalist Rabbi Yitzhak Luria and his students instituted a Tu BiShvat Seder (in the image of the Pesaḥ Seder), in which the fruits and trees of the land of Israel were given symbolic meaning (see below).

These customs have been renewed in modern Israel, and are widely celebrated by religious and secular alike, due to a deep connection to the land shared by many in Israeli society.

This day is also celebrated as an ecological awareness day, and trees are often planted in festive ceremonies.

TU BISHVAT FOR OUR TIME

The Stewardship Paradigm

Few texts have had a deeper influence on Western civilisation than the first chapter of Bereshit, with its momentous vision of the universe coming into being as the work of God. Set against the grandeur of the narrative, what stands out is the smallness, yet uniqueness, of humans, vulnerable but also undeniably set apart from all other beings.

The words of the psalmist echo the wonder and humility that the primordial couple must have felt as they beheld the splendour of Creation:

> When I consider Your heavens, the work of Your fingers,
> The moon and the stars, which You have set in place.
> What is humanity that You are mindful of it,
> The children of mortals that You care for them?
> Yet You have made them little lower than the angels
> And crowned them with glory and honour. (Tehillim 8:4–6)

The honour and glory that crowns the human race is possession of the earth, which is granted as the culmination of God's creative work: "Be fruitful and multiply; fill the earth and subdue it." This notion is fortified in Tehillim 115: "The heavens are the Lord's heavens, but the earth God has given to humanity." **While the Creation narrative clearly establishes God as master of the universe, it is the human being who is appointed master of the earth.**

Grappling with the challenging notion of humans as divinely ordained owners and subduers of the earth, we come face to face with the fundamental questions of our place in the universe and our responsibility for it. A literal interpretation suggests a world in which people may cut down forests, slaughter animals, and dump waste into the seas at their leisure, much like we see in our world today.

On the other hand, as Rav Kook, first chief rabbi of Israel, writes, any intelligent person should know that Bereshit 1:28 (the command to rule the world), "does not mean the domination of a harsh ruler who afflicts his people and servants merely to fulfil his personal whim and desire, according to the crookedness of his heart." Could God have really created such a complex and magnificent world solely for the caprice of humans?

Bereshit chapter 1 is only one side of the complex biblical equation. It is balanced by the narrative of Bereshit chapter 2, which features a

---

REFLECT

How does humanity demonstrate that they are "masters of the earth"? How do you demonstrate this in your everyday life?

"The honour and glory that crowns the human race is possession of the earth."

second Creation narrative that focuses on humans and their place in the Garden of Eden. **The first person is set in the Garden "to work it and take care of it."**

The two Hebrew verbs used here are significant. The first – *le'ovda* – literally means "to serve it." The human being is thus both master and servant of nature. The second – *leshomra* – means "to guard it." This is the verb used in later biblical legislation to describe the responsibilities of a guardian of property that belongs to someone else. This guardian must exercise vigilance while protecting, and is personally liable for losses that occur through negligence. **This is perhaps the best short definition of humanity's responsibility for nature as the Bible conceives it.**

We do not own nature – "The earth is the Lord's and the fullness thereof" (Tehillim 24:1). We are its stewards on behalf of God, who created and owns everything. As guardians of the earth, we are duty-bound to respect its integrity.

REFLECT

How is seeing our relationship with nature through the terms le'ovda *and* leshomra *like borrowing your parents' car?*

The mid-nineteenth-century commentator Rabbi Samson Raphael Hirsch put this rather well in an original interpretation of Bereshit 1:26, "Let us make the human in our image after our own likeness." This passage has always been puzzling, since the hallmark of the Torah is the singularity of God. Who would God consult in the process of creating humans?

The "us," says Hirsch, refers to the rest of Creation. Before creating the human, a being destined to develop the capacity to alter and possibly endanger the natural world, God sought the approval of nature itself. This interpretation implies that we would use nature only in such a way that is faithful to the purposes of its Creator and acknowledges nature's consent to the creation of humanity.

REFLECT

Do you think nature would have agreed to the creation of humanity if it could have seen how humanity would come to treat the planet in our generation?

The mandate in Bereshit 1 to exercise dominion is, therefore, not technical, but moral: humanity would control, within our means, the use of nature towards the service of God. Further, this mandate is limited by the requirement to serve and guard as seen in Bereshit 2. The famous story of Bereshit 2–3 – the eating of the forbidden fruit and Adam and Ḥava's subsequent exile from Eden – supports this point.

Not everything is permitted. There are limits to how we interact with planet Earth. The Torah has commandments regarding how to

sow crops, how to collect eggs, and how to preserve trees in a time of war, just to name a few. When we do not treat Creation according to God's will, disaster can follow.

We see this today as more and more cities sit under a cloud of smog and as mercury advisories are issued over large sectors of our fishing waters. Deforestation of the rainforests, largely a result of humanity's growing demand for timber and beef, has brought on irrevocable destruction of plant and animal species.

We can no longer ignore the massive negative impact that our global industrial society is having on the ecosystems of the earth. Our unbounded use of fossil fuels to fuel our energy-intensive lifestyle is causing global climate change. An international consensus of scientists predicts more intense and destructive storms, floods, and droughts resulting from these human-induced changes in the atmosphere. If we do not take action now, we risk the very survival of civilisation as we know it.

The Midrash says that God showed Adam around the Garden of Eden and said, "Look at My works! See how beautiful they are – how excellent! For your sake I created them all. See to it that you do not spoil and destroy My world, for if you do, there will be no one else to repair it."

Creation has its own dignity as God's masterpiece, and though we have the mandate to use it, we have none to destroy or despoil it. Rabbi Hirsch says that Shabbat was given to humanity "in order that he should not grow overweening in his dominion" of God's Creation. On the day of rest, "he must, as it were, return the borrowed world to its Divine Owner in order to realise that it is but lent to him."

Ingrained in the process of creation and central to the life of every Jew is a weekly reminder that **our dominion of the earth must be** *leshem Shamayim* – **for the sake of Heaven.**

The choice is ours. If we continue to live as though God had only commanded us to subdue the earth, we must be prepared for our children to inherit a seriously degraded planet, with the future of human civilisation put into question.

If we see our role as masters of the earth as a unique opportunity to truly serve and care for the planet, its creatures, and its resources, then we can reclaim our status as stewards of the world and raise our new generations in an environment much closer to that of Eden.

REFLECT

How have we allowed the situation to get to this point? Is it too late to save the planet?

REFLECT

What change can you make today to live by this message?

FROM THE THOUGHT OF RABBI SACKS

Judaism's ecological imperative is a delicate balance between "mastering and subduing" nature (Bereshit 1), and "serving and protecting" it (Bereshit 2). So we have Jewish laws that prohibit needless waste, the destruction of species, and the despoliation and overexploitation of the environment. The general principle is that we must see ourselves as the guardians of the world, for the sake of future generations.

A Letter in the Scroll, **165**

Though we must exercise caution when reading twenty-first-century issues into ancient texts, there seems little doubt that much biblical legislation is concerned with what we would call nowadays "sustainability." This is particularly true of the three great commands ordaining periodic rest: the Sabbath (Shabbat), the Sabbatical year (*Shemitta*), and the Jubilee year (*Yovel*). On the Sabbath, all agricultural work is forbidden, "so that your ox and your donkey may rest" (Shemot 23:12). It is a day that sets limits to our intervention in nature and the pursuit of economic activity. We become conscious of being creations, not creators. The earth is not ours but God's. For six days it is handed over to us, but on the seventh day we symbolically abdicate that power. We may perform no "work," which is to say, avoiding actions that alter the state of something for human purposes. Shabbat is a weekly reminder of the integrity of nature and the boundaries of human striving.

The Dignity of Difference, **167**

Shabbat reminds us that the universe is a creation – meaning that ultimately it belongs to God and we are merely its guardians. Adam was placed in the Garden to "serve and protect it," and so are we. One day in seven we must renounce our mastery over nature and the animals, and see the earth not as something to be manipulated and exploited, but as a thing of independent dignity and beauty. Our world is entitled to its rest and protection. More powerfully than any tutorial or documentary, Shabbat makes us aware of the limits of human striving. To put it another way, Shabbat is a day of ecological consciousness.

Faith in the Future, **136**

POINTS TO PONDER

1. *How do we find the balance between "mastering and subduing" nature (Bereshit 1), and "serving and protecting" it (Bereshit 2)?*

2. *How do the mitzvot of Shabbat,* Shemitta, *and* Yovel *help to protect the environment?*

3. *How can we internalise the inherent ecological message of Shabbat, so that we observe this throughout the week too?*

> "We must see ourselves as the guardians of the world, for the sake of future generations."

TOP TEN TU BISHVAT FACTS

1. Tu BiShvat is a date (not the type you can eat, though that is connected!).

2. Tu BiShvat is called Rosh HaShana (for trees) in the Mishna.

3. Beit Shammai taught that the date of the new year for trees should be on the first day of Shvat (which would have meant the festival would have become known as Alef BiShvat!).

4. Tu BiShvat is not mentioned in the Torah, only in the Talmud.

5. The original purpose of Tu BiShvat was a tax deadline (for tithing). Only later was it developed into a festival to celebrate trees and (eventually) the environment.

6. The almond tree is the first to blossom in Israel, around the time of Tu BiShvat, and this is considered a very early sign of the oncoming spring.

7. It is a Torah law that you are not allowed to cut down a fruit-bearing tree.

8. The Talmud describes a beautiful custom in which a tree is planted when a baby is born (a cedar tree for a baby boy and a pine tree for a baby girl). When the baby grows up and gets married, the tree's wood is used for the *ḥuppa* (Gittin 57a).

9. There is a custom to eat extra fruit on Tu BiShvat, especially fruit from the land of Israel, and some have the custom to eat a type of fruit they have not eaten that season (so that they can make the blessing *Sheheḥeyanu*).

10. The famous kabbalist teacher Rabbi Yitzhak Luria (the Arizal) had the custom to eat fifteen different varieties of fruit on Tu BiShvat.

IT ONCE HAPPENED...

The following story is inspired by the book "The Giving Tree" by Shel Silverstein. It has been adapted to reflect our current world.

Once there was a tree, and she loved a little boy. And every day the boy would come and play in her leaves, and climb her trunk and swing from her branches, and eat from her apples. And they would play hide-and-seek. And when he was tired he would sleep in her shade. The boy loved the tree very much, and the tree was happy.

But time went by. And the boy grew older. And the boy was given his first smartphone. And the boy loved to play games with his friends on his phone and his tablet and his video game console. Every day he would go to school, excited to talk to his friends about the games, and every day he would rush home to play the games again. And the tree was often alone.

One day they closed the schools, and they closed the offices, and they closed the shops, because of a dangerous virus. But he still had his smartphone, and his tablet, and his video game console. And the tree was still alone.

But the longer the boy had to stay at home (and the longer he had to attend school online), the more restless he became.

Until one day, out of the corner of his eye, the boy caught a glimpse of his old friend the tree through his window (which was just behind his computer screen). The tree had never looked more inviting or beautiful to him, and he ran to sit in her shade and play amongst her leaves and eat her apples.

And he promised never to forget the tree again.

And the tree was happy.

POINTS TO PONDER

1. *Why did the boy forget the tree?*

2. *Why did the boy remember the tree after he was stuck at home because of the virus?*

3. *What lessons do you think we can learn about looking after the environment from our experience during the coronavirus pandemic?*

ḤIDON ON THE ḤAG (A QUICK QUIZ)

Match the names of the Seven Species of the land of Israel to the corresponding images.

1 Wheat

2 Barley

3 Grapes

4 Figs

5 Pomegranates

6 Olives

7 Dates

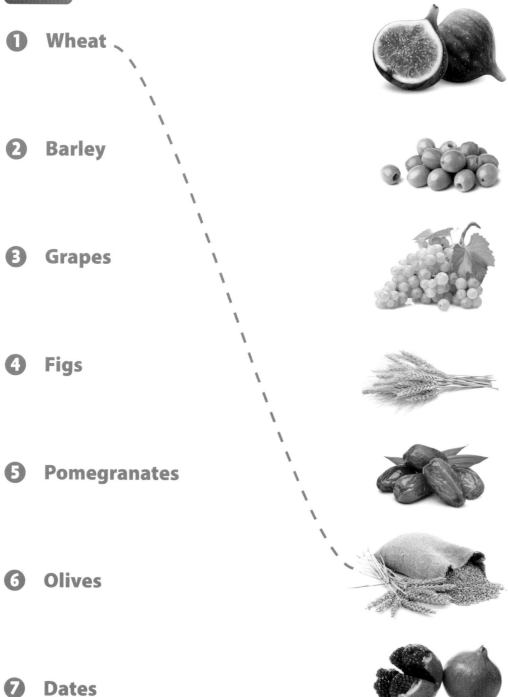

Match the pictures of these eight trees native to the land of Israel to the corresponding names and verses.

Terebinth

וַיֵּלֶךְ אַחֲרֵי אִישׁ הָאֱלֹקִים וַיִּמְצָאֵהוּ יֹשֵׁב תַּחַת הָאֵלָה וַיֹּאמֶר אֵלָיו הַאַתָּה אִישׁ הָאֱלֹקִים אֲשֶׁר בָּאתָ מִיהוּדָה וַיֹּאמֶר אָנִי.

And he went after the man of God and he found him sitting under a terebinth, and he spoke to him: "Are you the man of God who came from Yehuda?" And he replied: "I am he." (I Melakhim 13:14)

Oak

וְאָנֹכִי הִשְׁמַדְתִּי אֶת הָאֱמֹרִי מִפְּנֵיהֶם אֲשֶׁר כְּגֹבַהּ אֲרָזִים גָּבְהוֹ וְחָסֹן הוּא כָּאַלּוֹנִים וָאַשְׁמִיד פִּרְיוֹ מִמַּעַל וְשָׁרָשָׁיו מִתָּחַת.

And I destroyed the Amorites from before them, whose height is as the height of the cedar trees, and they are as strong as oaks, and I destroyed his fruit from above and his roots from below! (Amos 2:9)

Cedar

וַיִּבֶן שְׁלֹמֹה אֶת הַבַּיִת וַיְכַלֵּהוּ. וַיִּבֶן אֶת קִירוֹת הַבַּיִת מִבַּיְתָה בְּצַלְעוֹת אֲרָזִים מִקַּרְקַע הַבַּיִת עַד קִירוֹת הַסִּפֻּן צִפָּה עֵץ מִבָּיִת וַיְצַף אֶת קַרְקַע הַבַּיִת בְּצַלְעוֹת בְּרוֹשִׁים.

When Shlomo had completed the construction of the House, he built the walls of the House within boards of cedar; from the floor of the House till the joists of the ceiling, he covered them on the inside with wood; and he covered the floor of the House with boards of cypress. (I Melakhim 6:14–15)

Tamarisk

וַיִּטַּע אֶשֶׁל בִּבְאֵר שָׁבַע וַיִּקְרָא שָׁם בְּשֵׁם ה׳ קֵל עוֹלָם.

[Avraham] planted a tamarisk at Be'er Sheva, and invoked there the name of the Lord, the everlasting God. (Bereshit 21:33)

Cypress

כְּבוֹד הַלְּבָנוֹן אֵלַיִךְ יָבוֹא בְּרוֹשׁ תִּדְהָר וּתְאַשּׁוּר יַחְדָּו לְפָאֵר מְקוֹם מִקְדָּשִׁי וּמְקוֹם רַגְלַי אֲכַבֵּד.

The glory of the Lebanon shall come to you – cypresses, firs and box trees – and together, to glorify the place of My Sanctuary, and the place of My feet I will honour. (Yeshayahu 60:13)

Sycamore

וַיִּתֵּן הַמֶּלֶךְ אֶת הַכֶּסֶף בִּירוּשָׁלַםִ כָּאֲבָנִים וְאֵת הָאֲרָזִים נָתַן כַּשִּׁקְמִים אֲשֶׁר בַּשְּׁפֵלָה לָרֹב.

And the king made silver as common in Jerusalem as stones, and cedars as common as sycamores, which are in the low lands in abundance. (I Melakhim 10:27)

Acacia

וְעָשִׂיתָ אֶת הַקְּרָשִׁים לַמִּשְׁכָּן עֲצֵי שִׁטִּים עֹמְדִים.

You shall make the planks for the Mishkan out of acacia wood, upright. (Shemot 26:15)

Almond

וַיֹּאמֶר אֲלֵהֶם יִשְׂרָאֵל אֲבִיהֶם אִם כֵּן אֵפוֹא זֹאת עֲשׂוּ קְחוּ מִזִּמְרַת הָאָרֶץ בִּכְלֵיכֶם וְהוֹרִידוּ לָאִישׁ מִנְחָה מְעַט צֳרִי וּמְעַט דְּבַשׁ נְכֹאת וָלֹט בָּטְנִים וּשְׁקֵדִים.

So Yisrael, their father, said to them, "If so, then do this: take some of the choice products of the land in your vessels, and take down to the man as a gift, a little balm and a little honey, wax and lotus, pistachios and almonds. (Bereshit 43:11)

EDUCATIONAL COMPANION TO THE QUESTIONS

TU BISHVAT IN A NUTSHELL

1. We may not call them "New Years" but there are various annual cycles in the civil calendar also. For example, the academic year, the tax year, and sports seasons begin at various times during the year in different countries.

2. This festival was originally focused on the agricultural laws (which only apply when living in the land of Israel). After the exile began, these laws were no longer applicable for the majority of the people, and the festival had limited relevance. In order to continue to connect to both the festival and the land of Israel during the exile years, new meaning was found in the festival and new rituals were developed. A recent example of this is the reconnecting to trees and the land of Israel after the rise of Zionism and the establishment of the State of Israel.

3. In our generation, environmental awareness and conservation has become highly important and topical. This is a theme that connects naturally to Tu BiShvat and creates a new angle and relevance for us in the twenty-first century.

FROM THE THOUGHT OF RABBI SACKS

1. This is a very challenging question facing us, and finding the correct answer is more pressing than ever before. This is called environmentally sustainable development – where we continue to develop and use the natural resources of the earth for the betterment of humankind, but in an environmentally responsible way that allows our natural resources to regenerate, without causing permanent and long-term damage. To find the right balance, we (individuals and governments) must listen to the experts, including scientists, economists, and moral thinkers.

2. These three mitzvot force humans to take a step back from nature, ensuring they refrain from consuming and manipulating nature for a temporary period (one day in seven, or one year in seven, for example). This allows the earth's resources to replenish, but also, crucially, there is an educational impact on those observing these laws, reminding us that we are not the sole masters of nature and of the earth's natural resources. The universe belongs to its Creator, and we are tasked with maintaining it in a sustainable way in order to benefit from its resources without destroying them.

3. Shabbat gives us a weekly experience of spending a day taking stock and realising that there are boundaries that we cannot and should not cross. We are part of nature and not above it. When we recognise this, we can go into the week with a greater awareness of our duty to use the world's resources in an environmentally responsible way, preserving and protecting them where necessary. The message of Shabbat should impact the way we consume, develop, and grow as individuals and as a species.

IT ONCE HAPPENED ON TU BISHVAT...

1. The boy became distracted by other things in his life. To some extent this is a natural phenomenon. As children grow up, the things that are important to them and take up their time and energy change. However, this is also a metaphor for how we sometimes lose sight of the beauty all around us in the natural world when we become distracted by other things in life that become our priorities, such as technology or our careers.

2. During the pandemic, so much was taken away from us. The outdoors and nature suddenly became more important to us than ever before, and our appreciation of nature became heightened. While we couldn't go about our normal lives (school, work, shopping, etc.) we found ourselves heading outside to appreciate the natural world in a way we may not have done when we had more freedom but also more distractions.

3. During the early lockdowns around the world, there was no traffic on the roads, little air travel, dramatically less pollution in the air, less consumerism, and in general, the mad rush of life took a pause, as we began to appreciate the more important things in life, such as family, friends, and the environment. A silver lining from this challenging period would be if humanity learned this lesson and if we redrew our values and priorities with that in mind.

ḤIDON ON THE ḤAG (A QUICK QUIZ)

The Seven Species

Wheat – 6

Barley – 4

Grapes – 3

Figs – 1

Pomegranates – 7

Olives – 2

Dates – 5

Eight Trees Native to the Land of Israel

Terebinth – 7

Oak – 8

Cedar – 5

Tamarisk – 6

Cypress – 4

Sycamore – 2

Acacia – 1

Almond – 3

Purim

PURIM IN A NUTSHELL

Purim is the Jewish carnival of happiness, commemorating the rescue of the Jewish people during the ancient Persian Empire from the evil Haman (a descendant of the Jews' archenemy, Amalek), who tried "to destroy, kill, and annihilate all the Jews – young and old, women and children – in a single day" (Esther 3:13). The story is recorded in *Megillat Esther*. The word *"purim"* means "lots" in ancient Persian and became the name of the festival because Haman drew lots to determine when he would carry out his plot.

THE STORY

The Persian Empire of the fourth century BCE extended over 127 lands, and Jews were spread across the empire. When King Aḥashverosh had his wife, Queen Vashti, executed for failing to follow his orders, he arranged a beauty pageant to find a new queen. A Jewish girl named Esther found favour in his eyes and became the new queen, but she hid her nationality.

Meanwhile, the Jew-hating Haman was appointed prime minister of the empire. Mordekhai, the leader of the Jews, refused to bow to Haman – a direct defiance of the royal decree. Haman was furious, and he persuaded the king to issue a decree ordering the destruction of all the Jews on the thirteenth of Adar, a date randomly chosen by drawing lots.

Mordekhai urged Esther to confront the king and inform him of Haman's plans. Although reluctant at first for fear of her life, Esther agreed. She asked Mordekhai to gather all the Jews in Shushan and convince them to spend three days repenting, fasting, and praying to God. On the third day, Esther invited the king and Haman to join

> "Purim is the Jewish carnival of happiness."

her for a feast. At a second feast, Esther revealed her Jewish identity to the king and accused Haman of attempting to destroy her people. Haman was hanged, Mordekhai was appointed prime minister in his stead, and a new decree was issued, granting the Jews the right to defend themselves against their enemies.

On the thirteenth of Adar, the Jews mobilised and killed many of their enemies. On the fourteenth of Adar, they rested and celebrated. In the capital city of Shushan, they took one more day to finish the job, and so in areas which have been "walled cities" from the time of Yehoshua (like Shushan), Purim is celebrated on the fifteenth of Adar instead of the fourteenth. Today, this only applies to the city of Jerusalem, which celebrates "Shushan Purim" the day after all other Jewish communities.

HOW WE CELEBRATE PURIM

There are four mitzvot on the day of Purim, and they all begin with the letter *mem* in Hebrew. These are:

- *Megilla* – reading the Book of Esther, which tells the story of the Purim miracle. We listen to the *Megilla* once on the night of Purim and then again on the following day.
- *Matanot LaEvyonim* – giving gifts of money to at least two poor people.
- *Mishloaḥ Manot* – sending gifts of two kinds of ready-to-eat food to at least one person.
- *Mishteh* – eating a festive Purim feast (*Seudat Purim*), which often includes wine or other intoxicating beverages.

There is a general spirit of liveliness and fun on Purim that is unparalleled in the Jewish calendar. It is also customary for children especially (but adults also, if they desire) to dress up in costumes. This is because the role of God is hidden in the story of Purim (and in fact, even the name of God is starkly missing from the *Megilla*).

A traditional Purim food is hamantaschen (three-cornered pastries bursting with sweet fillings such as poppy seeds). "*Taschen*" means "pockets" in Yiddish and German, but some believe these pastries represent Haman's favourite three-cornered hat, and in Hebrew we call them "*oznei Haman,*" meaning "Haman's ears"!

On the day before Purim (or on the Thursday before, when Purim is on Sunday), it is customary for those over bar and bat mitzva age to fast. This commemorates Esther leading the people in fasting and prayer, begging God to save them.

POINTS TO PONDER

1. *What is the message behind the custom to dress up on Purim? How can we take this message into our everyday lives?*

2. *The word "purim" means "lots," which might imply that the destiny of the Jewish people is random. How is the message of the festival of Purim the opposite of this?*

3. *What do the four mitzvot of Purim have in common with each other? How is this connected to Purim?*

PURIM FOR OUR TIME: THE THERAPEUTIC JOY OF PURIM

There is a unique law in the approach to Purim. *"Mishenikhnas Adar marbim besimḥa,"* "From the beginning of Adar, we increase in joy." This is stated in the Talmud (Taanit 29a) and is based on the passage in the *Megilla* (Esther 9:21–22) in which Mordekhai sends a letter throughout the land instructing all Jews "to observe the fourteenth day of the month of Adar and the fifteenth day, every year – the days on which the Jews obtained rest from their enemies and *the month which for them was turned from sorrow into gladness and from mourning into a holiday."*

This in turn refers back to the text in which Haman decided on the timing of his decree: "In the first month, the month of Nisan, in the twelfth year of Aḥashverosh, they cast *pur* (lots) before Haman from day to day, and from month to month until the twelfth month, which is the month of Adar" (Esther 3:7).

The difficulties are obvious. Why do we increase our joy for an entire month? The key events were focused on a few days, the thirteenth to the fifteenth, not the whole month.

And why is this a time of *simḥa*? We can understand why the Jews of the time felt exhilaration. The decree sentencing them to death was rescinded. Their enemies were punished. Haman was hanged on the very gallows that he had prepared for Mordekhai, and Mordekhai himself was raised to greatness.

But is joy the emotion we should feel in perpetuity, remembering those events? The first warrant for genocide against the Jewish people (the second, if one counts Pharaoh's plan to kill all newborn Jewish males) was frustrated. But is *simḥa* the appropriate emotion? Surely, what we should feel is relief, not joy. Pesaḥ is the proof. The word "joy" is never mentioned in the Torah in connection with it.

Besides which, the Talmud asks why we do not say Hallel on Purim. It gives several answers. The most powerful is that in Hallel we say, "Servants of the Lord, give praise" – meaning that we are no longer the servants of Pharaoh. But, says the Talmud, even after the deliverance of Purim, Jews were still the servants of Aḥashverosh, still living in exile, under his rule (Megilla 14a). Tragedy had been averted but there was no real change in the hazards of life in the Diaspora.

> "Tragedy had been averted but there was no real change in the hazards of life in the Diaspora."

It seems to me therefore that the *simḥa* we celebrate throughout the month of Adar is different from the normal joy we feel when something good and positive has happened to us or our people. That is *expressive* joy. The *simḥa* of Adar, by contrast, is *therapeutic* joy.

Imagine what it is to be part of a people that had once heard the command issued against them: "To destroy, kill, and annihilate all the Jews – young and old, women and children – on a single day" (Esther 3:13). We who live after the Holocaust, who have met survivors, heard their testimony, seen the photographs and documentaries and memorials, know the answer to that question. On Purim, the Final Solution was averted. But it had been pronounced. Ever afterwards, Jews knew their vulnerability. The very existence of Purim in our historical memory is traumatic.

The Jewish response to trauma is counter-intuitive and extraordinary. You defeat fear with joy. You conquer terror with collective celebration. You prepare a festive meal, invite guests, give gifts to friends. While the story is being told, you make an unruly noise as if not only to blot out the memory of Amalek, but to make a joke out of the whole episode. You wear masks. You drink a little too much. You make a Purim *spiel*.

Precisely because the threat was so serious, you refuse to be serious – and in that refusal you are doing something very serious indeed. You are denying your enemies a victory. You are declaring that you will not be intimidated. As the date of the scheduled destruction approaches, you surround yourself with the single most effective antidote to fear: joy in life itself. As the three-sentence summary of Jewish history puts it: "They tried to destroy us. We survived. Let's eat." Humour is the Jewish way of defeating hate. What you can laugh at cannot hold you captive.

I learned this from a Holocaust survivor. Some years ago, I wrote a book called *Celebrating Life*. It was a cheer-you-up book, and it became a favourite of the Holocaust survivors. One of them, however, told me that a particular passage in the book was incorrect. Commenting on Roberto Benigni's comedy film about the Holocaust, *Life is Beautiful*, I had said that though I agreed with his thesis – a sense of humour keeps you sane – that was not enough to keep you alive in Auschwitz.

"On that, you are wrong," the survivor said, and then told me his story. He had been in Auschwitz, and he soon realised that if he failed to keep his spirits up, he would die. So he made a pact with another young man, that they would both look out, each day, for some occurrence they found amusing. At the end of each day they would tell one another their story and they would laugh together. "That sense of humour saved my life," he said. I stood corrected. He was right.

That is what we do on Purim. The joy, the merrymaking, the food, the drink, the whole carnival atmosphere, are there to allow us to live with the risks of being a Jew – in the past, and tragically, in the present also – without being terrified, traumatised, or intimidated. It is the most counter-intuitive response to terror, and the most effective. Terrorists aim to terrify. To be a Jew is to refuse to be terrified.

Terror, hatred, and violence are always ultimately self-destructive. Those who use these tactics are always, as was Haman, destroyed by their very will to destruct. And yes, we as Jews must fight anti-Semitism, the demonisation of Israel, and the intimidation of Jewish students on campus. But we must never let ourselves be intimidated – and the Jewish way to avoid this is *marbim besimḥa*, to increase our joy. A people that can know the full darkness of history and yet rejoice is a people whose spirit no power on earth can ever break.

REFLECT

What role do you think joy has played in the survival of the Jewish people throughout Jewish history?

FROM THE THOUGHT OF RABBI SACKS

I am proud to be part of a people who, though scarred and traumatised, never lost their humour or their faith, their ability to laugh at present troubles and still believe in ultimate redemption, who saw human history as a journey, and never stopped travelling and searching. I am proud to be part of an age in which my people, ravaged by the worst crime ever to be committed against a people, responded by reviving a land, recovering their sovereignty, rescuing threatened Jews throughout the world, rebuilding Jerusalem, and proving themselves to be as courageous in the pursuit of peace as in defending themselves in war.

A Letter in the Scroll, 228–229

POINTS TO PONDER

1. *How are humour and faith connected?*

2. *What is the "ultimate redemption"? Have we reached it yet?*

3. *What lessons can we learn both from Purim and from our ongoing journey through Jewish history?*

> "I am proud to be part of a people who, though scarred and traumatised, never lost their humour or their faith."

ḤIDON ON THE ḤAG
(A QUICK QUIZ)

1. What does the word "*purim*" mean?

2. What date did Haman select (via casting lots) for his planned execution of the Jewish people?

3. Which book of Tanakh tells the story of Purim?

4. What are the four mitzvot of Purim?

5. What does the congregation traditionally do when they hear the name Haman during the reading of the *Megilla*?

6. Why do we have the custom to dress up on Purim?

7. How many provinces did King Aḥashverosh rule over?

8. What were the names of the two guards who plotted to kill the king?

9. What are hamantaschen and what does the word mean?

10. What was Esther's Hebrew name (Esther was her Persian name)?

11. How many times is God mentioned in *Megillat Esther*?

12. When do we read the *Megilla*?

13. When and what is Shushan Purim?

14. What was the name of King Aḥashverosh's first wife?

15. Why do we fast on the thirteenth of Adar?

IT ONCE HAPPENED...

There is a story of a man named Eddie Jacobson that reminds us of the role Esther played in the Purim story. Eddie was an ordinary Jewish guy from the Lower East Side of New York. When Eddie was a child, his parents moved to Kansas City and there he met a boy named Harry. Soon they became close school friends, did military service together during the First World War, and decided that when the war was over, they would go into business together. They set up a clothing store in Kansas City, but the business was not a great success and soon they drifted apart. Eddie Jacobson went on to become a travelling salesman, selling clothes. His friend, Harry S. Truman, took a slightly different route and landed up as president of the United States.

In 1947–48, the Jews of the world needed the support of the United States of America for the State of Israel to be proclaimed and recognised. The State Department was against it and advised the president not to support the creation of the State of Israel. Jews and Jewish organisations tried their utmost to see the president in the White House, and every single attempt was refused. Even the leader of the Zionist movement, Chaim Weizmann, the man who would become the first president of the State of Israel, was refused a meeting.

As times became desperate, somebody remembered that Truman had a childhood friend called Eddie Jacobson. So they reached out to Eddie and asked if he could get the president of the United States to meet with Chaim Weizmann. Eddie phoned up President Truman and said he had to come and see him. Truman's officials tried to block the meeting, but Truman said, "This is my old friend, Eddie from school, Eddie from the army, Eddie from our shop together! How can I not see this man?"

When Eddie arrived at the White House, Truman said, "Eddie, you can talk to me about anything, except Israel." "Okay," said Eddie and he stood in the Oval Office, in front of the president of the United States, and began to cry. "Eddie, why are you crying?" asked the president. Eddie pointed to a marble statue in the room and asked, "Who is that, Harry?" "That's my hero, Andrew Jackson," Truman replied. "You really admire this man?"

asked Eddie. "Yes." "And he had an influence over you?" "Yes," said Truman. Then, said Eddie, "I have a hero. His name is Chaim Weizmann. Harry, for my sake, please meet this man." Harry looked at Eddie and he knew that he couldn't say no to his old friend. That is how Chaim Weizmann got to see President Harry S. Truman, and that is how America voted in favour of the creation of the State of Israel. If America had not voted, Israel would not have been brought into being. What's more, Harry S. Truman made the United States the first country in the world to recognise the state when David Ben-Gurion pronounced it.

Towards the end of the fourth chapter of *Megillat Esther*, we find Esther telling her uncle, Mordekhai, about all the problems there might be in interceding with King Aḥashverosh regarding the fate of the Jewish people. Mordekhai listens and then responds to her with the famous words, "*Im haḥaresh taharishi ba'et hazot, revaḥ vehatzala yaamod laYehudim mimakom aḥer,*" "If you are silent and you do nothing at this time somebody else will save the Jewish people." "*Umi yode'a im le'et kazot higaat lamalkhut?*" "But who knows, was it not for just this moment that you became a queen, with access to King Aḥashverosh in the royal palace?" Just like Eddie Jacobson and Esther HaMalka, Hashem is calling on each of us, saying there is a reason why we are here, because He has something for us to do, something that only we can do.

POINTS TO PONDER

1. *What did Esther and Eddie have in common?*

2. *Do you think they should be celebrated for their roles, or were they just carrying out God's plan?*

3. *Do you have a sense of what your calling is? How will you know it when you see it?*

THE GREAT PURIM SCAVENGER HUNT

One of the themes of Purim is the hidden role God played in the story of Purim, and this is the reason why we have the fun tradition to dress up ("hide" ourselves) in costumes on Purim. This is also one possible meaning of the name Esther. In this special Purim scavenger hunt, your task is to find the following Purim objects that are "hidden" somewhere in this chapter.

 Megilla

 Hamantaschen

 Mordekhai

 Matanot La'Evyonim

 Raashan

 Esther

 Mishloaḥ manot

 Mask

 Haman

 Seudat Purim

 Clown

 Aḥashverosh

EDUCATIONAL COMPANION TO THE QUESTIONS

PURIM IN A NUTSHELL

1. God's name is conspicuous in its absence from the Purim story. He is not mentioned at all in the text of *Megillat Esther*, and God plays no explicit role in the narrative. However, it is implicit and understood that all the intricate twists and turns of the story are engineered by God. This is the faith that Jews have. Even when it is not obvious, we have faith that God is backstage, engineering His plan for our lives. We dress up in costumes both to experience the joy and levity of the festival, and to remember that God was hidden in the story, yet very much present. When there are difficult times in our lives, or even (and perhaps more importantly) when life is going well, we must have faith that God is pulling the strings, that there is a larger picture, and even if we cannot see or sense the role God is playing, we have faith that He is always involved.

2. Lots are a cruel and random way to decide on the fate of a people. Perhaps this was Haman's message to the Jewish people. "There is no meaning to your national life. It is all random and there is no one protecting you or guaranteeing your destiny." Haman was proven completely wrong when God intervened in history, saving the Jews in dramatic (yet hidden) fashion. The message of Purim is that there is destiny, and God is behind the scenes ensuring it. There is nothing random about history!

3. All four mitzvot strengthen community and the relationships between people. Perhaps we can say that this was another victory of the Jewish people over their adversary Haman. The emphasis on community and unity within the Jewish people is devastating to our enemies, and the key to our strength.

FROM THE THOUGHT OF RABBI SACKS

1. Both humour and faith are an expression of the freedom contained in our hearts, despite those who may wish to take away our freedom. Survivors of the Holocaust (like Viktor Frankl and Edith Eger) often speak about the Nazis stripping away every freedom and vestige of dignity, but they could not take away people's freedom to choose how to respond and frame their experiences. Edith Eger called this "the choice" (and that is also the name of her famous book).

2. The ultimate redemption is the Messianic Age, when humankind will enter the final period of history, which will be one of peace for all. Judaism believes this has yet to happen in history, and that this is proven by the suffering and evil that still exists in the world.

3. Despite not experiencing an "ultimate redemption" (the Jews were still under the authority of Aḥashverosh after Haman had been defeated, and *Mashiaḥ* has not yet arrived), the joy of Purim tells us that redemption is a journey that must be travelled until the end. Yet there are many sources of joy on the way. Every day there are reasons for gratitude and joy. That is one of the messages of Purim, and modern Jewish history testifies to this. Despite the dark period of the Holocaust, the modern miracle of the establishment of the State of Israel occurred just a few years later, and although the redemption of Israel is not yet complete (we still need to fight for its very existence), there is still so much joy to be experienced and to be thankful for.

IT ONCE HAPPENED ON PURIM...

1. Both Esther and Eddie felt that they were average people without any particular power or influence. True, Esther became the queen with some limited influence (that she ultimately used to her and the Jewish people's benefit), but she probably felt like a nobody, an inconsequential Jewish girl who was picked off the street by random coincidence (or divine destiny) to be the king's wife. Eddie was an unremarkable Jewish travelling salesman from Kansas. Yet they both changed the course of Jewish history,

recognising their moment when it came, and playing their small role to help their people.

2. This is the classic question when a person achieves great things that we believe are part of the divine plan. Can they celebrate their achievement, or does all credit go to God? The message of the Purim story in particular, and Judaism in general, is that both exist concurrently. Esther and Eddie must be commended and celebrated for their courage and initiative and for the role they played. But the message of *Megillat Esther* is that God is always behind the scenes, pulling the strings, making sure His plan for history is fulfilled.

3. Some people sense their calling in life from an early age, and for some, like Eddie, it comes in an instant, much later in life. Our mission could be to make an impact continuously, in small moments and kind acts, through a career or through activism. Or it could be to make an impact in one single moment where we have the opportunity to change history, like Eddie and Esther. It is our responsibility to always look for this mission and to answer God's hidden call.

ḤIDON ON THE ḤAG (A QUICK QUIZ)

1. Lots (like in a lottery).
2. Thirteenth of Adar.
3. *Megillat Esther*.

4. The four *mems*:
   - *Megillat Esther* – reading the *Megilla*
   - *Matanot LaEvyonim* – giving gifts to the poor
   - *Mishloaḥ Manot* – sending gifts of food
   - *Mishteh* – eating a festive Purim feast
5. Make a loud noise (for example, booing, stamping their feet, or using a noisemaker known as a *raashan* or *gragger*).
6. To remind us that God was "hidden" in the Purim story, pulling the strings from backstage.
7. One hundred and twenty-seven.
8. Bigtan and Teresh.
9. Hamantaschen are three-cornered pastry treats that could represent Haman's three-cornered hat, his ears, or his pockets.
10. Hadassa.
11. He is not mentioned at all.
12. On the evening and morning of Purim.
13. This is the day that Jerusalem (and other cities walled at the time of Yehoshua) celebrates Purim. It falls on the fifteenth of Adar, the day after Purim for the rest of the world.
14. Vashti.
15. To remember the three-day fast that Esther proclaimed in response to Haman's plan to destroy the Jews.

Pesaḥ

PESAḤ IN A NUTSHELL

Seder night is a highlight of the Jewish calendar for parents and children alike. It is the night that revolves around children, and parents are reminded of the importance of their role as educators. (Thankfully, the Haggada gives them lots of tools and tips!)

Rabbi Sacks explains that on the eve of the original Pesaḥ, at the very moment when a new chapter in the life of the Jewish people began, we found out what it means to be a Jew: "About to gain their freedom, the Israelites were told that they had to become a nation of educators" (*A Letter in the Scroll*, 34). Being a Jew means being both a student and an educator, and Seder night is our opportunity to focus on both these roles.

This section serves as an educational companion to Seder night and will give you some ideas and thoughts on several of the core pages from the Haggada and how Rabbi Sacks understands them. As well as offering educational insights, like the other sections of this book, this Seder night companion also includes activities, stories, and reflection questions, designed to engage all the participants around your Seder table, young and old alike.

You will notice many extracts from Rabbi Sacks's writings, all sourced from *The Jonathan Sacks Haggada* (Koren). This guide is designed to be used in conjunction with a Haggada; it is not a replacement for one.

HA LAḤMA ANYA   הָא לַחְמָא עַנְיָא

IN A NUTSHELL

We start the Haggada, and with it the core of the Seder night, with the mitzva of *Maggid* (the telling of the story of the Exodus), which begins with this invitation to join the Seder. The language of this paragraph is Aramaic, because this was the vernacular (spoken language) at the time the Haggada was written. If this invitation is to be genuine, it is important that it is stated in a language that is understood.

DEEP DIVE

This is a strange invitation: "This is the bread of oppression our fathers ate in the land of Egypt. Let all who are hungry come in and eat." What hospitality is it to offer the hungry the taste of suffering? In fact, though, this is a profound insight into the nature of slavery and freedom. Matza represents two things: it is the food of slaves, and also the bread eaten by the Israelites as they left Egypt in liberty. What transforms the bread of oppression into the bread of freedom is *the willingness to share it with others*.

Sharing food is the first act through which slaves become free human beings. One who fears tomorrow does not offer his bread to others. But one who is willing to divide his food with a stranger has already shown himself capable of fellowship and faith, the two things from which hope is born. That is why we begin the Seder by inviting others to join us. Bread shared is no longer the bread of oppression. Reaching out to others, giving help to the needy and companionship to those who are alone, we bring freedom into the world, and with freedom, God.

REFLECT

What can you share in your life to show you are truly free?

> "Sharing food is the first act through which slaves become free human beings."

FURTHER THOUGHTS

This is the beginning of the Seder narrative, known as *Maggid*, from the word "*haggada*," "relate," "recount," "declare," "proclaim." The story of the Exodus is known as the Haggada because of the verse "You shall tell (*vehigadeta*) your child on that day, '[I do this] because of what the Lord did for me when I went out of Egypt'" (Shemot 13:8). However, the word "*haggada*" derives from a verb that also means "bind," "join," "connect." The story of the Exodus is more than a recounting (*sipur*) of things that happened long ago. It binds the present to the past and future. It connects one generation to the next. It joins us to our children. Jewish continuity means that each successive generation commits itself to continuing the story. Our past lives on in us.

REFLECT

Do you feel more connected to your parents and grandparents when you sit at the Seder table? Why do you think that is?

QUESTIONS TO ASK AT YOUR SEDER

1. *Why is it important to share your Seder table with people from outside your close family?*

2. *Does matza represent freedom or slavery to you?*

3. *How does Seder night connect you to other Jews?*

EXPERIENCING THE SEDER

If you have guests at your Seder table who are not from your immediate family, turn to them now and make sure they feel welcome.

A STORY FOR THE NIGHT OF STORIES

Primo Levi survived Auschwitz. In his book *If This Is a Man*, he describes his experiences there. According to Levi, the worst time of all was when the Nazis left in January 1945, fearing the Russian advance. All prisoners who could walk were taken on the brutal death marches. The only people left in the camp were those too ill to move. For ten days, they were left alone with only scraps of food and fuel. Levi describes how he worked to light a fire and bring some warmth to his fellow prisoners, many of them dying. He then writes:

When the broken window was repaired and the stove began to spread its heat, something seemed to relax in everyone, and at that moment Towarowski (a Franco-Pole of twenty-three, typhus) proposed to the others that each of them offer a slice of bread to us three who had been working. And so it was agreed.

Only a day before, a similar event would have been inconceivable. The law of the Lager [concentration camps] said: "eat your own bread, and if you can, that of your neighbor," and left no room for gratitude. It really meant that the law of the Lager was dead.

It was the first human gesture that occurred among us. I believe that that moment can be dated as the beginning of the change by which we who had not died slowly changed from Haftlinge [prisoners] to men again.

MA NISHTANA מַה נִשְׁתַּנָּה

IN A NUTSHELL

There are four places in the Torah where it speaks of children asking questions about Pesaḥ – and each of these four verses are the sources for the four children's questions (see below). This inspired a tradition that the story of the Exodus from Egypt must be told, wherever possible, in response to the questions asked by children, and this is where the idea for the four questions in *Ma Nishtana* comes from. The origin of the text is the Mishna (Pesaḥim 10:4), although the words have changed slightly over time to reflect our changing practices (for instance, since the destruction of the Temple, we can no longer bring the *korban*, so the fifth question, on serving roast meat, is no longer included in *Ma Nishtana*).

> "The story of the Exodus from Egypt must be told...in response to the questions asked by children."

DEEP DIVE

The Torah has two words for inheritance, *yerusha* and *naḥala*, and they represent the two different ways in which a heritage is passed on across the generations. The word *naḥala* comes from the root *naḥal*, which also means "river." It represents an inheritance that is merely handed down, without any work on the part of the recipient, as water flows in a river. *Yerusha*, by contrast, means active inheritance. Rabbi Samson Raphael Hirsch pointed out that *lareshet*, the verbal form of *yerusha*, sometimes means "to conquer" or "to capture." It means actively taking hold of what one has been promised. An inheritance for which one has worked is always more secure than one for which one has not. That is why Judaism encourages children to ask questions. When a child asks, they have already begun the work of preparing to receive. Torah is a *yerusha*, not a *naḥala*. It needs work on behalf of the child if it is to be passed on across the generations.

Commentary on *Ma Nishtana*, *The Jonathan Sacks Haggada*

REFLECT

How does Ma Nishtana *and the role of children asking questions affect your experience of the Seder?*

FURTHER THOUGHTS

Religious faith has often been seen as naive, blind, accepting. That is not the Jewish way. Judaism is not the suspension of critical intelligence. To the contrary: asking a question is itself a profound expression of faith in the intelligibility of the universe and the meaningfulness of human life. To ask is to believe that somewhere there is an answer. The fact that throughout history people have devoted their lives to extending the frontiers of knowledge is a compelling testimony to the restlessness of the human spirit and its constant desire to go further, higher, deeper. Far from faith excluding questions, questions testify to faith – that history is not random, that the universe is not impervious to our understanding, that what happens to us is not blind chance. We ask not because we doubt, but because we believe.

"The Art of Asking Questions," *The Jonathan Sacks Haggada*

REFLECT

How is asking questions "an expression of faith"? Doesn't it show a lack of faith?

QUESTIONS TO ASK AT YOUR SEDER

1. *Why do you think we encourage children to ask questions on Seder night?*

2. *Are there any bad questions?*

3. *Do all questions have answers? What do we do if no one we know has the answer to a question?*

A STORY FOR THE NIGHT OF STORIES

Isidor Rabi won the Nobel Prize in physics in 1944. When he was asked why he became a scientist, he replied: "My mother made me a scientist without ever intending to. Every other Jewish mother in Brooklyn would ask her child after school: 'So? Did you learn anything today?' But not my mother. 'Izzy,' she would say, 'did you ask a good question today?' Asking good questions made me a scientist."

> **REFLECT**
>
> *Are you more invested in your learning when you are encouraged to ask questions?*

AVADIM HAYINU   עֲבָדִים הָיִינוּ

IN A NUTSHELL

Avadim Hayinu is our response to the questions asked in the *Ma Nishtana*, and with this we begin the telling of the Exodus story, the main theme of the *Maggid* section of the Haggada. Before we delve into the depths of the story of the Exodus itself, the Haggada makes sure we realise how we are personally affected by this historical event. It reminds us that if not for the Exodus, we would still be slaves in Egypt! This passage also explains that the mitzva of telling the story of the Exodus is for everybody (even the old and wise), and the story should be told at length to make it impactful.

DEEP DIVE

One of the rules of telling the story on Pesaḥ is that each person must feel as if they had personally left Egypt. History becomes memory. The past becomes the present. At this stage, therefore, we speak of the continuing consequences of the past. Had the Exodus not happened, and the Israelites stayed in Egypt, none of the subsequent events of Jewish history would have occurred. What and where we are now is the result of what happened then.

There is a fundamental difference between knowing and telling the story. We do not tell the narrative of the Exodus to know what happened in the past. We do so because each telling engraves that event more thoroughly in our memories, and because each year adds its own insights and interpretations. Judaism is a constant dialogue

> **"History becomes memory. The past becomes the present."**

between past and present, and since the present always changes, there is always a new juxtaposition, a new facet of the story. The Sages said, "There is no house of study without *ḥiddush*, some new interpretation." The story of Pesaḥ never grows old, because the struggle for freedom never ends, and therefore each generation adds its own commentary to the old-new story.

Commentary on *Avadim Hayinu, The Jonathan Sacks Haggada*

FURTHER THOUGHTS

To be a Jew is to know that over and above history is the task of memory. As Jacob Neusner eloquently wrote: "Civilisation hangs suspended, from generation to generation, by the gossamer strand of memory. If only one cohort of mothers and fathers fails to convey to its children what it has learnt from its parents, then the great chain of learning and wisdom snaps. If the guardians of human knowledge stumble only one time, in their fall collapses the whole edifice of knowledge and understanding" (*Neusner on Judaism: Religion and Theology*). More than any other faith, Judaism made this a matter of religious obligation. Pesaḥ is where the past does not die, but lives in the chapter we write in our own lives, and in the story we tell our children.

"History and Memory," *The Jonathan Sacks Haggada*

Screenshot from the animated video **Being Jewish** *at rabbisacks.org*

EXPERIENCING THE SEDER

On Seder night we try to feel as if we ourselves are being freed from slavery in Egypt. During a point in the evening when the younger people seem less engaged (perhaps after we read of the Four Children, until it's time for the Ten Plagues), send them away from the table to find costumes and prepare their own play of the Exodus from Egypt.

They'll have to work quickly! To make it more challenging, you could ask the adults to choose a new genre for the play, such as adventure, science fiction, or fantasy. The play can then be performed later on, during the meal.

THE FOUR CHILDREN   אַרְבָּעָה בָּנִים

IN A NUTSHELL

The section of the Four Children in the Haggada is based on the four different verses in the Torah which describe children asking their parents about the story of the Exodus. Rather than seeing these as just four examples of asking the same question, the Rabbis noticed four distinctive personalities from the different ways the verses are phrased – and this inspired the idea for four kinds of children.

DEEP DIVE

The Four Children are a vignette of the Jewish people. One asks because he wants to hear the answer. A second asks because he does not want to hear the answer. A third asks because he does not understand. The fourth does not ask because he doesn't understand that he doesn't understand. Ours has never been a monolithic people.

Yet there is a message of hope in this family portrait. Though they disagree, they sit around the same table, telling the same story. Though they differ, they stay together. They are part of a single family. Even the rebel is there, although part of him does not want to be. This, too, is who we are.

The Jewish people is an extended family. We argue, we differ, there are times when we are deeply divided. Yet we are part of the same story. We share the same memories. At difficult times we can count on one another. We feel one another's pain. Out of this multiplicity of voices comes something none of us could achieve alone. Sitting next to the wise child, the rebel is not fated to remain a rebel. Sitting next to the rebel, the wise child may share his wisdom rather than keep it to himself. The one who cannot ask will, in time, learn how. The simple child will learn complexity. The wise child will learn simplicity. Each draws strength from the others, as we all draw strength from belonging to a people.

Commentary on the Four Children,
The Jonathan Sacks Haggada

REFLECT

Why do you think Jews argue so much with each other? Is this a strength or a weakness?

> "Though [the four children] disagree, they sit around the same table, telling the same story."

FURTHER THOUGHTS

Through the Haggada, more than a hundred generations of Jews have handed on their story to their children. The word "*haggada*" means "relate," "tell," "expound." But it comes from another Hebrew root [*a-g-d*] that means "bind," "join," "connect." By reciting the Haggada, Jews give their children a sense of connectedness to Jews throughout the world and to the Jewish people through time. It joins them to a past and future, a history and destiny, and makes them characters in its drama. Every other nation known to humankind has been united because its members lived in the same place, spoke the same language, were part of the same culture. Jews alone, dispersed across continents, speaking different languages and participating in different cultures, have been bound together by a narrative, the Pesaḥ narrative, which they tell in the same way on the same night. More than the Haggada is the story of a people, Jews are the people of a story.

"The Story of Stories," *The Jonathan Sacks Haggada*

REFLECT

How can a story link us to Jews across generations and across geography?

QUESTIONS TO ASK AT YOUR SEDER

1. *Which of the Four Children are you most like (it can be more than one)?*

2. *What do you see as the message of including four different children in*

the Haggada? What advice would you give to a teacher or parent who has many different types of children to teach?

3. *Why do you think that children are the central focus of such an important event as Seder night?*

A STORY FOR THE NIGHT OF STORIES

When I was a baby, I wouldn't talk. I was the youngest of five children, so I was surrounded by people who doted on me and gave me whatever I wanted. All I had to do was make a noise and point to get what I wanted. So it took me much longer to learn to talk. It worried my parents, and they took me to specialist doctors to make sure there was no deeper cause behind my late development.

When I started going to school, I couldn't sit still and focus for a minute. My mind would wander and then my body would wander, and next thing I knew, I was being told off, or worse, I would be sent to the headteacher's office. I wasn't trying to be mischievous or rude. I just couldn't sit in one place for long.

When I was a teenager, I got angry. Angry about all the injustices in the world, about the way the government didn't care enough about the environment, and angry that the school administration didn't do enough to make everyone feel valued and included in our school. I organised all sorts of demonstrations and one day I even led the

students in a strike. The school didn't like that one bit, and I almost got expelled for it!

Then I went to university, and I took my passion for making a difference in the world and channelled it into my studies. Today I am a lawyer who represents the underprivileged and disadvantaged in society, and my dream is to one day become a judge.

THE TEN PLAGUES עֶשֶׂר מַכּוֹת

IN A NUTSHELL

One of the most exciting and colourful parts of the story of the Exodus is the Ten Plagues. There is a custom to spill a drop of wine as we say the name of each plague. There are many reasons given for this, but the most beautiful is that of Abudraham (a fourteenth-century rabbi from Spain who is best known for his commentary on the Siddur), who interprets it in accordance with the verse "Do not rejoice when your enemy falls" (Mishlei 24:17). We give thanks for the miraculous plagues which brought our ancestors out of Egypt and granted them freedom, but at the same time, we also shed a symbolic tear for those who suffered.

> "We give thanks...but we also shed a symbolic tear."

DEEP DIVE

The plagues occupy the borderline, so common to the Torah, between the natural and the supernatural. Commentators have been divided between those who emphasise their miraculous character and others who have sought to provide a scientific account of the disasters in terms of a series of chain reactions to an initial ecological disaster, possibly the appearance of algae in the Nile, which turned the water red and caused the fish to die. Which view speaks more compellingly to us will depend on whether we understand the word "miracle" as a suspension of the laws of nature, or an event that occurs within nature but that, by happening when and to whom it does, reveals a providential pattern in history.

Commentary on the Ten Plagues, *The Jonathan Sacks Haggada*

FURTHER THOUGHTS

The plague of lice is a sardonic comment on the monumental scale of Egyptian architecture. The Egyptians believed the gods were to be found in things that are big. God shows them His Presence in something so small as to be almost invisible. The irony recurs in the division of the Red Sea, where Pharaoh's greatest military asset, the chariots, prove to be his undoing, as their wheels sink into the mud. The key to the plagues – as in God's covenant with Noaḥ – is the principle of reciprocity: "As you do, so shall you be done to." Those who harm others will themselves be harmed. Nations that begin by depriving others of their liberty in the end destroy themselves. Historically, this was so. Egypt never again recovered the greatness it had enjoyed in the earlier part of Ramesses II's rule.

Commentary on The Ten Plagues, *The Jonathan Sacks Haggada*

REFLECT

What is the message behind the plague of lice? How can we apply this lesson to our own lives?

QUESTIONS TO ASK AT YOUR SEDER

1. *Why do you think God chose these particular plagues?*

2. *In your opinion, which was the worst of the Ten Plagues?*

3. *Who were the plagues really for?*

EXPERIENCING THE SEDER

How many of the plagues can you simulate at your Seder table?
Here are a few ideas (some may require preparation in the days before Seder night):

1. Blood: Spill a little wine or grape juice onto everyone's plate, and/or (temporarily) confiscate all the bottles and jugs of water from the table.

2. Frogs: Get the children to jump around the table making frog noises.

3. Lice: Ask the children to check everyone's hair for lice. (If you plan this ahead of time, you could even plant some fake lice to find.)

4. Wild animals: Collect all the stuffed animals in the house and place them around the table.

5. Pestilence: Throw all of the stuffed animals on the floor and then bury them under the table.

6. Boils: Using forks, give all your guests boils (be gentle!).

7. Hail: Have a snowball/hail fight with cotton balls, pillows, pre-prepared hail made from paper, or other soft materials.

8. Locusts: Have the children lead everyone in making a humming, buzzing noise, and then increase the volume, like a swarm of locusts about to descend.

9. Darkness: Blindfold your guests (using scarves) and then try to play a game or continue with a section of the Haggada.

10. The striking down of the firstborn: Gather all the firstborn children together and take them outside.

DAYEINU   דַּיֵּנוּ

IN A NUTSHELL

Dayeinu is a song that explores the kindnesses of God to His people on the long journey from slavery to freedom. There are fifteen stages described between leaving Egypt, reaching the Promised Land, and building the Temple in Jerusalem. This song is a *tikkun*, a "putting-right," for the ingratitude of the Israelites in the wilderness. At almost every stage of their journey, they complained: about the water, the food, the difficulties of travelling, the challenge of conquering the land. It is as if we are saying: where they complained, let us give thanks. Each stage was a miracle. And each miracle would have been enough to convince us that Hashem is behind all the events in our history.

DEEP DIVE

Why is Shabbat specifically mentioned in *Dayeinu*? Shabbat is the ultimate expression of a free society, the antithesis of slavery in Egypt. On this day, all relationships of dominance and subordination are suspended. We may not work, or command others to work, "so that your manservant and maidservant may rest as you do" (Devarim 5:15). At many times in history, people have dreamed of an ideal world. The name given to such visions is "utopia," meaning "no place," because at no time or place have these dreams been realised on a society-wide basis. Shabbat is the sole successful utopian experiment in history. It is based on the simple idea that utopia (in Judaism, the Messianic Age) is not solely in the future. It is something we can experience in the midst of time, one day in seven. Shabbat became the weekly rehearsal of an ideal world, one not yet reached but still lived as a goal, of a world at peace with itself, recognising the createdness, and thus the integrity, of all people and all forms of life. If Egypt meant slavery, Shabbat is collective freedom, a "foretaste of the World to Come."

Commentary on *Dayeinu*, *The Jonathan Sacks Haggada*

FURTHER THOUGHTS

The Exodus was more than an event in the past. It was a precursor of redemption in the future. Israel, as Moshe warned, would not dwell securely in its land. It would forget its moral and spiritual vocation. It would be attracted to the pagan culture of its neighbours. By so doing it would lose its reason for existence and find itself unable, at times of crisis, to summon the shared vision and collective energy needed to prevail against neighbouring imperial powers. It would suffer defeat and exile. But despair would never prevail. In the past, God had brought His people from slavery to freedom and from exile to the land, and therefore He would do so again. The Jewish people never completely lost faith in God, because its prophets knew that God would never completely lose faith in His people. History intimated destiny. What happened once would happen again. That is what lies behind the words with which the Haggada begins: "Now we are here; next year in the land of Israel. Now – slaves; next year we shall be free." The Jewish people

> **"The Exodus was more than an event in the past. It was a precursor of redemption in the future."**

kept the vision alive. It is not too much to say that the vision kept the Jewish people alive....

That is what Pesaḥ was during more than eighteen centuries of exile and dispersion: a seed planted in Jewish memory, waiting to be activated, to grow. Without it, Jews would certainly have disappeared. Lacking hope of return – hope tempered by faith into a certainty-like steel – they would have made their peace with their condition, merged into their surrounding societies and ambient cultures, and vanished, like every other culture deprived of a home. Pesaḥ, like a seed frozen in suspended animation, contained the latent energy that led Jews in the twentieth century to create the single most remarkable accomplishment in the modern world, the rebirth of Israel, the land, the state, the nation, and the people. Mikha's vision, and Yeḥezkel's, and Moshe's, came true.

"Pesaḥ and the Rebirth of Israel," *The Jonathan Sacks Haggada*

REFLECT

Rabbi Sacks connects the Exodus to the modern return to Zion. How is this also connected to the poem Dayeinu?

QUESTIONS TO ASK AT YOUR SEDER

1. *Would it really have been "enough" if God had stopped at any of these stages?*

2. *What do you see as the message behind listing these fifteen stages in* Dayeinu?

3. *Where do you think the story of the Exodus actually ends?*

A STORY FOR THE NIGHT OF STORIES

Natan Sharansky is a hero of the Jewish people. Growing up in the Soviet Union, when it was almost impossible to live a Jewish life, he knew the term "Jew" only as something to hide. But then in 1967, following Israel's dramatic victory in the Six-Day War, Jews began to reconnect to their ancestral faith with pride. Many began to dream of returning to their homeland but were prevented by the Soviet authorities. They became known as Refuseniks. Sharansky, who was arrested at the age of twenty-nine for his Zionist activities, was arguably the most famous Refusenik, with thousands of people campaigning for his release from the Soviet gulag prison system in Siberia. He gained his freedom in 1986 and realised his lifelong dream to immigrate to the State of Israel.

At the beginning of the Coronavirus global pandemic, when many Jews around the world were facing the notion of a Pesaḥ Seder without their family around the table for the first time, he was interviewed about his experience of Pesaḥ in the gulag. The Soviet authorities knew the importance of Seder night, and cruelly ensured that Sharansky was in solitary confinement, where he was served nothing but three pieces of dry bread and three cups of water per day.

"I decided my three cups of water would be my wine and my three pieces of dry bread would be my matza," Sharansky recalled. "And my salt would be my *maror*. I found out that this is the great place to feel the unique struggle of the Jewish people – to be connected with every Jew in the world, and to enjoy thinking that this year we are slaves and next year we [will be] free people in Jerusalem."

Sharansky concluded his interview by emphasising that even if we are not with our family on Seder night, we are still connected, for we are one big family, a people with a shared history, a shared future, and a very special role in this world.

REFLECT

Natan Sharansky found meaning in the Pesaḥ story for his situation, both in the gulag and during the Covid pandemic. What meaning for this year can you find in the Pesaḥ story?

PESAḤ, MATZA, *MAROR*   פֶּסַח מַצָּה וּמָרוֹר

IN A NUTSHELL

These are the three mitzvot of the night that involve eating (we no longer eat the *korban Pesaḥ*, but while there was a Temple this was a biblical command). Normally, mitzvot are fulfilled by performing the required act with the intention of observing the commandment. To fulfil the duty of sukka, for example, we do not have to tell the story of the wandering of the Israelites in the desert. However, in the case of Pesaḥ two commands coincide: the first, to eat the festive meal, and the second, to tell the story. Rabban Gamliel argues that the two are connected. The story explains the food; the food allows us to relive the story.

The Torah states: "When you enter the land which the Lord shall give you as He promised, you shall observe this rite. And if your children should ask you, 'What is this service you observe?' you shall say, 'It is a Pesaḥ offering to the Lord, for He passed over the houses of the children of Israel in Egypt while He struck down the Egyptians, but saved those in our homes'" (Shemot 12:25–27). Thus, from the very outset, eating, asking, and explaining were connected, and it is this connection on which Rabban Gamliel bases his view that all three elements of the Pesaḥ meal must be explained.

> "The story explains the food; the food allows us to relive the story."

DEEP DIVE

The Pesaḥ lamb symbolises freedom. The bitter herbs represent slavery. Matza combines both. It was the bread the Israelites ate in Egypt as slaves. It was also the bread they ate when leaving Egypt as free people. Why do the symbols of freedom precede the bitter herbs of slavery? Surely slavery preceded freedom? The hasidic masters answered: only to a free human being does slavery taste bitter. Had the Israelites forgotten freedom, they would have grown used to slavery. "The worst exile is to forget you are in exile."

FURTHER THOUGHTS

In the Torah, the festival we call *Pesaḥ* is consistently described as *Ḥag HaMatzot*, the festival of unleavened bread (*Ḥag HaPesaḥ*, in the Torah, is confined to the fourteenth of Nisan, the day prior to the Seder, when the Paschal sacrifice was brought). Rabbi Levi Yitzḥak of Berditchev gave a beautiful explanation for this dual terminology. The name *Pesaḥ* signifies the greatness of God, who "passed over" the houses of the Israelites. The name *Ḥag HaMatzot* suggests the greatness of the Israelites, who followed God into the desert without any provisions. In the Torah, God calls the festival *Ḥag HaMatzot* in praise of Israel. The Jewish people, though, call the festival *Pesaḥ* in praise of God.

REFLECT

Was the story of Exodus a triumph for God or for the Israelites?

QUESTIONS TO ASK AT YOUR SEDER

1. *What is special about the educational methods used at the Seder table?*

2. *Do any other ḥagim have a similar aspect to them?*

3. *Do you think our educational institutions can learn anything from the educational methods of Seder night?*

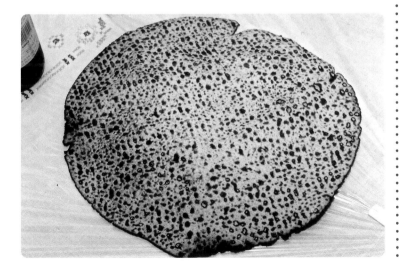

EXPERIENCING THE SEDER

At this point in the Seder, when we eat the matza and *maror* (and remember the Pesaḥ offering), we are experiencing the story we have been learning about. When you eat the matza and *maror*, close your eyes and be mindful about what your senses are feeling and experiencing. What do these foods smell and taste like? What emotions and feelings do they create in you when you eat them? Take a moment to imagine what the generation that left Egypt on the very first Pesaḥ must have felt as they ate these foods.

A STORY FOR THE NIGHT OF STORIES

A Jew was sent to Siberia by the Communist government for illegally maintaining a network of Jewish education during the years when it was against the law to practise Judaism openly. When he was finally let free he told his friends, "It was difficult to observe Pesaḥ in the labour camp. One year, we had no *matzot*. Another year, we had no wine. But of bitter herbs, we were never short!"

HALLEL הַלֵּל

IN A NUTSHELL

Now that we have finished telling the story of the Exodus, we feel an overwhelming need to thank and praise Hashem, just like the Israelites 3,300 years ago. So we begin to say Hallel (split into two sections, before and after the meal). This is one of the transitional moments of the Haggada, when we move from story to song, from prose to poetry, from recitation (*Maggid*) to praise (Hallel).

> "We move from story to song … from recitation to praise."

DEEP DIVE

Song plays a vital part in Judaism. At the end of his life Moshe gave the Israelites the last of the commands – that in every generation we should write a new *sefer Torah*. On that occasion he used an unusual word. He called the Torah a "song" (Devarim 31:19). Words are the language of the mind. Music is the language of the soul. Whenever speech is invested with deep emotion it aspires to the condition of song. Thus we do not say our prayers; we sing them. We do not read the Torah; we chant it. We do not study Talmud; we intone it. Each kind of text, and each period of the Jewish year, has its own melody. Thus Moshe was saying: to transmit Torah across the generations as a living faith, it must be not just a code of law, but also the song of the Jewish people.

FURTHER THOUGHTS

Hallel (Tehillim 113–118) is the great song of deliverance that, according to the Talmud, was sung at all the great triumphs of Jewish history. In our day we have added two new occasions when we say it: on Yom HaAtzma'ut, Israel's Independence Day, and Yom Yerushalayim, Jerusalem Day.

The late Rabbi Joseph Soloveitchik asked an interesting question about the recitation of Hallel at the Seder table. The Talmud states that we do not say Hallel on Purim because "the reading of the Megilla is equivalent to saying Hallel" (Megilla 14a). Why do we not apply the same reasoning to Seder night? We have recited the Haggada, the counterpart of the Megilla on Purim. Surely, then, the recital of Hallel is superfluous.

The answer I would give is that there are two different commands to say Hallel. The first is at the time of a miracle. The second is as a form of remembrance on the anniversary of the miracle. Thus, at the time of Ḥanukka, the Maccabees said Hallel at the moment of victory. The next year they established it as an annual obligation. The two forms of Hallel arise from different psychological states. The first is expressive, the second evocative. The first gives voice to an emotion we already feel. The second creates that emotion through an act of memory, recalling an event that occurred in the past.

Telling the story of a miracle, as we do on Purim, is equivalent to the second form of Hallel. It is an act of memory. On Pesaḥ, however, we do not merely tell the story. We relive it. We eat the bread of oppression and the bitter herbs. We taste the wine of freedom. We recline as free people. "Generation by generation, each person must see himself as if he himself had come out of Egypt." The Hallel we say on Seder night is therefore of the first kind, not the second. It arises out of the emotions we feel having lived through the event again. It is a "new song." This kind of Hallel is not cancelled by telling the story.

QUESTIONS TO ASK AT YOUR SEDER

1. *What do we have to praise and thank God for on Pesaḥ?*

2. *Is it better to use our own words to do this or the words of someone else (like King David's Tehillim)?*

3. *Do you connect more to words or song as a medium for expressing emotions?*

EXPERIENCING THE SEDER

Ask the guests around your Seder table to share as many tunes for the different parts of Hallel as they know. Spend a moment reflecting (either privately or in a conversation with the Seder participants) on how it feels to sing as opposed to saying or reading the words.

A STORY FOR THE NIGHT OF STORIES

Following the splitting of the Sea of Reeds when the Israelites were finally safe from the pursuing Egyptians, Miriam the prophetess took a timbrel in her hand, and all the women followed her, singing and dancing with their own timbrels, in praise and thanks to Hashem. The Rabbis in the Midrash ask why the women had musical instruments at all. (Was this really a priority to take with them when they left Egypt in haste?) They answer their own question by praising the women's faith in Hashem. They had deep faith that Hashem would perform miracles in the desert, to protect them and ensure their safe passage, and so they ensured that they had instruments and dances prepared so that they would be able to express their gratitude and praise of Hashem.

NIRTZA נִרְצָה

IN A NUTSHELL

Nirtza means "parting," and with this passage we reach the concluding section. We pray that next year we may be able to celebrate Pesaḥ in a rebuilt Temple according to the original biblical rituals (which we can no longer fulfil). This passage is taken from a liturgical poem (*kerova*) composed by Rabbi Joseph Tov Elem in the eleventh century CE. Originally, it was said in the synagogue on *Shabbat HaGadol*, the Shabbat preceding Pesaḥ, to conclude a detailing of the laws of Pesaḥ. It was transferred to the Haggada in the fourteenth century.

The Exodus by *Jacob Wexler*

DEEP DIVE

As at the conclusion of Yom Kippur, so here – at the two supreme moments of the Jewish year – we pray *"Leshana habaa biYerushalayim habenuya,"* "Next year in Jerusalem rebuilt." For eighteen centuries, Jews were scattered across the world, but they never forgot Jerusalem. They prayed toward it. They mourned it even during their celebrations. Each year, on the ninth of Av, the anniversary of the destruction, they sat and wept as if they had just been bereaved. Like the survivors of an earlier catastrophe, they said, "If I forget you, Jerusalem, may my right hand forget its skill. May my tongue cling to the roof of my mouth if I do not remember you, if I do not set Jerusalem above my highest joy" (Tehillim 137:5–6).

The French historian Chateaubriand, visiting Jerusalem in the early nineteenth century, was overcome with emotion as he saw for the first time the small Jewish community there, waiting patiently for the Messiah. Noting how this "small nation" had survived while the great empires who sought its destruction had vanished, he added, "If there is anything among the nations of the world marked with the stamp of the miraculous, this, in our opinion, is that miracle."

REFLECT

Why do you think the conclusion to these two important days in the Jewish calendar (Yom Kippur and Seder Night) end with these words?

FURTHER THOUGHTS

Jerusalem is a place, but it is more than a place. It became a metaphor for the collective destination of the Jewish people. A city is what we build together, individually through our homes, collectively through our public spaces. So Jerusalem became a symbol of what the Jews were summoned to build, a city of righteousness worthy of being a home for the Divine Presence. Its stones would be good deeds, and its mortar, relationships of generosity and trust. Its houses would be families; its defensive walls, schools and houses of study. Shabbat and the festivals would be its public parks and gardens. For Jews believed that, even in a violent and destructive world, heaven could be built on earth. It was their most daring vision. The architect of the city would be God. The builders would be ordinary men and women. It would be a Jewish city, but it would be open to all, and people from all faiths would come and be moved by its beauty.

So Jerusalem, the "faithful city" (Yeshayahu 1:27), became the destination of the Jewish journey, which began with Avraham and Sara

> "Jerusalem became a symbol of what Jews were summoned to build … a city of righteousness."

and will be complete only at the end of days. This is how the prophet Yeshayahu envisioned it, in words that for millennia have captured the human imagination:

> In the last days
> The mountain of the Lord's Temple will be established
> As chief among the mountains;
> It will be raised above the hills,
> And all the nations will stream to it.
> Many peoples will come and say,
> "Come, let us go up to the mountain of the Lord,
> To the house of the God of Yaakov.
> He will teach us His ways,
> So that we may walk in His path."
> For the Torah shall come forth from Zion,
> And the word of the Lord from Jerusalem.
> He will judge between the nations
> And settle disputes for many peoples.
> They will beat their swords into ploughshares
> And their spears into pruning hooks.
> Nation will not take up sword against nation,
> Nor will they train for war anymore. (*Yeshayahu 2:2–4*)

These words, among the most influential ever written, sum up much of Jewish faith. They epitomise what it might be like to "perfect the world under the sovereignty of God" (as described in the *Aleinu* prayer). And as they journeyed through the centuries and continents, Jews carried this vision with them, believing that their task was to be true to their faith, to be loyal to God, to exemplify His ways to humankind, and to build a world at peace with itself by learning and teaching how to respect the freedom and dignity of others.

REFLECT

What must the Jewish people do when they reach their final destination, Jerusalem?

QUESTIONS TO ASK AT YOUR SEDER

1. *Do you think Jews in Israel should still say this at the end of their Seder?*

2. *What does Jerusalem have to do with the Exodus story and Seder night?*

3. *Has anyone around your Seder table celebrated Pesaḥ in Israel? Was it special or different?*

EXPERIENCING THE SEDER

Close your eyes and imagine what celebrating the Pesaḥ Seder in Jerusalem would be like with a rebuilt Temple.

A STORY FOR THE NIGHT OF STORIES

It happened in Jerusalem, one Shabbat afternoon towards the end of the Gulf War. Our family had gone to the Holy City to find peace. Instead we found ourselves in the midst of war. Within weeks of our arrival it became clear that the Middle East was yet again about to be engulfed in conflict. Yet as we stepped out into the Jerusalem sunlight there was peace. The city breathed the stillness of Shabbat. The late afternoon sun was turning the houses of Jerusalem stone into burnished gold. As we looked across the valley to the walls of the Old City, we could understand why, long ago, people had called this the city of peace and why, even when it lay in ruins, Jews were convinced that the Divine Presence had never left Jerusalem.

We had been invited by our neighbours to *seuda shelishit*, the third Shabbat meal. When we arrived we discovered that they had also invited a group of Rumanian Jews who had recently come to make their home in Israel. They had made the journey as a group because they were a choir. In Rumania they had sung the songs of Jewish hope and longing. Now, in Jerusalem, they began to sing again, this time for all of us around the Shabbat table.

Then a rather moving thing happened. As the sounds of the choir reverberated around the alleyways of our quiet corner of Jerusalem, people from the neighbouring houses began to appear, drawn by the music. One by one they slipped in through the open door and stood around and, hesitantly at first, then with growing confidence, joined the singing. Here was an Israeli artist, there a new arrival from Russia, here an American investment banker, there a family from South Africa, and in the doorway a group of tourists who happened to be walking by and had stopped to see what was happening and then found themselves caught up by the embrace of the atmosphere. No one spoke; no one wanted to break the mood. We continued to sing the songs of Shabbat afternoon. As the sun began to set behind the hills, I could feel the Divine Presence among us, joining our words to those of a hundred generations of Jews, uniting them in a vast choral symphony, the love song of a people for God, and I sensed something of the mystery and majesty of the Jewish people, and I knew that it was this that I had come to Jerusalem to find.

We had come together, each of us as the result of a long journey, in some cases physical, in others spiritual, and in many, both. We each had stories to tell of how we came to be in Jerusalem that afternoon. But just as our individual voices had united to sing the words of our ancestors' songs, so our stories were part of a larger story. Our personal routes were stages on the most remarkable journey ever undertaken by a people, spanning almost every country on the face of the earth, and four thousand years of time. If we had been able, then and there, to trace back the history of our parents and theirs across the generations, we would have been awestruck at its drama and scope. Was there anything that could remotely compare to the long Jewish journey to Jerusalem? Was this, I thought, not the most vivid testimony imaginable to the power and endurance of faith?

As the singing ended, and Shabbat drew to a close, I understood that to be a Jew is to join the journey of our people, the story of Pesaḥ, and the long walk across centuries and continents from exile to homecoming. There is no story like it, and the journey is not yet complete.

ḤAD GADYA חַד גַּדְיָא

IN A NUTSHELL

This strange and haunting song seems simple on the surface but has hidden depths. Concluding one of Judaism's most important evenings of the year with a children's song tells us a lot about how important children are, especially on this night. The Jewish love of, and focus on, children means that we look forward to the future even more than we look back to the past. Just as we began the Seder with the questions of a child, so we end it with a nursery rhyme, reminding ourselves that what sustains a faith is not strength or power, but its ability to inspire successive generations of children to add their voices to their people's song.

DEEP DIVE

The theme of *Ḥad Gadya* is the destructive cycle of vengeance and retaliation. In one interpretation, the young goat represents Israel. The "father" who bought it for two coins is God, who redeemed Israel from Egypt through His two representatives, Moshe and Aharon. The cat is Assyria, which conquered the northern kingdom of Israel. The dog is Babylonia, which defeated the southern kingdom of Yehuda. The stick is Persia, which replaced Babylonia as the imperial power in the sixth century BCE. The fire is the Greeks, who defeated the Persians in the days of Alexander the Great. The water is Rome, which superseded ancient Greece. The ox is Islam, which defeated the Romans in Palestine in the seventh century. The slaughterer is Christianity – specifically the Crusaders, who fought Islam in Palestine and elsewhere, murdering Jews on the way. The Angel of Death is the Ottoman Empire, which controlled Palestine until the First World War. The song concludes with an expression of faith that "this too shall pass" and the Jewish people will return to their land. So it has been in our days.

"One Little Goat," *The Jonathan Sacks Haggada*

> "The theme of *Ḥad Gadya* is the destructive cycle of vengeance and retaliation."

The song, disarming in its simplicity, teaches the great truth of Jewish hope: that though many nations (symbolised by the cat, the dog, and so on) attacked Israel (the goat), each in turn has vanished into oblivion. At the end of days God will vanquish the Angel of Death and inaugurate a world of life and peace, the two great Jewish loves. *Ḥad Gadya* expresses the Jewish refusal to give up hope. Though history is full of man's inhumanity to man – dog bites cat, stick hits dog – that is not the final verse. The Haggada ends with the death of death in eternal life, a fitting end for the story of a people dedicated to Moshe's great command, "Choose life" (Devarim 30:19).

Commentary on *Ḥad Gadya, The Jonathan Sacks Haggada*

FURTHER THOUGHTS

Having earlier expressed the Jewish hope, "Next year in Jerusalem," we end our Seder night with the universal hope that the Angel of Death will one day be defeated by the long-overdue realisation that God is life; that worshipping God means sanctifying life; that God's greatest command is "Choose life" (Devarim 30:19); that we bring God into the world by reciting a blessing over life.

I find it almost unbearably moving that a people that has known so much suffering can summon the moral courage to end this evening of Jewish history on a supreme note of hope, and write it into the hearts of its children in the form of a nursery rhyme, a song. For what we give our children on this night of nights is something more and greater than the bread of oppression and the taste of Jewish tears. It is a faith that in this world, with all its violence and cruelty, we can create moments of redemption, signals of transcendence, acts of transfiguring grace. No people has risked and suffered more for a more slender hope, but no hope has lifted a people higher and led it, time and again, to greatness. So we end the night with a prayer and a conviction. The prayer: "God of life, help us win a victory over the forces of death." And the conviction? That by refusing to accept the world that is, together we can start to make the world that ought to be.

"One Little Goat," *The Jonathan Sacks Haggada*

EXPERIENCING THE SEDER

Ask every person at your Seder table in turn to share what their hopes for the next year are: hopes for themselves, for the Jewish people, and for the world.

EDUCATIONAL COMPANION TO THE QUESTIONS

HA LAHMA ANYA

1. As Rabbi Sacks explains in his Haggada, the root of the word "*haggada*" means not only "to tell" but also "to bind," and the Seder evening binds us together as a people. Jews from all walks of life and religious backgrounds will find themselves at a Seder table, and should be welcomed. In fact, the biblical command to sacrifice the Pesah lamb had to be done in a *havura*, which is more than one family coming together. The Exodus freedom is not just about leaving slavery, but also about journeying to the Promised Land and building a society based on the values of the Torah, where kindness to strangers will be a core value. This starts tonight.

2. The beauty of matza is that it can represent both. In fact, without slavery we would not appreciate our freedom, so both concepts can exist in this experience at the same time.

3. Although some families choose to have Seder night on their own (especially if they have young children, so the parents can focus on them) and this is perfectly okay, most people will find themselves at a Seder night with others from outside of their immediate family. People come together for this ritual. But more than this, it is a powerful thought that the entire Jewish people find themselves at a Seder table at the same time, and with some imagination, we can also feel connected to the generations that went before us who celebrated this festival in exactly the same way.

MA NISHTANA

1. Learning through questions makes the educational process engaging and empowering for the learner.

2. Any question asked out of a desire for knowledge, without a secondary agenda, is a good question. There are no bad questions in this case.

3. Not all questions have answers, or at least answers that humans with finite and limited understanding can arrive at. Some questions only the infinite God can answer. But we don't stop asking the questions. The questions are more important than the answers.

AVADIM HAYINU

1. As a nation, we have a national memory and identity. So when the Haggada speaks of our experience in Egypt as slaves, while this refers to a specific generation and historical time period, as a nation we have that experience implanted in our national memory and identity. The Haggada encourages us to re-experience this every year on Seder night, and *Avadim Hayinu* reminds us that the experience does impact us directly, for if God had not redeemed us, we would be slaves ourselves to this day.

2. A good story told well can have a big impact. Stories can be powerful when they are experiential, in that the listener can imagine that they are living the

story, or at least empathise and identify with the characters and their experiences. The longer and more detailed the story is, the better the chances are that this will happen. So the Haggada encourages us to tell the story at length, and deeply engage with it, so we can experience the story as fully as possible.

3. Because Seder night is not about "learning" or "reading" or "understanding" but rather about experiencing and living the story, the Haggada tells us that even wise and experienced people who have done this many times before still have to re-tell the story. Each year it is a new experience.

THE FOUR CHILDREN

1. Obviously all answers are legitimate, but in the ensuing discussion it is worth encouraging everyone to realise that each of us is all of the four children at different times in our lives (or even at different times of the day!).

2. All children are different and have different educational needs. Insightful parents and teachers realise this and try their hardest to cater to those individual needs.

3. Children are the main focus of the evening because this night more than any other is when we pass on our national heritage to the next generation. Even though the process of learning about and re-experiencing the Exodus is a task which takes a lifetime, it begins when we are children, laying the foundation of our Jewish identity and allowing the national narrative to become part of our very core. We take our cue from the Torah itself, which focuses on the questions children will ask about the Exodus.

THE TEN PLAGUES

1. Each plague attacked a different aspect of the physical and spiritual needs of Egyptian society. The Egyptians could probably have managed without one or two or even more of the elements that were attacked, but all ten plagues together was a systematic destruction of their way of life.

2. Every plague was terrible and designed to attack a different aspect of Egyptian society and cause problems for the Egyptians. If you have to choose one … it doesn't get more terrible than the final plague.

3. God could have taken the Israelites out of Egypt without any miracles or drama. But He chose to take the Egyptians on an educational journey, because the process was important. And even more important than the direct impact on the Egyptians was the impact on the world that was watching (or at least hearing reports) and the effect on the Israelites themselves. The plagues were as much for these other groups as they were for Pharaoh and the Egyptians, if not more so.

DAYEINU

1. Full redemption from Egypt was the establishing of a sovereign nation in the Promised Land, with the Temple at the centre of its religious and political life. If God had stopped short of this at any of the previous stages, then it would not have been complete redemption.

2. The message behind *Dayeinu* is that each individual stage was miraculous and magnificent, and worthy of praise and gratitude.

3. While the physical redemption ended with the liberation from slavery and leaving the geographical boundaries of Egypt, and the spiritual redemption took place at the Giving of the Torah on Sinai, the full religio-social redemption was only achieved once the Jews entered the land of Israel and built a society there based on the Torah.

PESAḤ, MATZA, MAROR

1. It is experiential. We don't just talk or learn or read about the story, we experience it through food and other rituals (such as leaning, pouring for each other, etc.) in order to relive the story.

2. Yes, all the *ḥagim* in Judaism do, although to a lesser extent than Pesaḥ. For example, we sit in the sukka, and we stay up all night learning to prepare to receive the Torah on Shavuot.

3. While some of our educational institutions do practise experiential education (camp is the best example) and some of our schools find opportunities to also do so (such as by having *shabbatonim*), perhaps institutions of formal Jewish education could find more creative ways to incorporate the methodology of experiential education.

HALLEL

1. It is hard to know where to start. But it is important to articulate all the things God did for the Israelites and how we benefit from these acts until this day. In the words of the Haggada itself, "And if the Holy One, blessed be He, had not brought our fathers out of Egypt – then we, and our children, and the children of our children, would still be enslaved to Pharaoh in Egypt."

2. If one is comfortable finding words that articulate genuine emotion, then there is room for that in our prayers. But for many this is a challenge, and so we fall back on the exquisite words of our greatest poets and spiritual leaders, to give us the words we need. Our challenge is then to channel our emotions through these words.

3. For some, words capture the feelings and emotions that we need to express. But for others, only music can connect to our soul to do this sufficiently. While Rabbi Sacks was a masterful wordsmith and orator, he acknowledged that music can take us further along when it comes to expressing what is in our soul.

NIRTZA

1. They should (and do) because this section refers to a rebuilt Jerusalem in Messianic times, when the Temple will exist (allowing us to celebrate Pesaḥ as originally described in the Torah) in a redeemed world of peace. This has clearly not been achieved yet, and so it is appropriate to pray for this at the end of the Seder night, even while sitting in the beautiful rebuilt modern city of Jerusalem.

2. The Exodus is the beginning of a journey that we are still on. The destination of this journey is rebuilt Jerusalem in a redeemed world of peace. We hope that this can be achieved in time for next year's Seder.

3. All the *ḥagim* are special and unique in Israel. There is something very powerful about celebrating a Jewish festival in a Jewish state. It is also easier to remember that we are closer to the final destination of the Jewish journey now than at any point in history, when sitting in the ancient Jewish homeland, rebuilt in modern times.

ḤAD GADYA

1. The whole of the Seder is focused on children, and on transmitting our heritage to the next generation. Like the other songs at the conclusion of the Seder, this song is fun to sing, and it also contains a strong educational message. This is a great way to end the Seder night journey.

2. The message of *Ḥad Gadya* is that while it may seem during our history that there are powerful forces who will dominate and even destroy us, these forces come and go, and only God decides who survives in the long term. And if you consider Jewish history, it is clear that He has decided that the Jewish people have a destiny to fulfil, and therefore we have outlasted all these powerful nations (represented in the song by the animals, etc.) that have tried to destroy us.

3. Modern Jewish history reflects this same message. In the twentieth century, an enemy of the Jewish people came closer than ever before to wiping them out, yet not only did the Jewish people survive, but in fact just three years later returned to their ancestral homeland, re-established sovereignty there, and are now thriving like never before. We are part of a generation that is living the fulfilment of the message of this song.

Yom HaShoah

IN A NUTSHELL

Yom HaShoah is Israel's official day of Holocaust remembrance when Jews around the world remember the six million Jewish victims of the *Shoah*, and the countless examples of Jewish heroism and resistance during those years. The following quotes have been taken from a series of videos recorded in 2020, in partnership with the Holocaust Educational Trust, to coincide with Yom HaShoah and the seventy-fifth anniversary of the liberation. You can watch the full video series at rabbisacks.org/holocaust.

FROM THE THOUGHT OF RABBI SACKS

GOD AND THE HOLOCAUST

The question: Why did God allow the Holocaust to occur?

Rabbi Sacks's answer: The first time I went to Auschwitz, I was simply overwhelmed. I asked, "God, where were You?" And words came into my mind…. "I was in the words 'You shall not murder.' I was in the words 'You shall not oppress a stranger.' I was in the words that were said to Kayin when he killed Hevel (the first murder in the Bible): 'Your brother's blood is crying to Me from the ground.'"

When God speaks and human beings refuse to listen, even God is helpless in that situation. He knew that Kayin was about to kill Hevel, but He didn't stop him. He knew Pharaoh was about to kill Israelite children. He didn't stop it.

God gives us freedom and never takes it back. But He tells us how to use that freedom. And when human beings refuse to listen, even God is powerless.

HUMANITY AND THE HOLOCAUST

The question: Do you have faith in humanity after the Holocaust?

Rabbi Sacks's answer: The Holocaust represented perhaps the greatest failure humanity has ever known. It featured the combination of technical brilliance and bureaucratic efficiency, but dedicated to the most evil of all purposes. This really is the greatest failure of humanity that I can think of…. [But] there's this very remarkable avenue called the Avenue of Righteous Gentiles, in Yad Vashem, in Jerusalem. Fourteen thousand people are honoured there, people whom any one of us would trust because they put their own lives at risk to save the lives of their neighbours and, in some cases, of strangers. These were beacons of light in the midst of one of the worst darknesses humanity has ever known, and therefore, yes, we can trust humanity if humanity shows itself capable of acting for the sake of others and taking risks to save others from death.

HOPE AND THE HOLOCAUST

The question: Considering the devastation of the Holocaust, how can we feel hope in the Jewish future?

Rabbi Sacks's answer: In the most uncanny evocation of the Holocaust, Yeḥezkel the prophet, twenty-six centuries ago, saw the Jewish people as a valley of dry bones, and God said to Yeḥezkel, "The people say our hope is lost… but it is not lost because I am going to take them out of their graves and bring them to the land of Israel."

I see three signs of hope today, and they're remarkable.

Today we have Israel, we have Judaism, and we have the Jewish people, all three of them stronger than they ever were before.

And I don't need any more grounds for hope than that.

Our hope is not destroyed.

REFLECT

1. *Which question do you think is harder to think about, where was God during the Holocaust or where was humanity?*

2. *What gave Rabbi Sacks hope? What hope can you find after the Holocaust?*

3. *Is it important to find hope in tragedies such as the Holocaust? What is the alternative?*

LEARNING LESSONS FROM THE HOLOCAUST

THE FAITH OF THE SURVIVORS

The following is an excerpt from the epilogue of Rabbi Sacks's book Future Tense.

It was the Holocaust survivors who taught me. I have read hundreds of books about the *Shoah*. I made a television programme from Auschwitz. To this day I cannot begin to imagine what they went through, how they survived the nightmare, and how they lived with the memories....

The survivors I came to know in the past twenty years were astonishing in their tenacious hold on life. Perhaps it's how they survived.

Some believed in God, others didn't, but they all believed in life – not life as most of us understand it, something taken for granted, part of the background, a fact that rarely holds our attention, but life as something to fight for, as a consciously articulated value, as something of whose fragility you are constantly aware. They had, in Paul Tillich's phrase, "the courage to be." Slowly I began to think about another phrase, not one that exists in the traditional literature, but one that was articulated in fateful circumstances and constituted a kind of turning point in modern Jewish history: *kiddush haḥayim*, the sanctification of life.

I had expected that trauma would turn the survivors inwards, making them suspicious of, even hostile to, the wider world.

It didn't, at least not those I knew, and by the time I came to know them.

Many of them had undertaken, fifty or more years after the event, to visit schools, talking to children, especially non-Jewish children.

What amazed me as I listened to them telling their stories was what they wanted to say. Cherish freedom. Understand what a gift it is to be able to walk in the open, to see a flower, open a window, breathe free air. Love others. Never hate. Practise tolerance. Stand up for others if they are being picked on, bullied, ostracised. Live each day as if it might be your last.

They taught the children to have faith in life. The children loved these elderly strangers from another world. I read some of their letters to them; they made me cry. Their courage kept me going through tough times. I count myself blessed to have known them.

REFLECT

1. *Would it be understandable if the trauma of their experiences made the Holocaust survivors "suspicious of, even hostile to, the wider world"? Why?*

2. *How was Rabbi Sacks's experience of the survivors he met different from his expectations? What impact did that have on him?*

3. *Have you ever met or heard a talk given by a survivor? What impact did it have on you?*

> "The survivors I came to know in the past twenty years were astonishing in their tenacious hold on life."

IT ONCE HAPPENED...

On August 11, 2017, the world's oldest living man passed away, just a month short of his 114th birthday – making him one of the ten longest-lived men since modern record-keeping began. If you knew nothing else about him than this, you would be justified in thinking that he had led a peaceful life, spared of fear, grief, and danger.

The actual truth is the opposite. The man in question was Yisrael Kristal, a Holocaust survivor. Born in Poland in 1903, he survived four years in the Lodz ghetto, and was then transported to Auschwitz. In the ghetto, his two children died. In Auschwitz, his wife Chaje was killed.

When Auschwitz was liberated, he was a walking skeleton weighing a mere 37 kilos. He was the only member of his family to survive.

He was raised as a religious Jew and stayed so all his life. When the war was over and his entire world destroyed, he married another Holocaust survivor, Batsheva. They had children. They made *aliya* to Haifa. There he began again in the confectionery business, as he had done in Poland before the war. He made sweets and chocolate. He became an innovator.

If you have ever had Israeli orange peel covered in chocolate, or liqueur chocolates shaped like little bottles and covered with silver foil, you have enjoyed one of the products he originated.

Those who knew him said he was a man with no bitterness in his soul. He wanted people to taste sweetness.

In 2016, at the age of 113, he finally celebrated his bar mitzva. A hundred years earlier, this had proved impossible. By then, his

mother was dead and his father was fighting in the First World War. On his bar mitzva he joked that he was the world's oldest tefillin-wearer. He gathered his children, grandchildren, and great-grandchildren under his tallit and said, "Here's one person, and look how many people he brought to life. As we're all standing here under my tallit, I'm thinking: Six million people. Imagine the world they could have built."

REFLECT

1. *What do you find most inspiring about this story?*

2. *What do you think was the secret of Yisrael Kristal's long life?*

3. *We now live in an age where we have fewer and fewer survivors alive among us to tell their story. How do you think we can continue their legacy?*

A PRAYER FOR YOM HASHOAH

Composed by Rabbi Sacks in 2013

Today, on Yom HaShoah, we remember the victims of the greatest crime of man against man –

the young, the old, the innocent, the million-and-a-half children, starved, shot, given lethal injections, gassed, burned, and turned to ash, because they were deemed guilty of the crime of being different.

We remember what happens when hate takes hold of the human heart and turns it to stone; what happens when victims cry for help and there is no one listening;

what happens when humanity fails to recognise that those who are not in our image are nonetheless in God's image.

We remember and pay tribute to the survivors, who bore witness to what happened, and to the victims, so that robbed of their lives, they would not be robbed also of their deaths.

We remember and give thanks for the righteous of the nations who saved lives,

often at risk of their own, teaching us how in the darkest night we can light a candle of hope.

Today, on Yom HaShoah, we call on You, Almighty God, to help us hear Your voice that says in every generation:

Do not murder. Do not stand idly by the blood of your neighbour. Do not oppress the stranger.

We know that whilst we do not have the ability to change the past, we can change the future.

We know that whilst we cannot bring the dead back to life,

we can ensure their memories live on and that their deaths were not in vain.

And so, on this Yom HaShoah, we commit ourselves to one simple act: Yizkor, Remember.

May the souls of the victims be bound in the bond of everlasting life. Amen.

Yom HaZikaron

IN A NUTSHELL

Yom HaZikaron (Israel's Memorial Day) is the day on which Israel pauses to remember all those who have given up their lives fighting for and defending the State of Israel, including victims of terrorism. It falls each year on the fourth of Iyar (the day before Yom HaAtzma'ut, Israel's Independence Day).

FROM THE THOUGHT OF RABBI SACKS

FAITH IN WAR

How do you live with the constant threat of violence and war? That takes faith. Israel is the people that has always been sustained by faith, faith in God, in the future, in life itself. And though Israel is a secular state, its very existence is testimony to faith: the faith of a hundred generations that Jews would one day return; the faith that led the pioneers to rebuild a land against seemingly impossible odds; the faith that after the Holocaust the Jewish people could live again; the faith that, in the face of death, continues to say: Choose life.

From the album **"Israel – Home of Hope"**
produced by Rabbi Sacks

FIGHTING FOR OUR VERY EXISTENCE

The journey is not yet over. Israel has not yet found peace. And after four thousand years Jews still find it hard to live their faith without fear. There is only one Jewish state, a country less than one quarter of one per cent of the land mass of the Arab world – the only place on earth where Jews form a majority, the only place where they are able to do what almost every other people takes for granted: to construct a society according to their values, and to be able to defend themselves. Jews still have to fight for the right to be.

From the album **"Israel – Home of Hope"**
produced by Rabbi Sacks

FIGHTING FOR LIFE, FIGHTING FOR PEACE

Jews fought, and never more so than in the State of Israel, with the courage that you find only in those whose ultimate aim is not victory but peace, not triumph but life. Let us acknowledge the heroes of *Medinat Yisrael*, the heroes not just of military battle, but also the heroes of the human spirit, who are willing to die so that we can live. They lit a flame in the Jewish heart that will never die. Let us remember them and their past, and look today at the Israel they have built: a land of freedom and energy and creativity and life.

From the album **"Israel – Home of Hope"**
produced by Rabbi Sacks

REFLECT

1. *Why do you think the State of Israel chose to remember its fallen on the day before Yom HaAtzma'ut, when it celebrates its independence?*

2. *How have we benefitted from the sacrifice of those who have given their lives for the State of Israel?*

3. *What are we still fighting for today?*

> "Let us acknowledge the heroes of *Medinat Yisrael*, heroes of the human spirit, who are willing to die so that we can live."

CARRYING THE PAST, TURNING DEATH INTO LIFE

At the end of the book of Bereshit, Yosef makes one deeply poignant request: Though I will die in exile, God will bring you back to the land, and when He does so, "*vehaalitem et atzmotai mizeh,*" "carry my bones" with you.

Moshe smashed the first set of tablets given to him by God at Mount Sinai, but the Israelites carried them in the Ark, together with the second set: the new tablets and the fragments of the old.

And so it has been throughout Jewish history; we carry with us all the fragments of our people's past, the broken lives, the anguished deaths. For we refuse to let their deaths be in vain. Our past lives on in us as we continue the Jewish journey to the future, to hope, and to life.

On Yom HaZikaron we remember the members of the Israel Defense Forces who fell in action, and also all those killed by terrorist attacks in Israel. What our enemies killed, we keep alive in the only way we can: in our minds, our memories, and in our land, the State of Israel.

There are cultures that forget the past and there are those that are held captive by the past. We do neither. We carry the past with us for as long as the Jewish people exist, as Moshe carried the bones of Yosef, and as the Levites carried the fragments of the shattered tablets of stone.

Those fragments of memory, of those no longer with us, help make us who we are. We live for what they died for, by walking tall as Jews, showing we are not afraid, refusing to be intimidated by the anti-Semitism that has returned, or the sustained assault on Israel.

On Yom HaZikaron, as we remember those who have fallen or been killed in defence of the State of Israel, we say to the souls of those lost: We will never forget you. We will never cease to mourn you. We will never let you down.

REFLECT

1. *Why is it important to remember each victim who has fallen defending the State of Israel?*

2. *How can we keep their memories alive?*

3. *How can we redeem their sacrifice and continue their legacy?*

A MESSAGE TO HONOUR THE LIVES AND MEMORIES OF OUR FALLEN LONE SOLDIERS

We remember the courage and the *mesirat nefesh* (self-sacrifice), the dedication and the bravery, of Israel's *ḥayalim bodedim* (lone soldiers), especially those who gave their lives defending *Medinat Yisrael* and *am Yisrael*.

We think of them as living examples of what it is to fight for the freedom of our people, and their safety, in the land of our beginnings, so that never again would *am Yisrael* be dependent on the goodwill of the nations.

Never again would we have to suffer the two thousand years of persecution of the centuries that preceded the birth of the State of Israel. These are among the great heroes of our people.

Let us honour the memory of those who died. Let us salute the example of those who live. And let us pray to Hashem to bless the State of Israel, the people of Israel, and the Defense Forces of Israel, and may He give all of us the blessing of health, and strength, and peace.

Amen.

Rabbi Sacks shared this message in 2020 to honour the lives and memories of our fallen lone soldiers at the annual Yom HaZikaron ceremony of the Lone Soldier Center in Memory of Michael Levin.

IT ONCE HAPPENED...

I met Yoni Jesner in Jerusalem in January 2002. He was nineteen years old, just beginning his second year in yeshiva. We had brought together a group of three hundred British students, but he stood out among them as a leader, a young man with quiet inner strength and a sense of humour that drew people to him and brought out the best in them. I knew of his reputation from the community in Glasgow where he had grown up. Already he was something of a legend. He worked with the young and the old, he took children's services in the synagogue, taught in its classes, ran the local youth group, and was a volunteer in the burial society, helping prepare the dead for burial with dignity. A brilliant student, he had decided to become a doctor and already had a place at medical school. His first priority was to dedicate his life to saving lives. Like many others in Jewish history, he saw medicine as a religious vocation.

Yoni was travelling on the number 4 bus in Tel Aviv on September 19, 2002, when the suicide bomber detonated his belt. Ari, his brother in London, caught the next flight to Israel. Yoni Jesner, of blessed memory, was a remarkable young man whose death at the hands of a suicide bomber devastated all who knew him.

It turned out, though, that Yoni had a last and yet more deeply moving message for us. After consulting Yoni's rabbi, his family came to a decision. Yoni had wanted to save lives. They would donate his organs. Among those whose lives were transformed was Yasmin Abu Ramila, a seven-year-old Palestinian girl from East Jerusalem who had been on dialysis for two years awaiting a compatible transplant. This is moral greatness of a high order – to create life out of death and turn a potential enemy into a friend. It takes exceptional courage to come to such a decision in the midst of grief, but acts like these are fragments of redemption.

A people is as great as its ideals, and Yoni lived those ideals to the limit. We will not forget him. We will cherish his memory as a blessing and inspiration.

***To Heal a Fractured World**, 208–209*

Yom HaAtzma'ut

YOM HAATZMA'UT IN A NUTSHELL

The State of Israel came into existence on May 14, 1948, as David Ben-Gurion, the first prime minister of Israel, read the Declaration of Independence in Tel Aviv on behalf of the provisional government. The Hebrew date was the fifth day of the month of Iyar 5708, and every year on this day we celebrate Yom HaAtzma'ut, Israel's Independence Day. In Israel, the day is celebrated with an official ceremony on Mount Herzl in Jerusalem, nationwide street parties at night, and hiking and picnicking during the day. Religious Jews conduct special prayer services to acknowledge and give thanks to God for His role in the miraculous story of the establishment and continued existence of the State of Israel.

FROM THE THOUGHT OF RABBI SACKS

THE MIRACLE OF THE STATE OF ISRAEL

The creation of the State of Israel was fraught with difficulty. Despite the Balfour Declaration of 1917, in which Britain, the new mandatory power in Palestine, promised Jews a national home, there was intense opposition – from the Arab world, from other international forces, from politicians in Britain, and at times from Jews themselves. For thirty years, various compromises were proposed, all accepted by Jews and rejected by their opponents. On the day the State of Israel was proclaimed, the country was attacked on all fronts by its neighbours. Since then, it has lived under constant threat of war, violence, terror, and delegitimisation. Yet Israel has achieved wondrous things.

Do you see God in the story of the establishment of the modern State of Israel? What role did humans play in this story?

Through it, Hebrew, the language of the Bible, was reborn as a living tongue. Jewish communities under threat have been rescued, including those like the Jews of Ethiopia who had little contact with other Jews for centuries. Jews have come to Israel from over a hundred countries,

> "No one, reviewing this singular history, can doubt ... that a nation's history is shaped by what it believes."

representing the entire lexicon of cultural diversity. A desolate landscape has bloomed again. Jerusalem has been rebuilt. The world of Torah scholarship, devastated by the Holocaust, has been revived and the sound of learning echoes throughout the land. Economically, politically, socially, and culturally, Israel's achievements are unmatched by any country of its age and size. The Sages said that, at the crossing of the Red Sea, the simplest Jew saw miracles that the greatest of later prophets were not destined to see. That, surely, was the privilege of those who witnessed Israel's rebirth and youth. The Messiah has not come. Israel is not yet at peace. The Temple has not been rebuilt. Our time is not yet redemption. Yet many of the prayers of two thousand years have been answered. No one, reviewing this singular history, can doubt that faith makes a difference, that a nation's history is shaped by what it believes.

Many of the heroes and pioneers of the return to Zion were not "spiritual," nor did they observe many of the commandments. But the vision of the prophets and the covenant of Jewish history flowed through their veins. God works through people; sometimes, so the prophets taught, without their conscious knowledge and consent. It is difficult to reflect deeply on the rebirth of Israel without sensing the touch of heaven in the minds of men and women, leading them to play their parts in a drama so much greater than any individual could have executed, even conceived.

Who, then, wrote the script of the Jewish drama? God or the Jewish people? Or was it, as the Sages taught, an inextricable combination of both: God as He was heard by the people, and the people as they responded to God? Isaac Bashevis Singer came close when he said, "God is a writer and we are both the heroes and the readers."

The Jonathan Sacks Haggada, 66–68

WHY A LAND?

[Jewish] destiny was to create a society that would honour the proposition that we are all created in the image and likeness of God. It would be a place in which the freedom of some would not lead to the enslavement of others.

Judaism is the code of a self-governing society. We tend to forget this, since Jews have lived in dispersion for two thousand years, without the sovereign power to govern themselves, and because modern Israel is a secular state.

Because Judaism is the code of a society, it is also about the social virtues: righteousness (*tzedek/tzedaka*), justice (*mishpat*), loving-kindness (*ḥesed*), and compassion (*raḥamim*). These structure the template of biblical law, which covers all aspects of the life of society, its economy, its welfare systems, its education, family life, employer-employee relations, the protection of the environment, and so on.

None of this is possible without a land. Judaism is the constitution of a self-governing nation, the architectonics of a society dedicated to the service of God in freedom and dignity. Without a land and state, Judaism is a shadow of itself. In exile, God might still live in the hearts of Jews but not in the public square, in the justice of the courts, the morality of the economy, and the humanitarianism of everyday life.

Jews have lived in almost every country under the sun. *In four thousand years, only in Israel have they been a free, self-governing people.* Only in Israel are they able, if they so choose, to construct an agriculture, a medical system, an economic infrastructure in the spirit of the Torah and its concern for freedom, justice, and the sanctity of life. Only in Israel can Jews today speak the Hebrew of the Bible as the language of everyday speech. Only in Israel can they live Jewish time within a calendar structured according to the rhythms of the Jewish year. Only in Israel can Jews live Judaism in anything other than an edited edition. In Israel, and only there, Jews can walk where the prophets walked, climb the mountains Avraham climbed, lift their eyes to the hills that David saw, and continue the story their ancestors began.

Future Tense, 135–136

REFLECT

Can God be found "in the public square, in the justice of the courts, the morality of the economy, and the humanitarianism of everyday life" in Israel today?

WHY THIS LAND?

Israel is not the Nile Delta or the Tigris-Euphrates valley. It is a land dependent on rain, and the rain in Israel is not predictable. But a message in Devarim (11:10–12) intimates a correlation between geography and spirituality. Israel is a place where people look up to heaven in search of rain, not down to earth and its natural water supply. It is a place where you have to pray, not one in which nature and its seasons are predictable.

That is part of a larger narrative. Because the terrain of Israel is such that it cannot become the base of an empire, it will constantly be at threat from larger and stronger neighbouring powers. Israel will always find itself outnumbered. It will need to rely on exceptional courage from its soldiers, and ingenuity in battle. That will take high national morale, which in turn will require from the people a sense of belonging to a just and inclusive society.

Commitment will be needed from every individual. They will need to feel that their cause is justified and that they are fighting for something worth preserving. So the entire configuration of the Torah's social ethics, whose guardians were the prophets, is already implicit in the kind of geo-political entity Israel is and will be. It would always be a small and highly vulnerable country, set in a strategic location at the junction of three continents, Europe, Africa, and Asia. As with its agriculture, so with its battles: Israel is a people that must lift its eyes to heaven.

Future Tense, 139–140

REFLECT

Are the things described in this passage still true of the modern State of Israel?

THE LAND OF HOPE

Twenty-six centuries ago, in exile in Babylon, the prophet Yeḥezkel had the most haunting of all prophetic visions. He saw a valley of dry bones, a heap of skeletons. God asked him, "Son of man, can these bones live?" Yeḥezkel replied, "God, You alone know." Then the bones came together, and grew flesh and skin, and began to breathe, and live again. Then God said: "Son of man, these bones are the whole house of Israel. They say, 'Our bones are dried up; our hope is lost (*avda tikvateinu*).' Therefore prophesy and say to them: 'This is what the Lord God says: "My people, I am going to open your graves and bring you up from them; I will bring you back to the land of Israel"'" (Yeḥezkel 37:1–14).

It was this passage that Naftali Herz Imber was alluding to in 1877, when he wrote, in the song that became Israel's national anthem, *HaTikva*, the phrase *"Od lo avda tikvateinu,"* "Our hope is not yet lost." Little could he have known that seventy years later, one-third of the Jewish people would have become, in Auschwitz and Treblinka, a valley of dry bones. Who could have been blamed for saying "Our bones are dried up; our hope is lost"?

Yet, a mere three years after standing face-to-face with the angel of death, the Jewish people, by proclaiming the State of Israel, made a momentous affirmation of life, as if it had heard across the centuries the echo of God's words to Yeḥezkel: "I will bring you back to the land of Israel."

And a day will one day come when the story of Israel in modern times will speak not just to Jews, but to all who believe in the power of the human spirit as it reaches out to God, as an everlasting symbol of the victory of life over death, hope over despair. Israel has taken a barren land and made it bloom again. It has taken an ancient language, the Hebrew of the Bible, and made it speak again. It has taken the West's oldest faith and made it young again. It has taken a shattered nation and made it live again. That remains the Jewish dream. Israel is the land of hope.

Future Tense, 152–153

REFLECT

How do you think Israel has managed to stay hopeful in the face of so many seemingly insurmountable challenges in its short history?

> "Israel has taken a barren land and made it bloom again. It has taken an ancient language … and made it speak again. It has taken a shattered nation and made it live again."

IT ONCE HAPPENED...

A personal retelling of the story of the State of Israel in the words of Rabbi Sacks:

In 1871, my great-grandfather, Rabbi Arye Leib Frumkin, left his home in Kelm, Lithuania, to go and live in Israel, following his father who had done so some twenty years earlier. One of his first acts was to begin writing a book, *The History of the Sages of Jerusalem*, a chronicle of the continuous Jewish presence in Jerusalem since Ramban arrived there in 1265 and began reconstructing the community that had been devastated during the Crusades.

In 1881, pogroms broke out in over a hundred towns in Russia. In 1882, the notorious anti-Semitic May Laws were enacted, sending millions of Jews into flight to the West. Something happened to my great-grandfather as a result of these experiences. Evidently, he realised that *aliya*, going to live in Israel, was no longer a matter of a pilgrimage of the few, but a vital necessity for the many. He moved to one of the first agricultural settlements in a new *yishuv*. It had been settled some three or four years earlier, but the original farmers had contracted malaria and left. Some were now prepared to go back to work the land, but not to live there. It was, they believed, simply too much of a hazard to health.

He led the return and built the first house there. When the settlers began to succeed in taming the land, they were attacked by local Arabs, and in 1894, he decided that it was simply too dangerous to stay, and he moved to London. Eventually he returned and was buried there. On his gravestone it records that he had built the very first house.

What fascinates me is the name the settlers gave to the village. I do not know why they decided on this particular name, but I have a guess. It was set in the Yarkon Valley, and when they discovered that it was a malarial swamp, it appeared to them as a valley of trouble. But they knew the Hebrew Bible, and they recalled a verse from the prophet Hoshea in which God promised to turn the "valley of trouble" into a "gateway of hope" (Hoshea 2:15). That is the name they gave the village, today the sixth largest town in Israel: Petach Tikva, the gateway of hope.

Since its establishment, Israel has done extraordinary things. It has absorbed immigrants from 103 countries, speaking 82 languages. It has turned a desolate landscape into a place of forests and fields. It has developed cutting-edge agricultural and medical techniques and created one of the world's most advanced high-tech economies. It has produced great poets and novelists, artists and sculptors, symphony orchestras, universities, and research institutes. It has presided over the rebirth of the great talmudic academies destroyed in Eastern Europe during the Holocaust. Wherever in the world there is a humanitarian disaster, Israel, if permitted, is one of the first to send aid. It has shared its technologies with other developing countries. Under immense strain, it has sustained democracy, a free press, and an independent judiciary. Had my great-grandfather seen what it has achieved, he would hardly have believed it. In truth, I hardly believe it when I read Jewish history and begin to understand what Jewish life was like when there was no Israel.

For me, more than anything else, Israel is living testimony to the power of Moshe's command, "Choose life."

Future Tense, 131–132

POINTS TO PONDER

1. *Why do you think Rabbi Sacks's great-grandfather left Europe to live in the land of Israel?*

2. *What do you think Rabbi Frumkin would say if he saw Petach Tikva today?*

3. *How does the modern-day city of Petach Tikva symbolise the miracle of the State of Israel?*

ḤIDON ON THE ḤAG (A QUICK QUIZ)

1. What was the exact date of the establishment of the State of Israel?

2. What is the population of the State of Israel today?

3. From which country have the most Jews made *aliya*?

4. How many trees has the Jewish National Fund (JNF) planted in Israel since it was founded in 1901: 40 million, 140 million, or 240 million?

5. The Israeli company Netafim, established in 1965, is the world leader in which type of technology?

6. Which countries have more startups per capita than Israel?

7. What is the name of Israel's Nobel laureate for literature?

8. Can you name Israel's nine universities?

9. How many elections were there in Israel from 2021 to 2022?

10. How many companies in Israel are using technology to combat Covid-19: more than twenty, more than fifty, or more than seventy?

EDUCATIONAL COMPANION TO THE QUESTIONS

IT ONCE HAPPENED...

1. Rabbi Frumkin was deeply religious, and so the opportunity to live in the land of his ancestors, fulfil the parts of Judaism that can only be fulfilled in Israel, and be a key part of the process of bringing the Messianic redemption, were no doubt factors in his decision. But equally, he was guided by the difficult living conditions in Eastern Europe, especially the anti-Semitism that Jews were facing every day. These were also the two main motivations for the majority of the Jews who moved to Israel at that time, what historians term "the First *Aliya*" (1882–1903).

2. He no doubt would struggle to recognise Petach Tikva today, a bustling Western city that in his day was a small, barely viable agricultural settlement. We can imagine that he would feel that this was the realisation of the dreams of the first pioneers (and the fulfilment of the biblical prophecies of the return to Zion). No doubt Petach Tikva of today is beyond the wildest dreams of the early pioneers.

3. The very name Petach Tikva demonstrates the deep faith and hope the Zionist pioneers had, that they were laying the foundation of a future Jewish state against all the odds. The fact that they succeeded, and today Petach Tikva is a bustling metropolis, is a wonderful example of the miracle of the creation and existence of the State of Israel. Modern-day Petach Tikva has a mix of religious and secular Israelis (like most cities in Israel), and this also represents two different approaches to the miracle of the State of Israel – was this achieved by the hand of God, or by human endeavour? It is most likely that the majority of Petach Tikva's inhabitants today see it as a combination of both.

ḤIDON ON THE ḤAG (A QUICK QUIZ)

1. Fifth of Iyar 5708/May 14, 1948.
2. 8,757,718 (at our last count).
3. Russia/Ukraine (FSU).
4. 240 million.
5. Drip irrigation (agricultural technology).
6. None. Israel has more startups per capita than any other country in the world!
7. Shmuel Yosef Agnon.
8. Hebrew University of Jerusalem, the Technion (Israel Institute of Technology), Weizmann Institute of Science, Bar-Ilan University, Tel Aviv University, University of Haifa, Ben-Gurion University of the Negev, Open University of Israel, Ariel University.
9. Four.
10. More than seventy.

Yom Yerushalayim

YOM YERUSHALAYIM IN A NUTSHELL

Yom Yerushalayim, which falls on the twenty-eighth of Iyar, celebrates the reunification of the city of Jerusalem in 1967. King David first made Jerusalem the capital city of the Jewish people three thousand years ago. It was conquered by the Romans in 70 CE, beginning a period of almost two thousand years of Jewish exile, mourning for Jerusalem, and yearning to return. In the late nineteenth century, the dream of returning to the land of Israel became a reality, but after the establishment of the State of Israel in 1948, and the end of the War of Independence in 1949, Israel only had sovereignty over West Jerusalem, with East Jerusalem, including the Old City and the Kotel, not in Jewish hands. Following the miraculous victory of the Six-Day War in 1967, the Israel Defense Forces captured the ancient, eastern part of the city, marking the first time in two thousand years that all of Jerusalem was under Jewish control. Finally, Jews once again had access to the holiest site for Judaism, the Kotel and the Temple Mount. Yom Yerushalayim is celebrated each year as a religious festival of thanksgiving, with special *tefillot* and celebrations held all around the world.

FROM THE THOUGHT OF RABBI SACKS

THE LOVE OF A PEOPLE FOR THEIR CITY

There has never been a love story like it in all of history: the love of our people for our city.

Jerusalem is mentioned approximately 660 times in Tanakh. History teaches us that the Temple was destroyed twice, and the city has been besieged 23 times and captured and reconquered 44 times. Yet in all those years, wherever Jews lived they never ceased to pray about Jerusalem, face Jerusalem, speak the language of Jerusalem, remember it at every wedding, in every home they built, and at all the high points of the Jewish year. Somehow it was where every Jewish prayer met and ascended to heaven.

Other cities and other faiths hold Jerusalem holy too, but they have holier places: Rome, Constantinople, Mecca, Medina. Jews only had this one city, a tiny city but somehow it was the place, said Maimonides, from which the Divine Presence was never exiled.

Never has a city had such power over a people's imagination. Never were a people more loyal than our ancestors who endured twenty centuries of exile and persecution so that their children or grandchildren or great-grandchildren could come home to Jerusalem, *ir hakodesh*, the holy city, the home of the Jewish heart.

From the 2017 video entitled "Rabbi Sacks on Jerusalem: The 50th Anniversary of Reunification"

> ### POINTS TO PONDER
>
> *Can you think of ways in which Jews have shown their yearning to return to Jerusalem over the past two thousand years?*

JERUSALEM: THE CITY OF PARADOXES

What's special about Jerusalem today is that despite all the very real tensions within and surrounding it, nonetheless it remains a city of peace. It is one of the very few places in the Middle East – indeed one of the very few places in the world – that is holy to three distinct faiths (Judaism, Christianity, and Islam), where those faiths pray together in freedom and in peace. That has only been made possible under Israeli rule in the last fifty years.

Somebody once said about Israel, and you could certainly say this about Jerusalem too, that it is not that long and it is not that wide, but it is very deep. Jerusalem is very deep. And somehow within its relatively narrow confines, it contains, in Walt Whitman's phrase, "multitudes."

Another incredible thing about Jerusalem is that something magical happens to our sense of time there. For instance, the walls of Jerusalem

> **"There has never been a love story like it in all of history: the love of our people for our city."**

were destroyed by every conqueror and then rebuilt using the very same stones. If you look at the stones of the walls around Jerusalem, they come from all the eras. Somehow, past and present, the old and the new, are all jumbled together. These bricks are a testament to how this city remains the oldest of the old, and yet it has also become one of the emerging high-tech cities of the world.

So it's the oldest of the old and it's the newest of the new. It is the living symbol of what Theodor Herzl titled his book about the return to Zion, *Altneuland*: the old new land, the old new city, for the old and renewed people.

From the 2017 video entitled "Rabbi Sacks on Jerusalem: The 50th Anniversary of Reunification"

POINTS TO PONDER

Which paradoxes found in Jerusalem are mentioned here? Can you think of any others? Do you think this adds or detracts from Jerusalem's holiness and beauty?

WE NEVER FORGET JERUSALEM

I used to ask myself: How could Jews believe so much in a city they had been exiled from for so long? The answer is very powerful, and it is contained in two words in the story of Yaakov. Recall, the brothers return home and show Yaakov the blood-stained coat of Yosef. Realising Yosef has gone, Yaakov weeps, and when the brothers move to comfort him, we are told, "*veyima'ein lehitnaḥen*," that Yaakov "refused to be comforted." Why? There are, after all, laws in Judaism about the limits of grief; there is no such thing as a bereavement for which grief is endless.

The answer is that Yaakov had not yet given up hope that Yosef was still alive. To refuse to be comforted is to refuse to give up hope.

That is what Jews did with Jerusalem. They remembered the promise that *am Yisrael* had made by the waters of Babylon, "*Im eshkaḥekh Yerushalayim tishkaḥ yemini*," "If I forget Jerusalem, may my right had lose its skill." We never forgot Jerusalem. We were never comforted. We never gave up hope that one day we would return and, because of that, Jews never felt separated from Jerusalem.

And when it happened in 1967, my Jewish identity was transformed as the world heard the announcement: "*Har HaBayit beyadeinu!*" "The Temple Mount is in our hands!" Those three words changed a generation.

From the 2017 video entitled "Rabbi Sacks on Jerusalem: The 50th Anniversary of Reunification"

POINTS TO PONDER

Why do you think Jews never forgot, or stopped yearning for, Jerusalem?

JERUSALEM OF TODAY CRIES OUT: *"AM YISRAEL ḤAI!"*

On Yom Yerushalayim a few years ago, standing on the streets of the city, I watched youngsters from around the world waving Israeli flags, singing and dancing with a joy that was overwhelming. As I watched the celebrations, I was overcome with emotion because suddenly I had a vision of the 1.5 million children who were killed in the *Shoah* not because of anything they had done, not because of anything their parents had done, but because their grandparents happened to be Jews. I remembered how twenty-six centuries ago, the prophet Yeḥezkel had a vision of the Jewish people reduced to a valley of dry bones. God asked, "Shall these bones live?" and Yeḥezkel saw them come together, take on flesh, and begin to breathe and live again. God promised Yeḥezkel He would open His people's graves and bring them back to the land.

I remembered the first reference to Israel outside the Bible on the Merneptah Stele, a block of granite engraved by Merneptah IV, successor to Ramesses II, thought by many to have been the Egyptian Pharaoh at the time of the Exodus. It was an obituary: "Israel is laid waste, her seed is no more."

I thought how some of the greatest empires the world has ever known – Egypt of the Pharaohs, Assyria, Babylon, the Alexandrian Empire, the Roman Empire, the medieval empires of Christianity and Islam, all the way to the Third Reich and the Soviet Union – were the superpowers of their day that bestrode the narrow world like a colossus, seemingly invulnerable in their time. And yet each tried to write the obituary of the Jewish people, and whilst they have been consigned to history, our people can still stand and sing *Am Yisrael Ḥai*. What I was seeing on that day in Jerusalem was *teḥiyat hameitim*, a collective people being brought back from death to life.

When we visit Jerusalem today and see a place of such beauty, it takes your breath away. Jerusalem is the place where all the prayers of all the Jews across all the centuries and from all the continents meet and take flight on their way to heaven. It is the place where you feel brushed by the wings of the *Shekhina*.

We have had the privilege to be born in a generation that has seen Jerusalem reunited and rebuilt. We have seen the Jewish people come home.

Today God is calling on us all to be Guardians of Zion. Never has this been more important. We must all stand up for the one home our people has ever known and the one city our people has loved more than any other. We are all *shagrirei Medinat Yisrael* (ambassadors for the State of Israel) and we must all make Israel's case in a world that sometimes fails to see the beauty we know is here. Let us all take on that task. With Hashem's help, we will succeed and we pray the world will make its peace with Israel so that Israel and Israel's God can bring peace to the world.

From the essay "We Never Forget Jerusalem," rabbisacks.org, May 15, 2015

POINTS TO PONDER

How does Jerusalem embody the story of Jewish history?

IT ONCE HAPPENED...

RABBI AKIVA, THE FOX, AND THE SIX-DAY WAR

In those critical, tense weeks before the Six-Day War, I was just coming near the end of my first year at Cambridge University. And for those three weeks we all felt that something terrible was going to happen, after all the troops were massed on the Egyptian and Syrian borders. All of my generation born after the Holocaust feared that we were about to witness a second holocaust. All the Jewish students, vast numbers of them, turned up in the little *shul* in Thompson's Lane to pray. I've never seen so many people there before or since. The atmosphere was absolutely intense. And for me it was life-changing.

As soon as we saw the paratroopers, as soon as we heard the words "*Har HaBayit beyadeinu*" ("The Temple Mount is in our hands"), I knew I had to go to Israel and see it for myself. I went there, and looking from Har HaTzofim (Mount Scopus), down on the Old City, I suddenly realised that I was standing at the very place that the Mishna and Gemara talk about at the end of Tractate Makkot, when R. Akiva and three of his rabbinical colleagues are standing on Har HaTzofim looking down on the ruins of the Temple. And the other Rabbis are weeping, and R. Akiva is smiling.

And he says, "Why are you weeping!?"

And they say, "Look at the Holy of Holies – it's all in ruins! A fox is walking through there! The place that only the holiest man, the high priest, could enter only on the holiest day, and now it is nothing but ruins. Of course we're weeping. Why are you *not* weeping?"

And R. Akiva says, "Because there were two prophets who gave prophecies. One, Mikha, saw the city in its destruction and another one, Zekharya, saw it rebuilt, and saw it as a place where '*od yeshvu zekeinim uzekeinot birḥovot Yerushalayim*,' where old men and women would sit at peace in the streets of Jerusalem, and the streets would be filled with the sounds of children playing.

"So if I have seen the fulfilment of the prophecy of destruction, am I not convinced that there will one day come true the prophecy of rebuilding and restoration?"

And as I stood where R. Akiva stood two thousand years earlier, I said to myself, "If he had only known how long it would take, would he still have believed?" And then I realised, of course he would still have believed, because Jews would never give up hope of Jerusalem. We never allowed it to escape our minds. In any of our prayers, at our weddings, we always remember Jerusalem. Every time we comfort mourners we say, "*HaMakom yenaḥem etkhem betokh she'ar avelei Tziyon viYerushalayim.*"

You know, Jews were a circumference whose centre was Jerusalem. And I knew then that a people who could never forget this holy city must one day return to it. And as I stood there, soon after the Six-Day War, I suddenly realised that faith brought back Jews to Jerusalem, and will one day rebuild its ruins. That is the most powerful testimony of faith I know.

> **"Jews would never give up hope of Jerusalem. We never allowed it to escape our minds."**

Jerusalem

hand drawn map

0   50

ḤIDON ON THE ḤAG
(A QUICK QUIZ)

1. Jerusalem is situated in the biblical portion of which of the twelve Tribes?

2. What is the name of the mountain that is the site of the Temple Mount?

3. According to Jewish tradition, which biblical story took place on this mountain?

4. Which animal is the symbol of the city, dating back to biblical times?

5. Who built the first Temple in Jerusalem?

6. Who built the walls that currently surround the Old City of Jerusalem?

7. What was the name of the first modern neighbourhood to be built outside of the walls of the Old City (in 1860)?

8. When was Jerusalem declared the capital of the State of Israel?

9. What are the four quarters of the Old City of Jerusalem?

10. Can you name all eight gates that lead into the Old City?

EDUCATIONAL COMPANION TO THE QUESTIONS

FROM THE THOUGHT OF RABBI SACKS

THE LOVE OF A PEOPLE FOR THEIR CITY

Yearning for Jerusalem has been cemented in Jewish practice and ritual through halakha and many customs. Three times a day we turn in the direction of Jerusalem and pray to God, because we believe that God has a stronger presence there, and because we have hope that someday we will return and re-establish the Temple as the focal point of Jewish worship. We always conclude the services on Yom Kippur and Seder night (the annual times when almost all Jews of all backgrounds come together, in synagogues and with family) with the words "Next year in Jerusalem." In our happiest moments we remember Jerusalem (such as breaking the glass and singing *Im Eshkaḥekh Yerushalayim* at weddings), and in our saddest moments we remember Jerusalem too (visiting mourners at a *shiva*, we ask that God comfort them "among the mourners of Jerusalem"). We build remembrance of the destroyed Jerusalem into our very homes, always leaving one cubit undecorated, because how can we have a complete home when God's home in this world has been destroyed? Through these examples and many others, we have maintained a love and yearning for Jerusalem for two thousand years.

JERUSALEM: THE CITY OF PARADOXES

While Jerusalem is a city of conflict, it is also a paradigm of peace, religious diversity, and tolerance. The city itself is a mix of ancient and modern, with the ancient worship found in the Old City and Me'a She'arim next to the high-tech hub of Har Ḥotzvim. Jerusalem has the most diverse population of any city in Israel, including religious and secular, Jewish and Arab. These dichotomies and paradoxes surely add to its complex beauty and are a reflection of humanity as a whole. These elements seem fitting for the city where God chose to make His earthly home.

WE NEVER FORGET JERUSALEM

Jews never lost hope. They never gave up believing that God would bring them back to their homeland one day. So generation after generation, they transmitted a love of Jerusalem to their children, and an active hope that they would be the generation to return.

JERUSALEM OF TODAY CRIES OUT: *"AM YIṢRAEL HAI!"*

Jerusalem tells the story of Jewish history. The kingdoms of David and Shlomo, with Jerusalem as their capital and seat of political, military, and religious power, tell of the origins of the Jewish people and their land. The destruction of Jerusalem in 70 CE at the hands of the Roman army signifies the beginning of a two-thousand-year exile and dispersion. Jews lost their home, but never stopped longing for her. Modern-day Jerusalem testifies to the miracle of the return and the fulfilment of the ancient prophecies that spoke of the day when the sound of children playing in the streets of Jerusalem would be heard once again, as it is today.

ḤIDON ON THE ḤAG (A QUICK QUIZ)

1. Yehuda.
2. Mount Moria.
3. *Akeidat Yitzḥak* (the Binding of Isaac).
4. A lion.
5. Shlomo HaMelekh.
6. Suleiman the Magnificent (1538).
7. Mishkenot Shaananim.
8. December 5, 1949 (by David Ben-Gurion).
9. Jewish, Christian, Muslim, and Armenian quarters.
10. Jaffa Gate, Lions' Gate, Damascus Gate, New Gate, Zion Gate, Dung Gate, Herod's Gate, and Golden Gate.

Shavuot

SHAVUOT IN A NUTSHELL

Shavuot is the second of the three biblical pilgrimage festivals (the *Shalosh Regalim*), falling on the sixth of Sivan (and continuing on the seventh of Sivan in the Diaspora). Shavuot celebrates the moment when, fifty days after the Exodus from Egypt, the Jewish people stood at *Har Sinai* for the Giving of the Torah. It also celebrates the wheat harvest in *Eretz Yisrael*.

Shavuot means "weeks," as it falls seven weeks (a "week of weeks") after Pesaḥ, the culmination of the forty-nine-day Omer period which began on the second night of Pesaḥ. Because of this, Shavuot is also known as "Pentecost," which means "fifty" in Greek (it is the fiftieth day, i.e. the day after the completion of the counting of forty-nine days). Other names for Shavuot found in the Torah are *Ḥag HaKatzir* (the Festival of Reaping) and *Yom HaBikkurim* (Day of the First Fruits), and in the Talmud it is also known as *Atzeret* ("refraining" or "holding back"). (This connects Shavuot to Pesaḥ in a similar way that Shemini Atzeret is connected to Sukkot). We also refer to Shavuot in our prayers as *Zeman Matan Torah* (the Time of the Giving of the Torah).

While there are no rituals associated with Shavuot in the Torah, there are several beautiful and meaningful customs that have developed to help us celebrate Shavuot. These include *Tikkun Leil Shavuot* (staying up all night to learn Torah), eating dairy foods, decorating the *shul* with flowers and greenery, and the reading of *Megillat Rut*.

FROM THE THOUGHT OF RABBI SACKS

TORAH: OUR GREATEST GIFT

On the face of it, Shavuot is a brief festival with few distinctive practices and, at least as far as the Torah is concerned, no specific historical content. But Shavuot is the festival of Jewish identity. Judaism is supremely a religion of the land – the whole of Torah from Avraham to the death of Moshe is a journey towards it – and Shavuot was the supreme festival of the land. There were agricultural elements on Pesaḥ and Sukkot also, but Shavuot was the time of the grain harvest and of bringing first fruits to the Temple and declaring: "My father was a wandering Aramean…. And the Lord brought us out of Egypt…. He brought us to this place and gave us this land, a land flowing with milk and honey."

However, from the outset Shavuot was also the festival of the Giving of the Law, seen as the culmination of the seven-week journey that began with Pesaḥ. But every nation had laws, and for much of the biblical era, other issues, political, military, and cultural, held centre-stage. The prophets tirelessly argued that without faithfulness to God and justice and compassion for their fellow humans, Israel would eventually suffer a momentous defeat, but all too few were listening, and the reforms of kings like Ḥizkiyahu and Yeshayahu proved too little too late.

Only with the experience of the Babylonian exile did people come to see that the law of Israel was unlike that of any other nation – not just because of its content but because of who gave it, when, and where. It was given not at Mount Zion in Jerusalem but at Mount Sinai in

the desert. The law came before the land. Therefore, though they had lost the land, they still had the law. Though they had lost the country, they still had the covenant. The law of Israel was not like the law of every other nation – the decree of kings or the edict of a legislative assembly. It came from God Himself, the Infinite Eternal. Therefore, it could never be lost or nullified.

This was when the full significance of Shavuot began to come clear. The real miracle was not the land but the law that preceded the land. Ezra and Neḥemiah understood this after the Babylonian exile, as did Rabban Yoḥanan ben Zakkai in the midst of the rebellion against Rome. Without them it is highly doubtful whether Jews or Judaism would have survived.

For the better part of two thousand years, Jews lost their land, and once again – as it was for the exile in Babylon – it was the Torah that sustained the people as a people, giving them the assurance that one day they would return. For in truth this always was our greatest gift: the Torah, our constitution of liberty under the sovereignty of God, our marriage contract with Heaven itself, written in letters of black fire on white fire, joining the infinity of God and the finitude of humankind in an unbreakable bond of law and love, the scroll Jews carried wherever they went, and that carried them. This is the Torah: the voice of heaven as it is heard on earth, the word that lights the world.

REFLECT

How did the Torah help the survival of the Jewish people after they were exiled from the land?

Adapted from "Shavuot Today," from the introduction to The Koren Sacks Shavuot Maḥzor *with commentary and translation by Rabbi Sacks.*

SHAVUOT FOR OUR TIME

At Mount Sinai, the Israelites made a covenant with God. He would be their God and they would be His people. But at key moments in Tanakh we find another phrase altogether.

Moshe says in the book of Devarim (7:9), "You shall know that the Lord your God is God, the faithful God, who keeps *habrit vehaḥesed* (the covenant and the loving-kindness)." When Shlomo HaMelekh dedicates the *Beit HaMikdash* (I Melakhim 8:23), he utters the following prayer: "There is no one like You, God, in the heavens above or the earth below, *shomer habrit vehaḥesed* (keeping the covenant and the loving-kindness)." Likewise, Neḥemiah, when he renews the covenant as the people come back from Babylon (Neḥemiah 9:32), says, "The great, mighty, and awesome God, *shomer habrit vehaḥesed* (He who keeps the covenant and the loving-kindness)."

That's a really puzzling phrase, "*shomer habrit vehaḥesed*," "the covenant and the loving-kindness." Look, for instance, at the Jewish Publication Society translation, which translates it just as "covenant" because the *ḥesed* is included in the covenant. If you look at the New International version (which is a very good non-Jewish translation), *habrit vehaḥesed* is translated as "the covenant of love." But of course it doesn't mean that, it means "covenant and love." Everyone had a problem in understanding what God does for the Jewish people other than making a covenant with them on Shavuot at *Har Sinai*. But if you think about it, the answer is really quite simple. A covenant is what sociologists and anthropologists call reciprocal altruism. You do this for me; I will do this for you. "You serve Me," says God, "and I will protect you." Covenant is always reciprocal and neutral. But that is terribly vulnerable, because what happens if we don't keep the covenant? The covenant is then rendered null and void.

The covenant is not enough. And that is what Moshe was saying, that is what Shlomo HaMelekh was saying, that is what Neḥemiah was saying. God does not just make a covenant with us. He has a relationship of *ḥesed* with us, an unconditional love that is translated into deeds of kindness to us. The covenant is conditional, but *ḥesed* is unconditional.

Maybe ultimately this is why we read the Book of Rut on Shavuot. The Book of Rut is the book of *ḥesed*. We received a covenant at Mount Sinai, but we also received something much more long-lasting and profound, which is God's unconditional love. And that's what the book is telling us, that God has love for us the way Rut had love for Naomi and the way Boaz had love for Rut. Acts of loving-kindness all define our relationship with God. And as the Book of Rut shows, they should be what define our relationship with one another.

This message resonates for us this year. Just as in *Megillat Rut*, tragedy and loneliness and isolation are healed by acts of loving-kindness, so has the isolation of so many of us been healed by acts of loving-kindness, acts of neighbourliness, people being in touch, helping us, getting things for us, phoning us up, connecting us by Zoom, showing that they care about us. Those acts of kindness have humanised and lightened our world. *Ḥesed* has a redemptive quality. It transforms tragedy into some form of celebration and despair into some powerful form of hope. Let what Rut did for Naomi and what Boaz did for Rut be with us as we try to reconnect with family and friends, and those who have been so terribly isolated during recent times.

And may we remember that, as well as giving us a covenant at *Har Sinai*, God gave us a bond of love that is unbreakable. He will never abandon us. Let us never abandon Him.

REFLECT

Why are laws not enough? Why do we need to also remember to be kind? How will you show ḥesed to someone today?

From a shiur *given on May 24, 2020, entitled "A Life of Vertical & Horizontal Responsibility: Shavuot During the Coronavirus Pandemic."*

DEEP DIVING INTO *MEGILLAT RUT*

BACKGROUND

The story of Rut is one of the most beautiful in the Bible. It begins in dislocation and grief. Famine leads Elimelekh, together with his wife Naomi and their two sons, to leave their home in Beit Leḥem, to go to Moav to find food. There, the sons marry Moabite women, but all three men die, leaving Naomi and her two daughters-in-law childless widows. Naomi decides to return home, and Rut, who had married her son Maḥlon, insists on going with her. There, in Beit Leḥem, in a field at harvest time, Rut meets a relative of Naomi's, Boaz, who acts kindly towards her. Later, at Naomi's suggestion, Rut asks him to act the part of a kinsman-redeemer. Boaz does so, and he and Rut marry and have a child. The book that begins with death ends in new life. It is a story about the power of human kindness to redeem life from tragedy, and its message is that out of suffering, if transformed by love, can come new life and hope.

The commentators make two primary connections between Rut and Shavuot. The first is seasonal. The key events in the book are set during the barley and wheat harvests, the time of the counting of the Omer and Shavuot itself. The second is substantive. Rut became the paradigm case of a convert to Judaism, and to become a convert you have to enter the covenant of Sinai with its life of the commandments: what the Israelites did when they accepted the Torah on the first Shavuot.

THE BOOK OF LOYALTY AND LOVE

All three *megillot* read on the pilgrimage festivals are about love: the stages of love as we experience it in our growth from youth to maturity to old age. Shir HaShirim, read on Pesaḥ, the festival of spring, is about love in the spring: the passion between two lovers that has nothing in it of yesterday or tomorrow but lives in the overwhelming intensity of today. The book is structured as a series of duets between beloved and lover, their voices loaded with desire. There is nothing in it about courtship, marriage, home-building, and having children: the world of adult responsibilities. The lovers long simply to be together, to elope.

Kohelet, read on Sukkot, the festival of autumn, is about love in the autumn of life, as the heat cools, light fades, the leaves fall, and clouds begin to hide the sun. "Live well, with the woman you love," says Kohelet (9:9). This is love as companionship, and it is rich in irony. Kohelet is written as the autobiography of Shlomo HaMelekh, the king who married seven hundred wives and three hundred concubines (I Melakhim 11:3), and in the end concluded, "And this is what I found: woman is more bitter than death, for she is all traps, with nets laid in her heart; her arms are a prison" (Kohelet 7:26). A thousand wives will not bring you happiness. Faithfulness to one will.

Rut is about the love at the heart of Judaism, the love of summer, when the passion of youth has been tamed and the clouds of age do not yet cover the sky. Rut is about love as loyalty, faithfulness, committing yourself to another in a bond of responsibility and grace. It is about caring for the other more than you care about yourself. It is about Rut setting her own aspirations aside to care for her mother-in-law Naomi, bereaved as she is of her husband and two sons. It is what Boaz does for Rut. The root *a-h-v*, "love," which appears eighteen times in Shir HaShirim, appears in Rut only once. By contrast, the words ḥesed, loving-kindness, and the verb *g-a-l*, "to redeem," do not appear at all in Shir HaShirim, but figure in Rut respectively three and twenty-four times.

The *megillot* are framing devices that force us into seeing the festivals themselves in a new light. When we read Shir HaShirim on Pesaḥ it transforms our understanding of the Exodus from a political event, the liberation of slaves into an elopement and honeymoon, which is precisely how the prophets portray it. Kohelet turns Sukkot into a philosophical reflection on the sukka as a symbol of mortality, the body as a temporary dwelling. It is the sobering story of how Shlomo, wisest of men, sought to deny death by taking refuge in possessions, wives, servants, and worldly wisdom, yet at every step he found himself face to face with the brevity and vulnerability of life. Only at the end did he discover that joy is to be found in simple things: life itself, dignified by work and beautified by love.

> "The covenant at Sinai was a bond of love whose closest analogue in Tanakh is the relationship between Boaz and Rut."

Rut likewise invites us to reframe Shavuot, seeing the making of the covenant at Sinai not simply as a religious or political act, but as an act of love – a mutual pledge between two parties, committing themselves to one another in a bond of responsibility, dedication, and loyalty. The covenant at Sinai was a marriage between God and the children of Israel. The covenant at Sinai was a bond of love whose closest analogue in Tanakh is the relationship between Boaz and Rut.

One of the most sustained libels in religious history was Christianity's claim that Judaism was a religion not of love but of law; not of compassion but of justice; not of forgiveness but of retribution. The Book of Rut, read on Shavuot, is the refutation. Judaism is a religion of love, three loves: loving God with all our heart, our soul, and our might (Devarim 6:5); loving our neighbour as ourselves (Vayikra 19:18); and loving the stranger because we know what it feels like to be a stranger (Devarim 10:19).

Judaism is, from beginning to end, the story of a love: God's love for a small, powerless, and much afflicted people, and a people's love – tempestuous at times to be sure – for God. That is the story of Rut: love as faithfulness, loyalty, and responsibility, and as a marriage that brings new life into the world. That is the love that was consecrated at Sinai on the first Shavuot of all.

Adapted from "Ruth: The Book of Loyalty and Love," an extract from the introduction to The Koren Sacks Shavuot Maḥzor *with commentary and translation by Rabbi Sacks.*

POINTS TO PONDER

1. *What are the thematic connections between* Megillat Rut *and Shavuot?*

2. *Why is Shavuot compared to the wedding day of Israel and God?*

3. *How is this connected to* Megillat Rut*?*

IT ONCE HAPPENED ON SHAVUOT...

There are two famous midrashic accounts of the Giving of the Torah that paint very different pictures of what led to the Israelites receiving the Torah on *Har Sinai*. They are retold here:

When Hashem was ready to give the Torah to the children of Israel, He offered the Torah to all the other nations as well. First Hashem went to the children of Esav and asked them, "Will you accept the Torah?" They replied to Him, "Master of the universe, what is written in it?" He said, "You shall not murder." They replied to Him, "Killing has always been part of our way of life. We cannot accept the Torah!"

Then He went to the children of Amon and Moav, and asked them if they would accept the Torah. They asked Him, "Master of the universe, what is written in it?" He told them, "You shall not commit adultery." They replied to Him, "Adultery has always been part of our way of life. We cannot accept the Torah!"

Then He went to the children of Yishmael, and asked them if they would accept the Torah. They asked Him, "Master of the universe, what is written in it?" He told them, "Do not steal." They replied to Him, "Theft has always been part of our way of life. We cannot accept the Torah!"

Finally He came to Israel. They simply said, "We will do and we will listen" (na'ase venishma) (Shemot 24:7).

Pesikta Rabbati, 21

The Israelites actually stood underneath the mountain, as Hashem held the mountain upside down above their heads like a gigantic barrel, and He said to them: "If you accept the Torah, excellent, but if not, I will drop the mountain on top of you and this will be where you are buried!"

But if this is true then the Jewish people can claim they had no choice and were forced into accepting the Torah! Does this mean we don't need to keep it if we do not want to today? Ah, but then the people re-accepted it voluntarily at the end of the Purim story.

Talmud Bavli, Shabbat 88a

POINTS TO PONDER

1. Do you find anything troubling about these two stories?

2. What lessons can we learn from the ways the Rabbis told the story of the Giving of the Torah on Mount Sinai in these midrashim?

3. Which of these two stories best articulates how you see the relationship between the Jewish people and the Torah?

> "Finally He came to Israel. They simply said, 'We will do and we will listen.'"

MAKE A DOUBLE-CHOCOLATE CHEESECAKE FOR YOUR WHOLE FAMILY!

INGREDIENTS

Graham cracker crust

- 4 oz. graham crackers (see note)
- 2 tbsp melted dark chocolate
- 4 tbsp (½ stick) butter, melted

Cheesecake top

- 12 oz. full-fat soft cheese (such as Philadelphia cream cheese)
- 100 grams caster sugar (½ cup granulated sugar)
- ¾ cup thick plain or vanilla yoghurt (plain Greek yoghurt)
- 300 ml or ½ pint double cream (1¼ cups whipping cream)
- 6 oz. (1 cup) dark chocolate, melted
- 6 oz. (1 cup) white chocolate, melted
- 1 chocolate bar such as Elite's *mekupelet*, optional

METHOD

Part 1: Graham cracker crust

1. Line an 8-inch baking tin with baking paper (use either a spring-form tin or loose-bottom tin).
2. Place the graham crackers in a sealed plastic food bag, and crush them using a rolling pin until you have a bag full of very small chunks.
3. Mix the crushed graham crackers, melted chocolate, and melted butter in a bowl.
4. Pour the mixture immediately into the tin and smooth it down with a spoon, so that it's spread evenly over the bottom of the tin. This is your crust. Now you just need to leave it to set.

Part 2: Cheesecake top

1. Mix the cheese and sugar with a wooden spoon until the mixture is smooth.
2. Pour in the yoghurt (still using your wooden spoon) and mix well.
3. Whisk the cream separately (using either a hand whisk or electric beaters) until the cream is just holding its shape. Then fold the cream into the sugar-cheese mixture.
4. Divide the mixture into two equal bowls and get ready to add the chocolate.
5. Mix all the melted white chocolate into one of the bowls and all the melted dark chocolate into the other bowl.
6. Take the tin with the biscuit base and create a rough chess-board pattern by spooning alternate tablespoonfuls of the two cheesecake mixtures. Then add a second layer, continuing to alternate your spoonfuls of white and dark, but this time also try to place white on top of dark and vice versa. Continue layering until all the mixture in both bowls has been used.
7. Very gently, pull a fork through the mixture in the tin to create a "marbled" effect.
8. Level the top with a knife or palette knife, then have fun creating a pattern by raking a fork across the top.
9. If using the *mekupelet*, crush and sprinkle it on top.
10. Refrigerate for at least 90 minutes, until you are ready to serve your cake.

Note: Biscuits or toasted oat cereal can be used instead of graham crackers. If you choose one of those options, omit the melted chocolate from the crust.

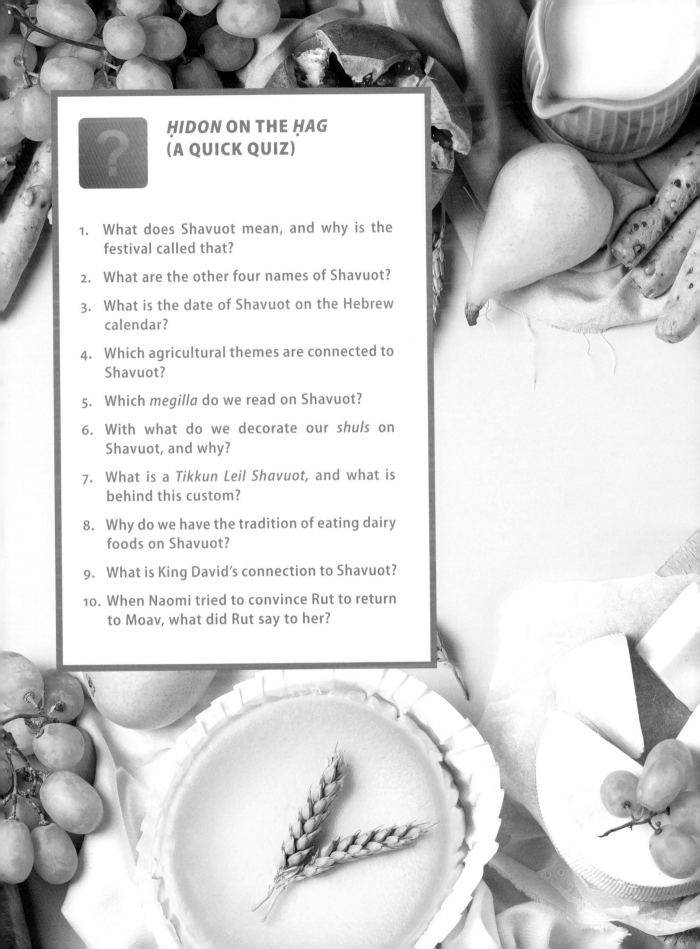

ḤIDON ON THE ḤAG
(A QUICK QUIZ)

1. What does Shavuot mean, and why is the festival called that?

2. What are the other four names of Shavuot?

3. What is the date of Shavuot on the Hebrew calendar?

4. Which agricultural themes are connected to Shavuot?

5. Which *megilla* do we read on Shavuot?

6. With what do we decorate our *shuls* on Shavuot, and why?

7. What is a *Tikkun Leil Shavuot,* and what is behind this custom?

8. Why do we have the tradition of eating dairy foods on Shavuot?

9. What is King David's connection to Shavuot?

10. When Naomi tried to convince Rut to return to Moav, what did Rut say to her?

EDUCATIONAL COMPANION TO THE QUESTIONS

DEEP DIVING INTO MEGILLAT RUT

1. The story took place at the time of the grain harvests in early summer, which is the time in the calendar when Shavuot falls. But there are several additional themes that are present in the story that are also linked to the themes of the festival. Rut is a model example of a convert to Judaism, entering voluntarily into the covenant of Sinai, which is what the Israelites did when they accepted the Torah on the first Shavuot. The themes of love and *ḥesed* are also central to Shavuot and *Matan Torah* (see also "Shavuot for Our Time," p. 169). Finally, *Megillat Rut* ends with the birth of Rut's great-grandson, David HaMelekh, who was born (and died) on Shavuot.

2. The wedding metaphor helps us to understand the covenantal love between God and the Jewish people. Just as marriage is a covenant based on love, with both parties having contractual obligations to each other (the contract being the *ketubba*), so the covenant of Sinai is a contract based on love and mutual obligation between God and Israel (with the Torah serving as the contract). There are even some who suggest that the aggadic story found in Talmud Bavli, Shabbat 88a (see "*It Once Happened on Shavuot*," p. 174), where God suspends Mount Sinai above the heads of the Israelites, represents the *ḥuppa* (the wedding canopy).

3. The recurring themes of *Megillat Rut* are love, loyalty, and contractual obligations. The relationship between Rut and Naomi is an example of love and loyalty, and while the relationship between Boaz and Rut becomes one of love also, its foundation is contractual (as he redeems her as the next of kin).

IT ONCE HAPPENED ON SHAVUOT...

1. The first story seems to suggest that Israel was the only people willing to enter into a covenant with God and accept the obligations of the Torah, rather than God choosing the Jewish people to be His *am segula* (treasured people). The second story suggests that the Israelites had no choice but to accept the Torah at Sinai, because God was threatening their very lives. Apart from the question of fairness and coercion, this would cause many theological and legal problems. For example, how can Jews be held responsible for not observing the mitzvot if they did not readily commit to them from a position of free choice? This is why the story ends with a national voluntary recommitment to the Torah at the end of the Purim story in *Megillat Esther*.

2. These midrashic retellings of the events at Sinai are not necessarily to be taken as historically factual, but rather as a pedagogic tool to teach us theological lessons. For example, if there is discomfort caused by the chosenness of the Jewish people (why would God choose one nation above all the others?) this story suggests that it is actually the Jews who chose God. It is a complimentary text that praises the Israelites for accepting the Torah unconditionally without even fully understanding what its content or obligations are. This can also be a lesson to us, to accept all the contents of the Torah, even the difficult parts or the parts that do not make sense to us. The second story articulates the binding obligation to keep the Torah and join with the destiny of the Jewish people. It hints at the ramifications for disobedience that are explicitly described in the Torah itself.

3. For some people it is clear that all Jews have a binding obligation to keep the Torah in its entirety, and this was a covenantal relationship initiated between God and our ancestors. However, for some, Torah observance feels like something that each individual recommits to themselves in the modern age of freedom and competing lifestyles.

HIDON ON THE *HAG* (A QUICK QUIZ)

1. Weeks, because Shavuot falls seven weeks after Pesah.
2. *Zeman Matan Torah, Hag HaKatzir, Yom HaBikkurim, Atzeret.*
3. Sixth of Sivan (and the seventh of Sivan also, in the Diaspora).
4. The wheat harvest and the bringing of the first fruits.
5. *Megillat Rut.*
6. Greenery and flowers, because the Midrash says that *Har Sinai* blossomed with flowers in anticipation of the Giving of the Torah.
7. *Tikkun Leil Shavuot* translates literally to the "rectification for Shavuot night." It is the custom to stay up all night learning Torah to make amends for the Israelites, who according to the Midrash went to sleep to be well rested for the next day, but then overslept and had to be woken by Moshe.
8. Because before the receiving of the Torah it wasn't clear which meat was kosher, and so to be safe, the Israelites only ate dairy meals. Additionally, the Torah is compared to milk (Shir HaShirim 4:11), and the *gematria* (numerical value) of the word *halav* (milk) is forty, signifying the number of days and nights that Moshe spent on Sinai.
9. King David was born on Shavuot (and seventy years later, he died on that same day) and his great-grandmother was Rut, who we read about in *Megillat Rut* on Shavuot.
10. "Wherever you go, I will go; wherever you stay, I will stay; your people will be my people, and your God my God."

The Three Weeks

THE THREE WEEKS IN A NUTSHELL

The period known as the Three Weeks (known in Hebrew as *Bein HaMetzarim* – "Between the Straits/ Days of Distress") is the saddest period in the Jewish calendar. Customs of mourning are observed during this time to commemorate the destruction of the First and Second Temples. This three-week period of mourning begins on the seventeenth day of Tamuz, with the fast of Shiva Asar BeTamuz, and concludes on the ninth day of Av, which is the fast of Tisha B'Av.

SHIVA ASAR BETAMUZ

On this day we commemorate the breach of the walls of Jerusalem before the destruction of the Second Temple in the year 70 CE. According to the Mishna (Taanit 4:6), there were four other historical calamities that occurred on this day:

1. Moshe broke the Tablets of Stone upon descending Sinai and seeing the Israelites worshipping the Golden Calf.
2. The daily *tamid* offering ceased to be brought in the Temple (during the First Temple period).
3. An idol was erected inside the Temple (during the First Temple period).
4. Prior to the Bar Kokhba revolt, the Roman military leader Apostomus burned a *sefer Torah*.

Fasting on the seventeenth of Tamuz begins at dawn and ends at nightfall.

LAWS AND CUSTOMS OF THE THREE WEEKS

Different communities have different customs of mourning during this period, including prohibitions on: haircuts and shaving; listening to live music; weddings and other celebrations; and buying/wearing new clothes. The intensity of mourning increases from the first of Av until midday on the tenth of Av (the period called the Nine Days), when in addition to the mourning customs of the Three Weeks, no freshly laundered clothes may be worn, and meat and wine are not consumed (except on Shabbat). Many Sephardim only observe these extra stringencies from the Sunday before Tisha B'Av. The Three Weeks are also considered to be a time of misfortune, and therefore some are careful to avoid all dangerous situations including swimming, undergoing a major operation, or engaging in a court case that could be postponed until after Tisha B'Av.

TISHA B'AV

This is the saddest day in the Jewish calendar, when the destruction of both the First and Second Temples is commemorated. According to the Mishna (Taanit 4:6), the following tragic events occurred on this day in Jewish history:

1. The twelve spies sent by Moshe to scout the land of Israel returned, with ten of them bringing a damaging report that led to forty years of *benei Yisrael* wandering in the desert until the entire generation had died out.

2. The First Temple, built by King Shlomo, was destroyed by the Babylonian King Nevukhadnetzar in 586 BCE, and the population of the kingdom of Yehuda was sent into exile.

3. The Second Temple was destroyed by the Romans in 70 CE, scattering the people of Judea and signifying the beginning of a two-thousand-year exile.

4. The subsequent defeat of the Bar Kokhba revolt and destruction of the city of Beitar, killing over 500,000 Jewish civilians in 135 CE.

5. Also in 135 CE, following the Bar Kokhba revolt, the Roman commander Turnus Rufus ploughed the site of the Temple and the surrounding area of Jerusalem.

The fast observed on Tisha B'Av begins at sundown at the end of the eighth of Av, and lasts for twenty-five hours until nightfall on the ninth of Av. As well as all the customs of the Nine Days, Tisha B'Av shares the five prohibitions of Yom Kippur, which are:

1. no eating or drinking
2. no washing or bathing
3. no applying creams or oils
4. no wearing leather shoes
5. no marital relations

Additionally, there are several customs of mourning associated with Tisha B'Av. These include: eating a hardboiled egg dipped in ashes, and a piece of bread dipped in ashes during the pre-fast *seuda hamafseket* meal; refraining from studying Torah (apart from sad portions) until midday on the ninth of Av (because of the enjoyment it provides); removing the *parokhet* (curtain of the ark) and dimming the lights in the synagogue; and sitting on low stools or on the floor (as is done during *shiva*) until midday. *Megillat Eikha* and special *kinnot* (sad poems) are read during the synagogue service, and the custom is to not put on tefillin or a tallit at the Shaḥarit morning service of Tisha B'Av, but rather at Minḥa instead.

POINTS TO PONDER

1. *What do all the historical events that occurred on the seventeenth of Tamuz and the ninth of Av have in common?*

2. *What do you think is the objective behind the laws and customs of the Three Weeks?*

3. *Why do you think Tisha B'Av and Yom Kippur share the same five prohibitions?*

THE THREE WEEKS FOR OUR TIME

REMEMBER THE PAST, BUT DO NOT BE HELD CAPTIVE BY IT

Judaism is a religion of memory. The verb *zakhor* appears no fewer than 169 times in the Hebrew Bible. "Remember that you were strangers in Egypt"; "Remember the days of old"; "Remember the seventh day to keep it holy." Memory, for Jews, is a religious obligation. This is particularly so at this time of the year. We call it the "Three Weeks" leading up to the saddest day in the Jewish calendar, Tisha B'Av, the anniversary of the destruction of the two Temples, the first by Nevukhadnetzar, king of Babylon in 586 BCE, the second by Titus in 70 CE.

Jews never forgot those tragedies. To this day, at every wedding we break a glass in their memory. During the Three Weeks, we have no celebrations. On Tisha B'Av itself, we spend the day fasting and sitting on the floor or low stools like mourners, reading the Book of Eikha. It is a day of profound collective grief.

Two and a half thousand years is a long time to remember. Often I am asked – usually in connection with the Holocaust – is it really right to remember? Should there not be a limit on grief? Are not most of the ethnic conflicts in the world fuelled by memories of perceived injustices long ago? Would not the world be more peaceable if once in a while we forgot?

My answer is both yes and no, for it depends on how we remember.

Though the two are often confused, memory is different from history. History is someone else's story. It's about events that occurred long ago to someone else. Memory is my story. It's about where I come from and of what narrative I am a part. History answers the question "What happened?" Memory answers the question "Who, then, am I?" It is about identity and the connection between the generations.

In the case of collective memory, it all depends on how we tell the story. We don't remember for the sake of revenge. "Do not hate the Egyptians," said Moshe, "for you were strangers in their land." To be free, you have to let go of hate. Remember the past, says Moshe, but do not be held captive by it. Turn it into a blessing, not a curse; a source of hope, not humiliation.

To this day, the Holocaust survivors I know spend their time sharing their memories with young people, not for the sake of revenge, but its opposite: to teach tolerance and the value of life. Mindful of the lessons of Bereshit, we too try to remember for the future and for life.

In today's fast-moving culture, we undervalue acts of remembering. Computer memories have grown, while ours have become foreshortened. Our children no longer memorise chunks of poetry. Their knowledge of history is often all too vague. Our sense of space has expanded. Our sense of time has shrunk.

That cannot be right. One of the greatest gifts we can give to our children is the knowledge of where we have come from, the things for which we fought, and why. None of the things we value – freedom, human dignity, justice – were achieved without a struggle. None can be sustained without conscious vigilance. A society without memory is like a journey without a map. It's all too easy to get lost.

I, for one, cherish the richness of knowing that my life is a chapter in a book begun by my ancestors long ago, to which I will add my contribution before handing it on to my children. Life has meaning when it is part of a story, and the larger the story, the more our imaginative horizons grow. Besides, things remembered do not die. That's as close as we get to immortality on earth.

An excerpt from an article first published by The Times *(UK) in July 2004.*

TISHA B'AV FOR OUR TIME

WE ARE THE PEOPLE THAT BUILD

The great prophets of doom were also the supreme prophets of hope. For example, let us look at Yeshayahu, whose words we say on *Shabbat Ḥazon* immediately prior to Tisha B'Av. He delivers a devastating critique of Jerusalem: *"As you spread your hands out towards Me (in prayer) I will close My eyes,"* says God. *"The more you pray the less I will listen"* (Yeshayahu 1:15).

Yet in the very next chapter, Yeshayahu delivers some of the most famous words of hope, of vision, of peace, that the world has ever known. These words are engraved opposite the United Nations building in New York: "Many peoples will come and say, 'Come, let us go up to the mountain of the Lord, to the house of the God of Yaakov. He will teach us His ways, so that we may walk in His path.' For the Torah shall come forth from Zion, and the word of the Lord from Jerusalem. He will judge between the nations and settle disputes for many peoples. They will beat their swords into ploughshares and their spears

> "The great prophets of doom were also the supreme prophets of hope."

into pruning hooks. Nation will not take up sword against nation, nor will they train for war anymore" (Yeshayahu 2:3–4).

Yeshayahu, of all the prophets in the Bible, is the poet laureate of hope. So somehow the man who announced the doom of the city also announced the new age that would someday be greater in its blessings than the destruction.

Likewise Yirmeyahu gives us two of the three *haftarot* leading up to Tisha B'Av, and of all the prophets he was the one who most vividly foresaw the terrible events that would soon happen. In chapter 3 of Eikha, he says, "I actually saw it. I didn't just foresee it the way other people did – I actually lived through it."

But it was Yirmeyahu who also said in the name of God, "There is hope for your future" (Yirmeyahu 31:16). And "just as I threw Myself into destruction, I will take that same energy and use it to build and to plant" (Yirmeyahu 31:27). And Yirmeyahu says something else in chapter 31 that nobody else says in all of Tanakh: "Thus says the Lord who gives the sun to give light by day and the moon and the stars by night … only if these things cease to be, will the children of Israel cease to be" (Yirmeyahu 31:34–35). Yirmeyahu is the person who says the Jewish people will be the eternal people.

How is it that these supreme prophets of doom also became supreme prophets of hope?

Because they relied on God's promise in *Parashat Beḥukotai* that "even when they are in the land of their enemies, I will not so despise them as to destroy them, thus invalidating My covenant with them" (Vayikra 26:44). God says, "I will keep My promise. I will never let them be destroyed." The prophets had God's word, and that gave them hope.

We have here a unique phenomenon. The Jews gave to the world this idea of time as a narrative of hope, which meant that what is lost can be regained, what is destroyed can be rebuilt, and what disappears may one day return. Our prophets were able to see beyond the horizon of history, so that where everyone else saw doom, they also saw the hope that lay just over that horizon, and they understood that there was a route from here to there. That really is a remarkable vision.

We are the people who gave the concept of hope to the world. We kept faith, we never gave up, and for twenty-six centuries, we honestly observed, without a single pause, the line in Tehillim 137, "*I will never forget you, O Jerusalem.*" And because we never gave up hope, we finally came back to Jerusalem.

Hope rebuilds the ruins of Jerusalem. The Jewish people kept hope alive, and hope kept the Jewish people alive.

POINTS TO PONDER

1. *How can we learn hope from the prophets of doom?*

2. *How have Jews taught the world the art of hope?*

3. *Since we have the modern State of Israel, do you think we should still be mourning on Tisha B'Av?*

"The Jewish people kept hope alive, and hope kept the Jewish people alive."

FROM THE THOUGHT OF RABBI SACKS

Jews are the people who refused to be comforted because they never gave up hope. Yaakov did eventually see Yosef again. Raḥel's children did return to the land. Jerusalem is once again the Jewish home. All the evidence may suggest otherwise: it may seem to signify irretrievable loss, a decree of history that cannot be overturned, a fate that must be accepted. Jews never believed the evidence because they had something else to set against it – a faith, a trust, an unbreakable hope that proved stronger than historical inevitability. It is not too much to say that Jewish survival was sustained in that hope. And that hope came from a simple – or perhaps not so simple – phrase in the life of Yaakov. He refused to be comforted. And so – while we live in a world still scarred by violence, poverty, and injustice – must we.

From "Refusing Comfort, Keeping Hope," *in Covenant & Conversation: Genesis, Vayeshev, 257*

REFLECT

How would Jewish history have been different if Jews had found comfort in their history instead of hope?

As at the conclusion of Yom Kippur, so here – at the two supreme moments of the Jewish year – we pray "*Leshana habaa biYerushalayim habenuya*," "Next year in Jerusalem rebuilt." Nothing in the imaginative life of peoples throughout the world quite compares to the Jewish love for, and attachment to, Jerusalem. A psalm records, in unforgettable words, the feelings of the Jewish exiles in Babylonia two and a half thousand years ago: "By the rivers of Babylon we sat and wept as we remembered Zion.… How can we sing the Lord's song on foreign soil? If I forget you, O Jerusalem, may my right hand forget its skill. May my tongue cling to the roof of my mouth if I do not remember you, if I do not set Jerusalem above my highest joy" (Tehillim 137:1–6).

Wherever Jews were, they preserved the memory of Jerusalem. They prayed towards it. They spoke of it continually. At weddings they broke a glass in its memory. On Tisha B'Av they sat and mourned its destruction as if it were a recent tragedy. They longed for it with an everlasting love.

The French historian Chateaubriand, visiting Jerusalem in the early nineteenth century, was overcome with emotion as he saw for the first time the small Jewish community there, waiting patiently for *Mashiaḥ*. "This people," he wrote, "has seen Jerusalem destroyed seventeen times,

yet there exists nothing in the world which can discourage it or prevent it from raising its eyes to Zion. He who beholds the Jews dispersed over the face of the earth, in keeping with the Word of God, lingers and marvels. But he will be struck with amazement, as at a miracle, who finds them still in Jerusalem and perceives even, who in law and justice are the masters of Judea, to exist as slaves and strangers in their own land; how despite all abuses they await the King who is to deliver them." Noting how this "small nation" had survived while the great empires who sought its destruction had vanished, he added, "If there is anything among the nations of the world marked with the stamp of the miraculous, this, in our opinion, is that miracle."

The Jonathan Sacks Haggada, 150–151

REFLECT

How did Jews remember Jerusalem every day of their history, and what did this achieve?

Ours is the only civilisation I know whose canonical texts are anthologies of arguments. The prophets argued with God; the Rabbis argued with one another. We are a people with strong views – it is part of who we are. Our ability to argue, our sheer diversity, culturally, religiously, and in every other way, is not a weakness but a strength. However, when it causes us to split apart, it becomes terribly dangerous because whilst no empire on earth has ever been able to defeat us, we have, on occasions, been able to defeat ourselves.

It happened three times. The first was in the days of Yosef and his brothers, when the Torah says, "They could no longer speak peaceably together." The brothers sold Yosef as a slave and yet eventually they all, as well as their grandchildren, ended up in slavery. The second followed the completion of the First Temple. Shlomo HaMelekh died, his son took over, and the kingdom split in two. That was the beginning of the end of both the northern and the southern kingdoms. The third was during the Roman siege of Jerusalem when the Jewish men and women besieged inside were more focused on fighting one another than the enemy outside. Those three splits within the Jewish people caused the three great exiles of the Jewish people.

> **"Our ability to argue, our sheer diversity, culturally, religiously, and in every other way, is not a weakness but a strength."**

How then do we contain that diversity within a single people, bound together in fate and in destiny? I think there are seven principles that can help:

1. Keep talking.
2. Listen to one another.
3. Work to understand those with whom you disagree.
4. Do not think in terms of victory or defeat. Think in terms of the good of the Jewish people.
5. If you seek respect, give respect.
6. You can disagree, but still care.
7. Remember that God chose us as a people.

God chose us as a people, and it is as a people that we stand before God and before the world. The Sages said a very striking thing. They said, "Great is peace, because even if Israel is worshipping idols, as long as there is peace among them, God will never allow harm to happen to them." That is a powerful idea to reflect upon. So the next time you are tempted to walk away from some group of Jews that you think have offended you, make that extra effort, that gesture to stay together, to forgive, to listen, to try and unite. Because if God loves each of us, can we justify failing to strive to do this too?

From the video "Seven Principles for Maintaining Jewish Peoplehood," 2017

REFLECT

Why do Jews argue so much? How then have we kept united as one people?

The Siege and Destruction of Jerusalem *by David Roberts*

IT ONCE HAPPENED...

WHY THE TEMPLE WAS DESTROYED

The Talmud tells us that Jerusalem was destroyed by the Romans because of the story of Kamtza and Bar Kamtza. There once was a man who had a friend called Kamtza and an enemy named Bar Kamtza. He was planning a big party, so he gave his servant a list of all the people he wanted to invite, including his good friend Kamtza. The servant mistakenly delivered the invitation to Bar Kamtza instead.

When the host saw that Bar Kamtza had arrived at his party, he was furious. In front of all the other guests he confronted him, asking, "What are you doing here? We are enemies! Get out!" Bar Kamtza said to him, "I now realise you didn't mean to invite me. But since I am already here, please don't embarrass me by throwing me out. Let me stay and I will pay for whatever I eat." But the host refused, and again insisted that he leave immediately. Bar Kamtza said, "Let me stay and I will pay for half of the party!" But the host continued to demand that he leave his house. Bar Kamtza pleaded with him one more time, "Let me stay and I will pay for the entire party!" The host refused again, and this time dragged him out onto the street.

Bar Kamtza could not forgive this harsh treatment. He thought to himself: The Sages were at the party too, and they didn't say a thing to the host about the way he spoke to me and humiliated me, so I can only assume they supported his actions. I am going to get my revenge on them and convince the emperor they are rebelling against the Roman Empire.

He travelled to Rome and met with the emperor, where he told him that the Jews had rebelled against him. The emperor asked him, "How do I know what you are telling me is the truth?" Bar Kamtza replied, "Let's set a test to see if I am right. Send them an animal offering to be brought in their Temple in honour of the government and see whether they will sacrifice it." The emperor agreed and sent him off with a perfect three-year-old calf as an offering, but on the journey back to Jerusalem, Bar Kamtza made a small cut on the calf's upper lip, knowing that this would render the animal invalid as an offering in the Temple. When Bar Kamtza brought the animal to the Temple, the priests noticed the blemish and could not accept the calf.

When word got back to the emperor, he was furious, and this is how the war between the Jews and the Romans began, ultimately leading to the destruction of the Temple and the exile of the Jews from Jerusalem.

Based on Talmud Bavli, Gittin 55a–b

THE LEGEND OF NAPOLEON

A legend is told of Napoleon Bonaparte, the French emperor in the early nineteenth century, who took a stroll through the streets of Paris with his advisors one Tisha B'Av during his reign. As his entourage passed a small synagogue they heard wailing and crying coming from within. Puzzled by the commotion, Napoleon sent an aide inside to inquire as to what had happened.

The aide returned after a few minutes and told Napoleon that the Temple of the Jews had been destroyed and they were in mourning over its loss.

Napoleon was outraged. "How can it be that I have no knowledge of this event? Where in the empire did this occur? When did this befall the Jews of that community and who were the perpetrators?"

The aide responded, "Sir, the Temple was lost in Jerusalem on this date more than 1,700 years ago."

Napoleon stood in silence and shock for a moment, and then said, "A people who can mourn for Jerusalem so long will one day have it restored to them!"

EDUCATIONAL COMPANION TO THE QUESTIONS

THE THREE WEEKS IN A NUTSHELL

1. All these events were national calamities that significantly impacted the Jewish people. Some were more symbolic (e.g., the idol in the Temple, and the burning of a *sefer Torah*) and some were tragic events that caused a catastrophic shift in Jewish history (e.g., the story of the twelve spies, or the destruction of the Temples). It is tempting to describe each event as a negative destructive force in Jewish history, and this is certainly how these were all experienced at the time. However, Jews believe in God's involvement in history, and have faith in a divine plan, and with the hindsight of thousands of years of Jewish history we can see that these events led us to the point we are at today.

2. These laws are connected to the laws of mourning, designed to focus our thoughts and feelings towards our national sadness for what has been lost. They take our focus away from our individual concerns and joy, allowing us to focus on the bigger themes of national mourning.

3. Both these days are deeply serious, and both encourage introspection. However, there are also significant differences between the two days. Yom Kippur is not a sad day, but rather one of prayer and personal reflection and growth. Tisha B'Av is the saddest day in the Jewish calendar, when we consider tragic events that have befallen the Jewish people. The prohibitions of these days are designed to help with the process of introspection and reflection by

taking our focus away from our personal needs and desires (e.g., our appearance and physical needs), allowing us to focus on spiritual and national needs and growth.

THE THREE WEEKS FOR OUR TIME

1. One can become obsessed with the past and the injustices that have occurred to our people. This can lead to a victim mentality, or to thoughts of revenge. Too much grief can be paralysing and prevent us from moving forward and fully living life. These are not healthy emotions or a positive outlook on life.

2. But on the other hand, remembering the past is vital to understanding national identity. Rabbi Sacks draws a distinction between memory and history. History happened long ago to someone else. Memory is my story. It's about where I come from and who I am. Remembering our national collective past connects us to previous generations and is critical to understanding who we are and what we hope our future to be.

3. The Holocaust survivors Rabbi Sacks met in his life taught him how experiences of tragedy and trauma can be used for healing. The survivors ensured that we remember their story by sharing their memories with young people, not for the sake of revenge, but to teach tolerance and the value of life, to build a life for our people and for the world in which they hope to live.

TISHA B'AV FOR OUR TIME

1. Although the biblical prophets prophesied doom, they also predicted a future of hope, because they had faith that God would keep His promises and never abandon His people. So while they believed in a shared vision of destruction and catastrophe, they also reminded the people of a brighter future, and the idea that, if we keep faith with God, this future can be achieved.

2. Jewish history is one of terrible trauma, enough to justify any nation giving up all hope. But the Jewish people never ceased to hope and dream of a brighter future, as promised by God through the prophets. They never gave up hope of returning to their land and rebuilding their nation there. The Jewish story is an inspiration to millions.

3. While we live in a generation that has been privileged to return to our land and rebuild there, the story is not complete. We are still fighting for our existence in Israel, and we have still not fulfilled our national destiny. The lessons of Tisha B'Av are as relevant today as they ever were, if not more so.

IT ONCE HAPPENED ON TISHA B'AV...

1. The unnecessary hatred between two Jews, and perhaps more importantly the leadership of the time who turned a blind eye to it, led to this tragic, destructive end. Jewish society as described in the story of Bar Kamtza was not a society of unity. The people were unkind and acted with hatred. We often use this story to learn about *sinat ḥinam* (baseless hatred) and the Rabbis tell us that this was the underlying reason why we were punished with exile, and why the Temple was destroyed.

2. The antidote to *sinat ḥinam* is *ahavat ḥinam* (unconditional love) and if and when we achieve this as a nation, and spread this message to the world, we will be able usher in the Messianic Era, which will in turn bring a rebuilt Third Temple.

3. The message of this story is the impressive emotional connection that these (and all) Jews had to their history, so much so that they mourned the 1,700th anniversary of the destruction of their Temple as if it had just happened. A nation that remembers its past as if it were recent history, experiences its national pain, and continues to yearn for a brighter future will one day achieve that future. Our takeaway from this is the importance of reliving and experiencing our past, learning the lessons from it, and never giving up hope in our future.

Bibliography

Works by Rabbi Jonathan Sacks cited

A Letter in the Scroll (The Free Press, 2000)
Celebrating Life (Continuum, 2019)
Ceremony & Celebration (Maggid Books, 2017)
The Dignity of Difference (Continuum, 2002)
From Optimism to Hope (Bloomsbury, 2004)
Faith in the Future (Darton, Longman & Todd Ltd, 1995)
Future Tense (Hodder & Stoughton, 2009)
The Great Partnership (Hodder & Stoughton, 2011)
To Heal a Fractured World (Schocken, 2005)
The Jonathan Sacks Haggada (Koren Publishers, 2017)
The Koren Sacks Pesah Mahzor (Koren Publishers, 2013)
The Koren Sacks Shavuot Mahzor (Koren Publishers, 2016)
The Koren Sacks Sukkot Mahzor (Koren Publishers, 2015)
The Koren Sacks Yom Kippur Mahzor (Koren Publishers, 2012)
The Koren Sacks Rosh Hashana Mahzor (Koren Publishers, 2011)
Morality (Hodder & Stoughton, 2020)
Ten Paths to God (https://www.rabbisacks.org/curriculum-resources/ten-paths-to-god/)

Image Credits

All images are copyright © Koren Publishers Jerusalem Ltd., except:

Other works by the author:

A Letter in the Scroll

Arguments for the Sake of Heaven

Celebrating Life

Community of Faith

Crisis and Covenant

The Dignity of Difference

Faith in the Future

From Optimism to Hope

Future Tense

The Home We Build Together

Morality

Morals and Markets

Not in God's Name

One People?

The Persistence of Faith

The Politics of Hope

Radical Then, Radical Now

To Heal a Fractured World

Tradition in an Untraditional Age

Will We Have Jewish Grandchildren?

The Covenant & Conversation Series:

Genesis: The Book of Beginnings

Exodus: The Book of Redemption

Leviticus: The Book of Holiness

Numbers: The Wilderness Years

Deuteronomy: Renewal of the Sinai Covenant

Ceremony and Celebration

Ethics in Essays

Lessons in Leadership

Judaism's Life-Changing Ideas

Studies in Spirituality

I Believe

graphics
in new
dimensions

stereo
graphics

edited &
published
by
viction:ary

viction:ary™

Stereographics
Graphics In New Dimensions

First published and distributed by viction:workshop ltd.

viction:ary™

Unit C, 7th Floor, Seabright Plaza,
9-23 Shell Street, North Point, Hong Kong
URL: www.victionary.com
Email: we@victionary.com

Edited and produced by viction:workshop ltd.

Concepts & art direction by Victor Cheung
Jacket, cover and images on P.1, 3, 5 by Jean Jullien
Preface by Shirley Surya

ISBN 978-988-98229-0-3

EUR & US edition
Printed and bound in China

AD   Advertisement

BN   Banner

CL   Collateral

ED   Editorial

EX   Experimental

ID   Identity

PK   Packaging

PO   Poster

Intro [006]
Behind the Scenes [009]
Stages Set [033]   Objects Installed [097]
Types Constructed [153]
Biography [220]
Acknowledgement [224]
. . .

Content

Intro

Going beyond the two-dimensional (2-D) world of backlit screens, modern image-makers are getting their hands dirty making products of a graphic quality and dabbling with spatial layout for their final designs using paper, wires, foam boards and other everyday objects. How visual communication is breaking out of the confines of digital 'flatland' has certainly caught the attention of designers, media and the public. As the fruit of an ongoing trend, where the breadth of contemporary visual culture makes its mark on the three-dimensional (3-D) realm – of products, interiors and the great outdoors – this book presents its subset, focusing on the exploration of 3-D skills and styles to be realised in the 2-D medium. Entitling the book 'Stereographics,' with reference to the geometric term 'stereography' (art of picturing 3-D solid bodies on a 2-D plane) alludes to designers translating captured moments of 3-D collages in space into traditional 2-D print, video or web images. But in these transitory times, when any trend has lived and died before we know, "Stereographics" is not just an invitation to move along with a trend, but also about taking a step back to reflect on the phenomenon.

The surge in 3-D graphic application is often attributed to designers' love-and-hate relationship with the ubiquitous digital technology. While computer-aided creative techniques have enabled the flexibility for experimentation and the merging of various media, there is a growing desire for authenticity through the materialisation of graphic design. This led to artists and designers taking their signature craft, forms and styles into the third dimension, where the imperfect handmade qualities are favoured over the slickness of increasingly monoculture products of vector design. Such inclination is just as evident outside of the design community. With the prevalent virtualisation of our world, we also have a great desire for a tactile and spatial experience. Objects of fantasies made of varying materials and entire fairy-tale like settings are no longer realised as personal artistic endeavours, but also as commercial projects where businesses seek to create sensorially comprehensible experiences to capture everyone's imagination.

While the driving factors reflect the designer's intention and desires, it is also significant to consider what this development could mean for the design world. The most obvious is perhaps how it has led to an enriched design process. Beginning this book with the chapter "Behind The Scenes" is an emphasis on how design visions are translated into the 3-D realm and back, which demands more time, skills and creativity. Its four case studies show how the final work is often made possible by tapping on the resources of artists, production crew and photographers. If left alone, the designer would have to possess a diverse set of skills – from a knack for materials, 3-D model-making skills, to the expertise and aesthetic sensibilities in lighting and shooting – to create a world of make-be-er. More than encouraging a similar graphic application, such laborious process in conception and execution should inspire image-makers to go beyond plain digital work, and to flex both physical and creative muscles for a process that could be just as rewarding as the final product. With the injection of allusions, surrealism or abstraction in the visual narrative of 3-D still lifes, graphic design has also taken on a more cerebral potential to communicate concepts and philosophies, taking them beyond its normally commercial and utilitarian nature. Hybrid forms that combine graphic and 3-D stylistic elements also give a narrative quality that can change perceptions in a much more powerful way, as it turns reality on its head to present an out-of-the-world pictorial language.

The above possibility of reinforcing the bond between the creator, the work and the viewer on a 2-D format, which may be considered as a limited medium, is what "Stereographic" sets to prove. Following the stories of the ideation, production and implementation process in "Behind The Scenes" are three chapters to show how the spirit of play and imagination still reigns in the 3-D world translated into the 2-D medium, in the form of objects installed, stages set, and typography constructed – which have inspired the chapter titles. "Objects Installed" presents handmade and found objects as well as assemblages, realised from abstract and playful thoughts. "Stages Set" features bizarre and comic landscapes of narrative qualities made out of constructed hybrid forms and characters. "Types Constructed" covers various projects characterised by their 3-D typographic sculptures and installations made out of the most common or unusual of material. All of which have enhanced the texture and meaning of print campaigns, video format, website interface and album covers. The conquest of space is full of possibilities even within the virtual layers and dimensions of the 2-D surface – a medium that one may not be able to literally touch or walk through, but spells more permanence and accessibility to a larger group of audience.

"Stereographics" certainly hopes that the diverse creative expressions in this book can inspire the possibilities of stretching the designer's medium of representation. Yet an entire book of projects with similar graphical treatment can also be a precarious move, especially if it is taken to promote a particular approach. There is a fine line between adventurous creative exploration and meaningful creativity. Constructing letters in the most unlikely forms and materials to adorn a poster for adornment's sake may well produce an attention-grabbing yet inflated image possibly falling flat in the face of smart and effective communication. The quality of a work is becoming more obvious to today's design-literate viewer, who can tell if all the time and materials spent for a particular treatment is necessary or redundant, effective or ineffectual in conveying its intended message.

Mark Gowing's "Hopscotch Compendium" is one of the many exemplary works in this book that demonstrates a fitting use of 3-D treatment in 2-D format. Here, abstract sculptures in different materials were the focus of the posters to provoke thought on the role of films as an art form, which aptly promotes Hopscotch Films as a leader in the art-house cinema scene. By having the figure of singer Kate Nash superimposed on the images of a series of rooms within a hand-built dollhouse, artist Chrissie Macdonald created a backdrop with every element and illustration of each room included, for her album cover that perfectly reflects her song lyrics and the personal and home-grown musical inspiration. But not every work is worthy of attention only for its tight link between agenda and execution. Oscar and Ewan's typographic installation of the word 'Agency' constructed with wooden dowel sticks, being both the client's studio signage and an image for their website, is innovative in its use of material, and beautiful for its lyrical shadow under the light. The haptic qualities are certainly what such treatments can convey more than plain vector lines. But when the discerning eye can tell what is more quality than gimmicky, perhaps it is better to be true to content and intention. Is it just the trend and desire for spatial and material play that justifies all the labour and resources? We hope the works in this book reveal more reasons than these.

Behind the Scenes

One of the features that gives prominence to projects translating designers' vision between 3-D and 2-D realm is the amount of work that goes in dealing with space and physical materials. Personal anecdotes and shots about the brief, the idea and the production process behind the four selected projects reveal the skills and manpower needed as designers work with distinct materials of wood, paper, leaves and photography equipments to construct assemblages and settings of make-belief. Instead of saving the best of documentation to the last, we begin with these four distinctive works as the lens to imagine the labour and joy behind the scenes of stretching disciplinary boundaries for graphic endeavours.

red design

Album design for Quantic's album 'An Announcement to Answer.' It is believed that the raw nature of the paper-made installation favourably brought warmth to the whole design, which could hardly be found in vector-based illustration.

01

Sopp Collective

Album design for The Fall's 'Long Time Coming.' Complete creative freedom and trust from clients were found precious and treasurable for experimenting new design approach and techniques, even more than financial support.

02

CoDesign Ltd

Identity for the RTHK Designers Abroad TV program and art direction for its promotional items. The first and yet the only presented idea was well-accepted due to a good understanding of the client's requirements and expectation.

03

Dan Tobin Smith Studio Ltd

Magazine cover for Creative Review Annual. The installation shooted in trickery perspective has become a favourable reference to the studio's portfolio which led several advertising jobs afterwards.

04

quantic
an announcement
to answer

Project / Quantic – An announcement to answer
Client / Quantic, Tru Thoughts (Record label)
Design / red design
Media / Paper, Communication cables
Camera / Nikon D200

01

Assignment

The artist Quantic and his record label Tru Thoughts operate in the crowded marketplace of independent leftfield dance music. They electrify their audience with the symbiotic relationship between music and art, which spreads globally across Europe, USA and Asia, primarily aged from 20 to 35. The target group has been growing up and getting much bigger than the one from the commercial music sector. red design was entrusted to create strong impact and distinguishable features for the album package within tight budgets and timescales.

The brief was to design the sleeve for Quantic's album 'An Announcement to Answer' exploring its theme on cross-cultural communication. 'Soul,' 'craft' and 'innovation' were chosen to be the key words to develop further as agreed with the client.

Having numerous illustrated album covers, the client wanted a different design in a fresh creative angle. Additionally, red design was also required to include an image of the artist. With a trusting relationship with Will Holland, the soul of Quantic, as well as the label, the team could just enjoyed the freedom to experiment and inject new techniques to create something remarkable for both the client and their own sake.

Ideas

In this album, Quantic produced his own potent musical brew of the 21st century funk through collaborations with other musicians, or playing different instruments himself.

To echo this approach and capture the soul and craft of Quantic's music, red design came up with the idea of creating an evocative yet emotive scene with paper-cuts and layered settings.

It has long been a technique that red would like to work on. Limited budget from the client in a way stopped them from offering different and time-consuming visual solutions. Realising how much time and cost could be saved by building a set out of paper, red decided to go for the simple yet inexpensive materials such as white card, string, tape and glue. Without the need to commission expensive set builders and hence making it a more personal approach, Will bought the idea immediately.

Process

red design challenged the normal production methods and created a point of difference by developing an reminiscent and emotive scene with a non-culturally specific landscape in paper crisscrossed with communication cables constructed with a silhouetted figure of Will Holland in the middle.

They initially made a detailed scene in Illustrator for a good and balanced composition. It was followed by experiments with small-scale models of the setup, to learn about the process, find out what problems they might encounter, and understand how lights should be set during the photoshoot. This step was also very useful in letting the client visualise how the end result might look.

When red design began to execute their plan, they cut out different paper shapes by hand, which was seen as the most painful part in the process – the grass in particular was a laborious job. They experimented with various weights of cards to strike a balance between accurate paper-cut with details and tensile strength which could reinforce some of the more delicate areas like the meticulous telegraph posts and avoid any drooping or sagging.

Review

red design was highly satisfied with the project as they had never done anything similar before and since, marking it a highlight of red's design approach as well as a very good reference to their portfolio. They enjoyed the physical process of producing the set and were pleasantly surprised by the end results. Both the record label and the artist were very happy with the outcome who received a great deal of positive feedback from their supporters and audience. People were often unsure how it was made, whether it's real, painted or computer-generated which red design took them as a great compliment.

In this digital age, it's all too easy to make perfect vector illustrations. Through this project, red design now understands and recognises this means of production, without a physical process of creation, could only mean a lack of a certain soul and warmth which is fragile and flimsy.

"We cut out different paper shapes by hand, which was the most painful part in the process – the grass in particular was a laborious job."

Project / The Falls 2006
Client / The Falls (Simon Rudston-Brown,
Melinda Kirwin)
Design / Sopp Collective
Media / Leaves
Camera / Nikon DX1

02

Assignment

The initial brief for this project was very loose. The client, The Falls, is a Sydney indie/folk rock/country band, led by Simon Rudston-Brown and Melinda Kirwin. They approached Sopp in 2006 for the package design of their upcoming release 'Long Time Coming.' Their brief for the sleeve was simply something in line with their music inclusive of their portrait (and possibly the rest of their supporting live band) on the artwork.

The budget was very limited. Usually, record labels would not get involved in the production of a release. There were very little existing photographic materials, only a few band shots in urban and nature set-

tings were provided. Plus, Sopp was not given any photographic budget for additional photography. In terms of print production, Sopp was also restricted to a cover solution in a pre-existing template.

Sopp felt that photography could not really capture the warmth that was needed for the band, no matter how nice the outdoor settings could be. The team also found it too weak to present a concept and draw attention for the release. So the real brief for Sopp was to come up with some sort of a fitting, a unique treatment or illustration that could reflect the beauty of the band's natural and honest sounds.

Ideas

The music of the band was a great inspiration to Sopp. Listening to the beautiful and honest songwritings played with acoustic instruments, the team began with explorations revolved around loose, natural collage treatments in different illustration styles. However, it either seemed to lack a visual impact or appear too artificial for a sense of natural beauty and warmth that Sopp felt for the band and their music.

The team was totally stuck and Katja Hartung from the group found the need for a break. Together with her colleague Thorsten Kulp, they went for a coffee and a walk in a close-by park, which was only three minutes away. (But Sopp has moved since. Katja really misses the park; she believes that it is a really

important part as in a creative space, to have somewhere peaceful to go to.) It was autumn at the time; lying on the grass, looking at the sky, talking through and rationalising the brief, the solution slowly grew!

Triggered by the leaves on the ground and the band's name, the idea soon emerged from the mist. The two thought it was worth trying to create an actual portrait just from leaves. To further work on the concept, they played around with the idea and made the band's portrait into a black-and-white illustration. Tp avoid tonality, they decided to fill in the dark areas of the faces only. The duo then collected some leaves and headed back to the studio. By then, the key was to explore on the vague idea in mind and make it real!

Process

As the very first step, Katja converted an image of Melinda's face into a bitmap image and printed it in A3 size. A clear foil was laid on top and the dark areas of the print were filled out with dried leaves. The leaves were difficult to be positioned because they were not really flat and weighty. They moved easily when other leaves were placed on top, under or on the side. Hence she had to use Blue Tack to hold them in place, and looked at the work from the above.

Initially, Katja used leaves in various colours in a random mix. However, they encountered two main problems. The first was that she could not recognise the overall shape simply by her eyes because the focus was always put straight on each individual leaf. She did not want to loose the colour spectrum as a whole and hence the solution of creating the

'gradient' of leaf colours throughout the portrait. The other problem was the scale. The first test was too small to create the details that were needed to make the faces recognisable, so at least a double of the original scale was needed.

Sopp presented the concept and the initial test to the client, Melinda and Simon who both got very excited about it right away and approved Sopp to go ahead with the idea. The rest of the process was more straightforward in terms of creative problem solving, but it proved quite tricky of how Sopp started on the execution.

To begin, Katja created the basic portrait graphic and printed it at the scale needed. It turned out to be 2x3 meters, not massive but quiet large for the

Process

15-square-meter studio indeed. The next task was to collect dried leaves, from yellow to pale green and deep red. Unfortunately, leaves in Sydney city did not come in the variety of colours and shapes needed, so the collection was done on a weekend trip to the Blue Mountains. Sopp collected leaves from different kinds of trees including eucalyptus and bamboo. In order to create an even depth with details around the edges, leaves in just-the-right size was a key to emphasise on, as small leaves could fail to create the depth while large leaves would have been too hard to work with.

After that, Katja sorted the different kinds of leaves by colour, which took up a little more space in the studio, and started working on the floor piece. Time became a crucial point to pay attention to as the dryness of the leaves would change easily and hence affect the colours! To make the best use of the leaves collection and keep its quality, she needed to work quickly and finish the floor piece in limited time. It took her three days to complete the whole piece. Not to mention the need to change her viewpoints constantly between working on the ground and standing over it to check the finished angle. Sponges strapped to her knees came in very handy after the first day.

Upon the completion of the collage, Sopp went on to photography. However, Katja realised that Sopp did not have well enough equipments to produce the quality they were hoping for, particularly the lighting.

The image they tried with their limited resources was too flat and it did not look like a piece with actual dimensions. Luckily, Sopp got help from their professional photographer friend, Richard Dobson. He shot the work from a ladder with two lights bounced off the sidewalls, with his Nikon DX1. Brilliant depth and shadows were perfectly exposed and demonstrated through his images forming the key visual of the whole design.

After the creation of the key visual, the remaining work fell into place quite quickly. To keep it consistent, all other elements on the album cover would have to support the core concept and tell the same story. A strong contrast in scale and colour seemed to be the best solution for the inside cover, and therefore, the close-up image of dried leaves. The type used on the cover, also as a base font for the logotype, was 'Italia,' a very round and friendly serif/slab serif. Extending on the idea of 'actual objects,' the type was made to appear in the form of a little worn paper tag which corresponded the overall tone of the artwork. It was also 'traditional' enough to sit on a paper tag. The logo font was slightly tweaked for a better flow to integrate the letters to a logotype. The only other application of the key visual was the band poster, which followed the same design as the album cover.

Review

In retrospect, Sopp was lucky enough to have lots of creative freedom and trust from the client on this project. This allowed a tailor-made solution based on the client and project's need in unique expression without excessive pressure.

The project took on a life on its own. After looking at the first test and realising that the collage could really work, Sopp was happy to stretch budget and timing constraints to proceed. Though, they were not quite sure how long the process might take.

Needless to say, the budget would not compensate for all the time spent on executing the piece. The

result, however, turned out to be quite rewarding for The Falls as well as very rewarding for Sopp as a creative. Not every project would have such result and the team finds it very important, as a design force, to have the creative freedom and excitement by an idea through trying something new every now and then. Even though the process may not be smooth and the project may lack financial support, Sopp believes that it is what makes design worthwhile: to have the opportunity to play and explore!

"The problem with dried leaves was that they weren't really flat but really light, they moved when other leaves were placed on top, under or on the side."

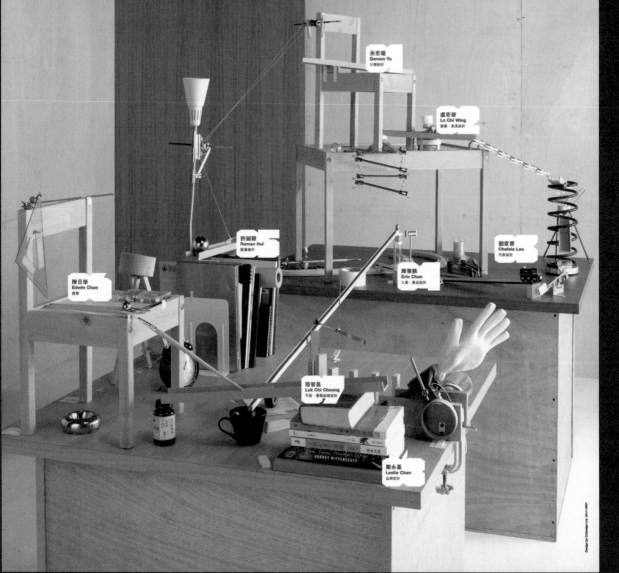

Project /	Designers Abroad 2007
Client /	RTHK
Design /	CoDesign Ltd
Media /	Office stationery, everyday objects
Camera /	Hasselblad H1D

Assignment

'Designers Abroad' was a TV series about design, a collaboration between the Radio Television Hong Kong (short-named 'RTHK') and the Hong Kong Design Centre. The target audiences were the general public as well as the designers. RTHK was expecting the related identity and promotional materials designed in a different yet refreshing perspective.

The TV series consisted of eight half-hour episodes about eight renowned Chinese designers living and working abroad. One thing they have in common is that they were all born and educated in Hong Kong before they went for further studies and pursued their

career overseas. The project aimed to reveal what inspires these creative minds, the passion and driving force behind, the goals they try to achieve, the design principles fuelled in their work and the belief they hold most sacred. The series documented their everyday life, daily work and the path they went through to get where they stand right now. So, CoDesign had to deliver the spirit of this program to the audiences.

Ideas

The program introduced eight designers who achieved great success in a specialised field of design. Apart from the boundless creativities, wide knowledge base is also vitally important in any design process. By understanding more about their inspirations, believes and visions, the three artists, Woolingling, Thomas L., and Esther Kwok M.Y. were inspired to create such 'mechanism' of the installation. With the same token, the creation of the 'mechanism' also started from careful observation to detailed mathematical and physical calculations, and went through repetitive testing and experiments.

The setup of the show prologue, a delicate Pythagorean Device installation made with various office stationery and everyday items, had already been created by the three artists prior to awarding the art direction part of the project. CoDesign found such installation very interesting to be used as a unique ground for the main visual elements of the promotional materials. After numerous meetings with the client gaining a good understanding of their requirements and expectations, the first yet the only presented idea of adopting its form and choice of material onto the design of the logotypes and promotional materials was well-accepted by the client.

Process

The basic concept had been formed and the mechanism of the installation had already been tested preliminarily when Hung Lam from CoDesign made his first visit to their studio. Hung was very impressed by the set and so he started to explore by anticipating the size and outlook of the finished structure, the possibility and the feasibility of using it as the main visual element of the campaign.

Unlike other promotional campaigns of the client's previous shows, where conventional backdrops were usually used to present the show info at public areas, CoDesign suggested the client to make the installation the main feature and focal point for the program's identity and related promotions. Despite of the big challenge for the client to handle the compli-

cate logistics of transporting the delicate setup from one exhibition location to another, the move proved it's worthwhile as it successfully drew attention from the general public.

The installation had well-delivered the theme of the TV program. It was made up of various daily objects that appeared in a genuine and unpretentious way. They were neither polished nor painted. It was the naturalness that Hung wanted to capture and retain, and that's why the use of the wood material and its colour tone for the whole design.

Photos of the installation were used to create a consistent look and feel instead of plain graphics. Professional photographer CK Wong was hired for the

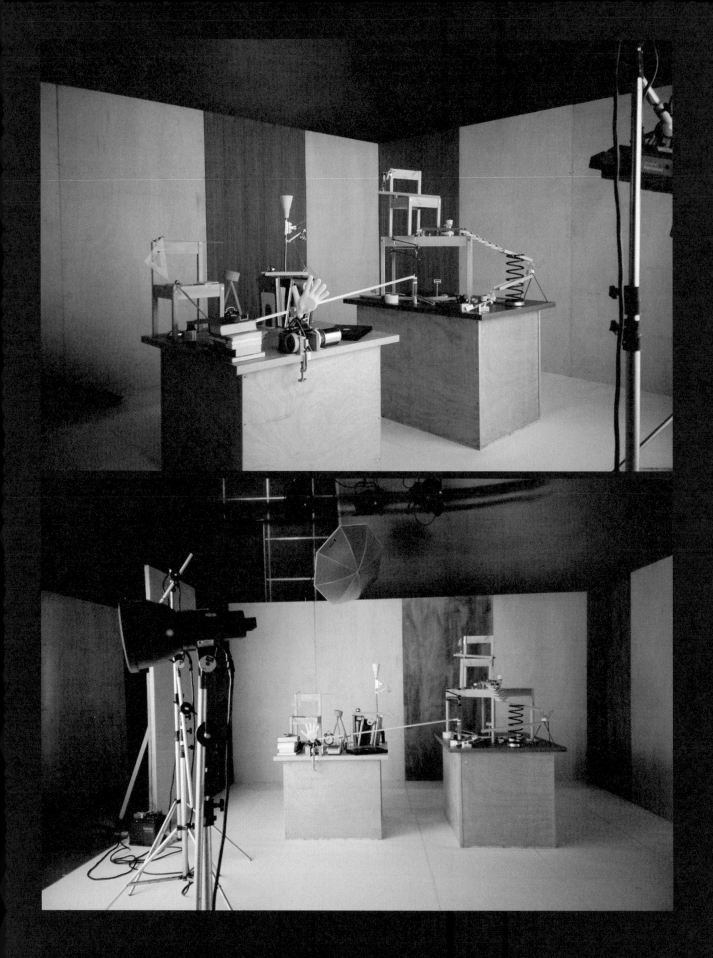

"The backdrop for the installation was made of wooden panels in various colour shades; it's perfect to correspond to the installation's back-to-basics connotation."

Photo-shooting of the installation took place at a
TV studio by photographer CK Wong .

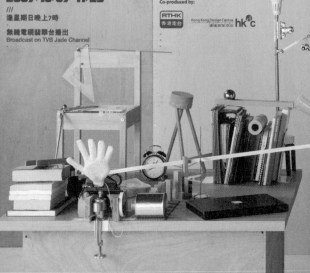

Process

photoshoot, which took place at a TV studio. The backdrop for the installation was made of wooden panels in various colour shades; it's perfect to correspond to the installation's back-to-basics connotation. Inspired by the focus of the TV program introducing Hong Kong designers abroad, Hung also created an ambience of a loft through the use of bounce light rousing a soft and warm atmosphere for the installation.

Time management was tricky though. Since the original production plan for the show prolog did not quite intersect with the design of promotional materials for the show, the idea of bringing in the installation as the main visual element implied an influential requirement – very skillful time management. Close collaborations and careful coordination between RTHK, the three artists and the TV producer were needed. CoDesign was proud to say that it was successfully achieved. The design schedule aligned with the shooting schedule as well as the setup schedule processed perfectly in a tight timeframe.

Working on the identity of the RTHK Designers Abroad TV program and art direction for its promotional items, it included a logotype, an invitation card, a set of postcards, a poster, a DVD box set and roving exhibition.

Instead of using ordinary offset printing, the invitation card was made of wood with laser engraving. It seemed to bring the element of the set directly to the audiences. The invitation card received a lot of attention as expected and the awareness of the show was then drawn. The tailor-made logotype, which imitated the shapes of objects used in the installation, was also an element for the continuation of the consistent yet varied designs of the identity and promotions. The unified look and feel for the campaign was hence successfully delivered, and that resulted in a consistent yet variant user experience.

Review

The receptiveness of the client, who was surprisingly open-minded to accept new ideas and suggestions as a public service broadcaster, was very much appreciated.

Yet, it was not an uncommon media nor very much different from Hung's other works. To him, design is all about innovating ideas, manipulating space, colours, texture and the composition of them.

CoDesign likes the final result very much. The process was a very smooth one. From idea formulation to execution, the process had been smooth and under control. The feedbacks were good too.

Instead of using ordinary offset printing, the invitation
card was made of wood with the custom-made
logotype laser engraved on it.

Project /	Creative Futures 2005, Creative Review Annual 2006-07	
Client /	Creative Review Magazine	
Design /	CF 2005: Dan Tobin Smith Studio Ltd (Photography), The Projects (Set Design) CR 2006: Dan Tobin Smith Studio Ltd	
Media /	Photography Equipment	
Camera /	Sinar P2	

04

Assignment

In 2005, Creative Review asked The Projects to design and create a set for the magazine front cover to celebrate the Creative Futures prize. The prize was given to upcoming talents in design schools. The Projects took inspiration from the logo of Creative Review and made a 'CF' to stand for Creative Futures; for that, they represented it with light bulbs. The setting was shot from exactly the same distance from the two sides on a Sinar P2 5x4 camera with the 150mm lens. One with the light bulbs on in a dark room was used as the front cover while the other one with the light bulbs off in a room with lights on was used as the back cover.

Aiming to celebrate the innovation and hard work for a year with the CR readers, and especially with all related people within the design industry, Creative Review commits one artist or photographer to interpret the letter 'A' for the Photography Annual Awards every year. In the year of 2007, they approached Dan again to submit his and that would be used for the front and back cover of the Creative Review Photography Annual 2007.

Dan only had two days to complete the work, including the construction of the letter 'A' and the photoshooting of it. The budget was also very small and he needed to shot it in the dark as they used multiple flashes.

Ideas

It was up to Dan on how to interpret the letter 'A.' The only requirement was that Dan must use the specific CR font used on their front cover, 'Helvetica.' To study more about the brief, Dan realised this particular issue associated with the awards for craft. Therefore he wanted to construct the 'A' out of things that are related to his craft, photography.

Dan has long been a fan of perspective trickery and he likes the idea of doing it all within camera. The idea was to use the objects he uses within his practice as a photographer to make the actual 'A' itself. This included everything from large-scale such as

flash lighting, stands and softboxes through to small-scale items like Polaroid boxes, gaffa tape (a kind of sticky tape) and light meters.

Since lots of equipment Dan uses are in dark colour or simply black, Dan needed to use all of the flash lighting within the construction of 'A' to light up the floor as well as the background surrounding the 'A' to silhouette it. This arrangement could make the 'A' stand out from the background and nicely highlighted all the objects used to make up the letter 'A.'

Process

It was fairly informal of how Dan presented the idea to a client, which was all done verbally. He explained to CR that he was going to make up the 'A' from all sorts of photography and lighting equipment in a simple studio space; and how it would be lit. CR's response was very positive. They had faith that Dan would produce a great image. Dan finds it a great magazine and they have worked together for many times.

There were two installations of 'A' in total. The first was commissioned earlier on for the promotional poster for the upcoming awards while the second larger 'A' was made for the front and back cover of the annual publication. 'A' was made twice in two different scales where the latter one was supposed

to hold a linkage to the first one but in a bigger and better presentation.

Not only the size of the installation of two 'A's but also the scale of the kit included within the 'A's were bigger. Due to limited budget, Dan needed to hire part of the flash lighting kits he planned to use for the construction of the big 'A' and that actually made him exceeded the budget at the end. For the whole construction, there was about 60% of Dan's own equipment while the rest of 40% of flash light was rented along with some stands and flash packs.

"I have long been a fan of perspective trickery and I like the idea of doing it all within camera. The idea was to use the objects I use within my practice as a photographer to make the actual 'A' itself."

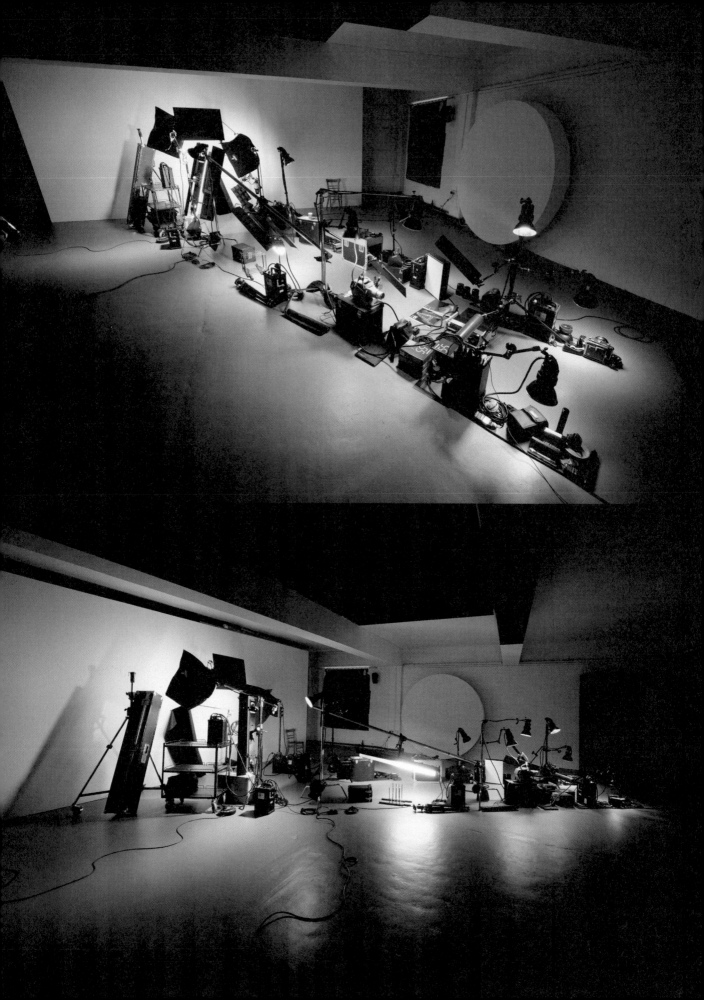

Process

Dan believed that the quality of the transparency produced was fantastic on the scale of 10x8, and so the installation began with marking down where the line of the 'A' fell into shot by projecting an 'A' through a Sinar P2 10x8 camera with 150mm Schneider Super-Symmar lenses. Once that was done in the studio, the area inside the 'A' was gradually filled up with all prepared equipment.

Since it was shot on 10x8 scale, Dan could project through the lens easily as the image circle is very big. Towards the back of the image, it was easier to fit in the large scale photography equipment within the 'A.' While towards the front, the space was very tight so it was harder to fit in the lights, hence Dan managed to use the small scale equipment like the 10x8 Polaroid processor, pens and gaffa instead. The process went quite smooth and not many problems came up throughout the time, it just took time. Though, some objects were too big to fit in a certain space that Dan needed to move it further away; others were in a wrong shape, slipped out of place, or just did not look good.

The final image was done in only one shot and just a small amount of colour work and retouching was done in the postproduction.

Review

Dan received a very good respond from CR who found it very clever and creative. He finds it very satisfying starting with an image of a letter as it is already in a beautiful yet simple shape. Enlarging it to a grand scale enabled Dan to realise how well the font has been designed.

The work has been used as reference for other jobs that Dan have done afterwards. He has got advertising jobs partly from referencing these images. For instance, there was a shoot done for Spring Studios, a rental studio in London UK, for their website and promotional material.

elow:
eft) The front cover of Creative
eview Annual 2006
Middle & Right) The front and back
over of Creative Future 2005

Stages Set

Some say space and material promise maximum originality. Designers go beyond the use of materials to construct elaborative settings across a 3-D space in numerous hybrid forms, characterised by a pictorial language and narrative quality. While someone in a white jumpsuit becomes a makeshift mountain, a floor is strewn with objects to represent a hypersomniac's apartment, all to be photographed for eventual collaterals like album covers and promotional posters. Experiments with spatial layout have resulted in images that deliberately juxtapose real life and constructed reality. With these bizarre and comic landscapes, graphic design becomes more cerebral than commercial conveying layered messages.

Pg. 033 – 096

open days

University of Brighton

Undergraduate Open Days in the
Faculty of Arts and Architecture

30/01/08
06/02/08

– Fine Art Painting
– Critical Fine Art Practice
– Fine Art Sculpture
– Screen Studies
– Photography
– Graphic Design
– Illustration

– Culture and Society
– History of Decorative Arts
  and Crafts
– Humanities
– Culture and Historical Studies
– Fashion and Dress History
– Museum and Heritage Studies

– Fine Art Print Making
– Textiles With Business Studies
– Fashion With Business Studies
– Digital Music
– Performance and Visual Art:
  Music, Theatre, Dance
– Moving Image

– Interior Architecture
– Architecture
– Three Dimensional Design
– Material Practice / Wood Metal
  Ceramics and Plastic
– Visual Culture
– History of Design

University of Brighton

Open Days
Ciara Phelan
An innovative identity proposal for the University
Brighton's Open Days 2008.

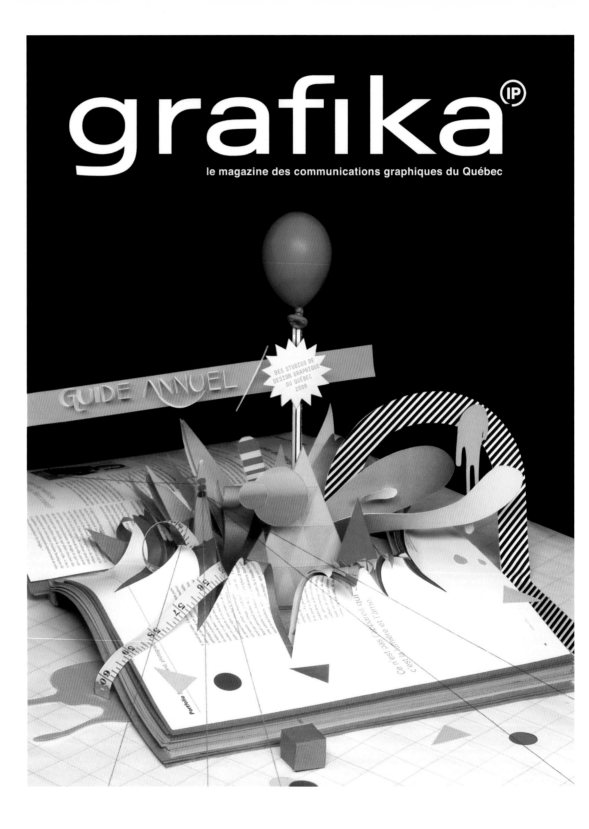

2008 Quebec's Annual Graphic Studios Guide
Julien Vallée

Magazine cover of the 2008 Quebec's annual graphic design studios guide for Grafika. The exploding colours from the open book represents the creativity of the most talented Quebec design studios, all regrouped in one guide.

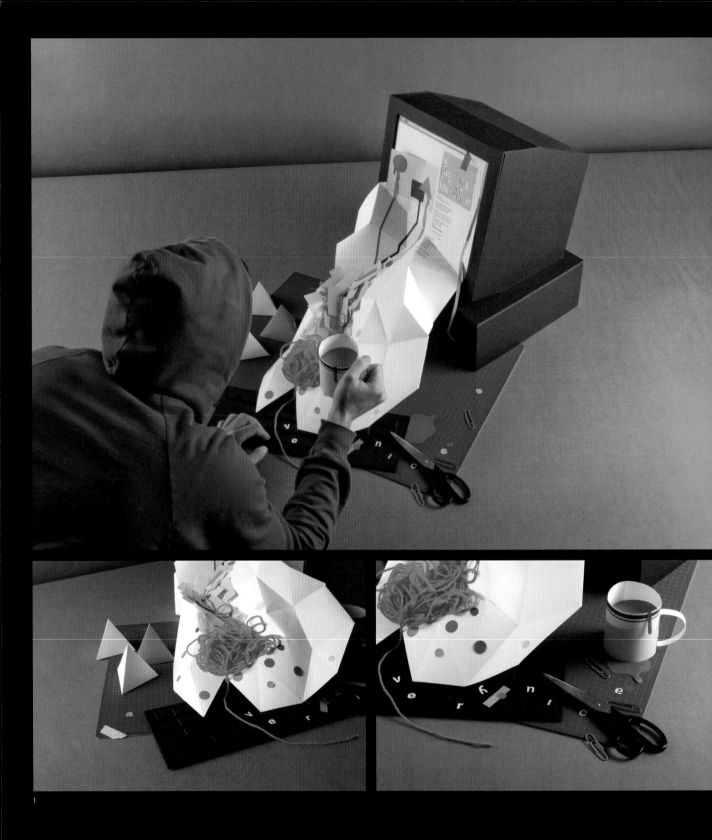

Very Nice - Manystuff[1]

Julien Vallée

Print project created in response to a brief set by a French
online visual communication blog, Manystuff. The design
studio hoped to make something by hand with a clean,
almost digital aesthetic appeal. The unfolding computer
screen and realised digital information reflected the
translation from Manystuff's website into print.
Design: Nicolas Burrows

PK

Disco Drive - Things
To Do Today[2]

Nous Vous

The composition of 3D elements was a decision made in
response to the music of the album. Individual letters and
items were made followed by various configurations
before final shots were taken.

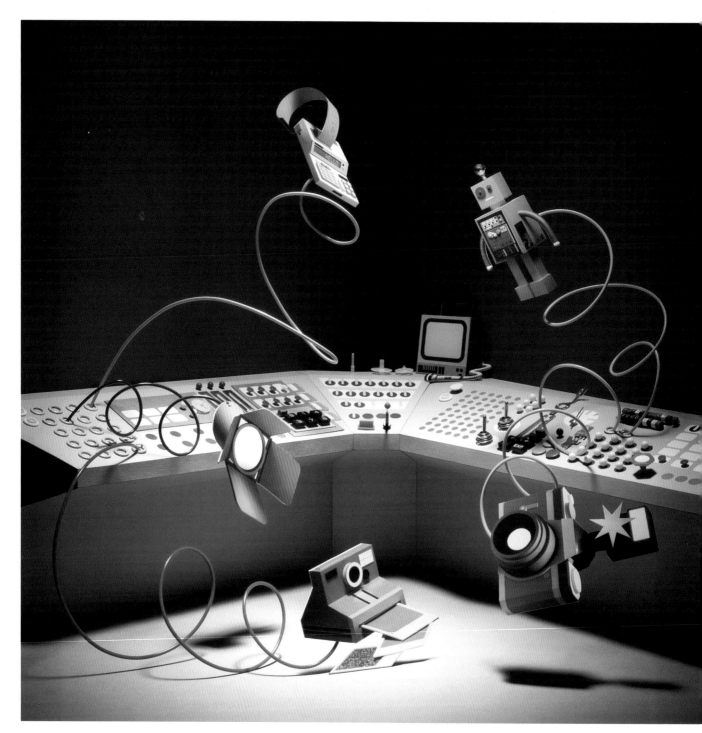

 ED

Creative Review Front
and Back Covers August 2008
Chrissie Macdonald (Peepshow Collective Ltd)
Images to illustrate an article about design director
Naoto Fukusawa.
Photography: John Short

 ED

Um Was Es Nicht Geht
Pixelgarten

A photography project composing 3D illustrations
in real space with studio members as well as the
use of paper and other objects in the studio.

PO

Laforet - Grand Bazar (Summer 2008)
Pixelgarten

In cooperation with Masaya Asai and Takayu-ki Nizawa from TBWA\Hakuhodo, Pixelgarten created the visuals for 'Laforet Grand Bazar Summer 2008' for Laforet Harajuku Departe-ment Store in Tokyo. The team had built two 3D-settings with real comic elements attached to 2 1.8-meter wooden frames, as the base of the poster designs.

1

Garorock Project[1]
Alice Guillier

Project done in response to the entry invitation for the
visual identity of Garorock festival. The project was
composed of photography and set design made
of coloured papers and figurines. This is a piece of
unselected work.

Paper Profiles[2]
Dan Tobin Smith Studio Ltd

Originally commissioned by M-real magazine, Dan
Tobin Smith Studio Ltd took women's profile to create
various images solely with papers in various colours
and tones. The shape was laser-cut and hung into
different positions. Images were made through varied
light and paper with subtle changes in camera angle.
Set Design: Rachel Thomas

NOUS VOUS PRÉSENTS
MAN ALIVE!
AT THE BRUDENELL SOCIAL CLUB
ENTRY £4
+ FREE CD
WEDNESDAY 19th SEPTEMBER
WELCOME TO THE BRUDENELL
7:00pm
JOIN US FOR A NIGHT OF POP MUSIC IN THE WOODS WITH:
NAPOLEON IIIRD + MECHANICAL OWL +
VEST FOR TYSSO + GLACIERS + DINOSAUR PILE-UP
+ ARTWORK FOR SALE BY NOUS VOUS + OTHER LOCAL ARTISTS
NOUS VOUS PRESS
www.nousvous.eu

Opulent presents

Bounce

Moving to
Miss Libertine

Friday, November 9

Ooh-Ee, CWD, Young Steezy, Tranter, Skeetparty

www.opulentmagazine.com

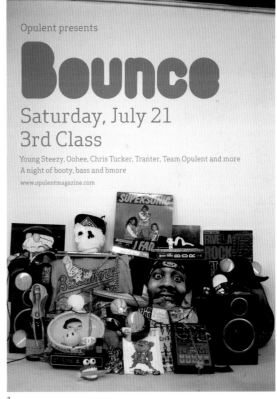

Opulent presents

Bounce

Saturday, July 21
3rd Class

Young Steezy, Oohee, Chris Tucker, Tranter, Team Opulent and more
A night of booty, bass and bmore
www.opulentmagazine.com

3

Man Alive!¹
Nous Vous

Poster produced for a Nous Vous event that involved the music, which was more than just a show. Nous Vous wished to convey an imaginary atmosphere of the special night. The initial idea was to decorate and photograph the venue. However, due to time and personnel constraints, Nous Vous had to come up with an alternative solution and hence the miniature version.

Bounce Poster #4²
Aesthetically Loyal

The fourth Bounce poster represented a major geographical and conceptual shift as the night was moving away from its original home at Third Class. To celebrate the occasion, Aesthetically Loyal created a miniature diorama in a scale of 1/250 based around the venue and its iconic naïve neon graffitied walls. The packed bags not only represented Bounce's departure, but also the propositional end of Third Class as one of Melbourne's premier club night venues.
Construction assistant: Jade Butler

Bounce Poster #1³
Aesthetically Loyal

An introduction to the public of the night-series run by the Opulent Magazine family. Constructing and photographing it over the course of a day in the corner of their Melbourne studio, Aesthetically Loyal collected a cluster of objects which personified the direction of the night.
Construction assistant: Jade Butler

Rodeo[1, 3]
Damien Poulain

One of the six images created by Damien Poulain, commissioned by Rodeo magazine. Given a total freedom to approach the theme 'Rodeo,' Poulain made use of the fragility of paper as a way to oppose the popular perception of Rodeo, as a rough, violent and macho sport.

B.A.C. System (Bacteriological Artificial Chromosome)[2]
Damien Poulain

This piece was based on the Bacteriological Artificial Chromosome system, the duplication and proliferation of the chromosome. The work later became a comment on the nature of globalisation within the modern world.

AD For The 'Festival Du Mot'

Merci Bernard

The aim of this ad was to put 'words' as the principal
character of the festival in a 3-dimensional way, whereas
the city with simple decoration was left 2-dimensional.
All the elements featured in the ad were handmade with
paper, the traditional support of words.

ED

Enroute Cover
Illustration
HORT

Illustrations done through paperwork for
magazine cover story. The artwork should
speak for itself.
Client: Enroute Magazine

Form
Pixelgarten

The cover design, poster and five illustration spreads created for the 50th anniversary issue of 'Form,' the oldest Swiss-based design magazine in Europe, if not worldwide. The finished illustrations were a combination of photography and vector-illustration.

Booka Shade / Dj Kicks[1]
HORT
CD/Vinyl artwork.
Client: K7! records

Prof. HORT Poster[2]
HORT
A notification poster of lectures invited by Eike König, creator of HORT.
Client: HFG Offenbach

Der Hort
lädt ein

Adrian
Shaughnessy
20.12. '05

Kesselskramer
6.12. '05

Hi-Res!
10.01.'06

Antoine
et Manuel
22.11. '05

Ralf
Hiemisch
8.11. '05

Hort
25.10.'05

19.30
Raum
101

hfgOF_MAIN

die vorträge finden jeweils um 19.30 uhr
in raum 101 im hauptgebäude der hfg offenbach,
schlossstraße 31, statt

heinz und gisela friederichs stiftungsprofessur
prof. eike könig

weitere informationen finden sie unter
www.prof.hort.org.uk oder
www.hfg-offenbach.de

 PK

Neuser
HORT

Concept for record sleeve design.
A 'Pop-Theater-Neuser-World'
made from everyday objects.

NEUSER
VON VORN ANFANGEN

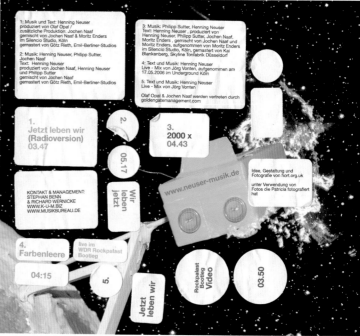

 PK

Neuser
HORT

(Continue from previous spread)
Concept for record sleeve design.
A 'Pop-Theater-Neuser-World'
made from everyday objects.

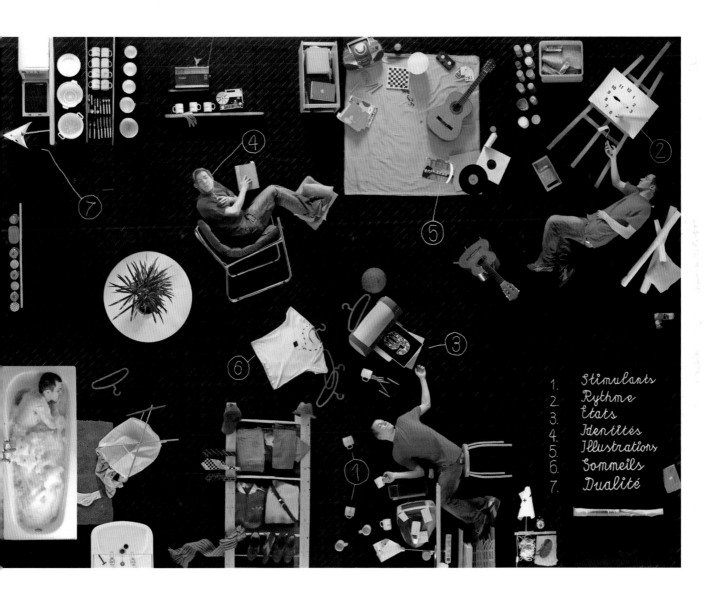

1. Stimulants
2. Rythme
3. États
4. Identités
5. Illustrations
6. Sommeils
7. Dualité

Appartement De L'hypersomnique
(Hypersomniac's flat)
repeatafterme

Designer Jonathan Prêteux was working on hypersomnia, an illness that puts hypersomniac to sleep a lot and hardly stay awake during the daytime. As he spent a big part of his 'life' lying on the floor, all objects in the flat were installed on the ground. Lemoine and his workmate Guillaume Ninove set a camera on the room's ceiling, recreated various parts of the flat and laid for photography.

 Kate Nash - 'Made Of Bricks'

Chrissie Macdonald (Peepshow Collective Ltd)

Doll house sets and rooms created and photographed for Kate Nash's debut album, representing the artist's musical inspiration, which was very personal and home grown. Elements and illustrations used were depictions of the lyrics of Kate's songs.

Kowloon Motor Bus Year Planner
Gwen Yip

A collectible year planner to be sold to bus fans. The planner appeared as a children's story book with 12 illustrations, one for each month, telling how a little bus had got along with a family and the neighbourhood.
Design: Chan Tsang Wong Chu & Mee Advertising, Hong Kong
Photography: Connie Hong

Print Campaign for
Hong Tai Sesame Sauce
Gwen Yip

A print campaign to build an wholesome image
appealing to young ladies who like healthy diets.
Photography: Connie Hong

Branding for
Makui Jewellery Ltd.
wen Yip

branding campaign to build a playful and young image
r Makui, an accessories brand targeting teenage girls.
hotography: Connie Hong

Funk Sinatra[1]
pleaseletmedesign

A 'physically' combined, double-sided album sleeve for Funk Sinatra's double albums. Objects used in the images were directly or subtly related to the lyrics.

Two Faced[2]
Grandpeople

Two Faced was a project bringing together the 90 most influential creatives from various professions. The idea was to pair the invited ones, which was then asked to create a portrait of each other. Grandpeople made this portrait of Syrup Helsinki from Finland, while they were portrayed the other way round. The collection was later presented in a book and an exhibition around the world.

1

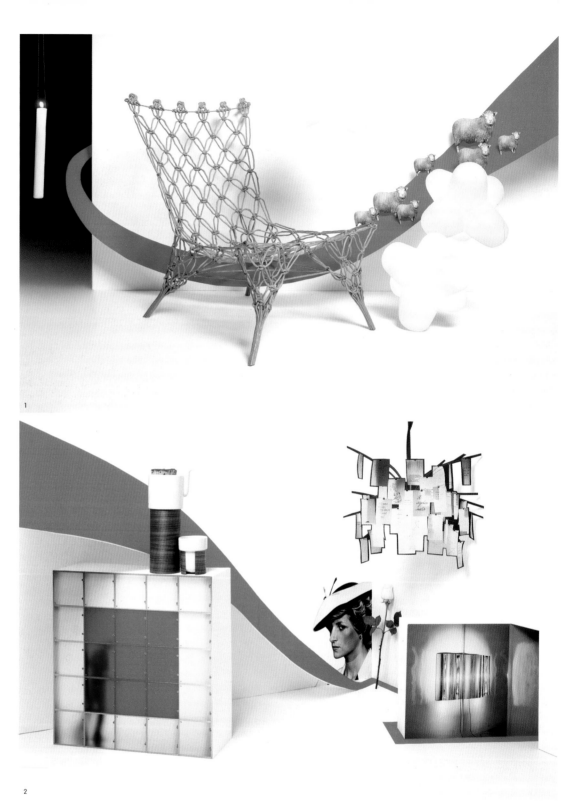

A Decade of Design
Bela Borsodi

A series of symbolic designs to feature 10 iconic events over the decade, and celebrate Wallpaper's 10th anniversary in 2006. A red line was introduced to indicate the chronology of events and interact with the designs. The scenes were a tricky combination of photography and concrete display of real objects, overall resulting in a good balance, scale and flow on each spread.

1/ First cloned mammal born, Dolly the Sheep (1996); 2/ Diana, Princess of Wales died in Paris (1997); 3/ Petronas Towers, Kuala Lumpur, completed as world's tallest building (1998); 4/ Human population passed 6 billion (1999); 5/ Big Brother on TV (2000); 6/ Apple launched iPod (2001); 7/ Golden Jubilee of Queen Elizabeth II (2002); 8/ Arnold Schwarznegger became governor of California (2003); 9/ Tsunami strikes Asia (2004); 10/ Pope Benedict XVI became head of the Catholic church (2005)

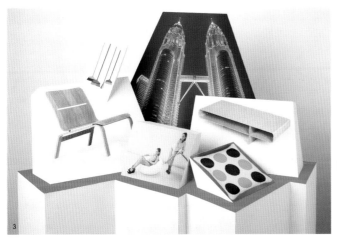

3

4

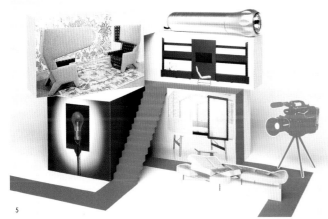

5

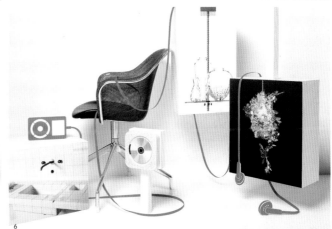

6

7

8

9

10

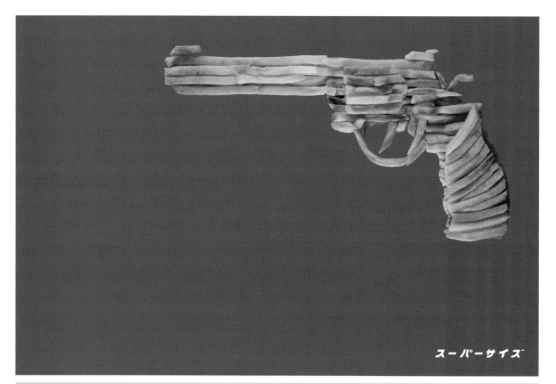

スーパーサイズ

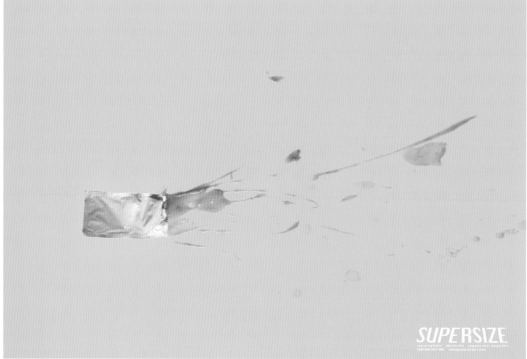

SUPERSIZE

1

 ED

Supersize[1]
PLAZM

Magazine spreads and posters series originally designed for Japanese design magazine IDEA, for the issue 'Made In America.' PLAZM's response examined what pernicious effects American designs had brought to the Japanese culture, such as gun violence and fast food.

Art direction: Joshua Berger, Niko Courtelis
Design: Enrique Mosqueda
Photography: Dan Forbes
Client: IDEA Magazine

 PO

Les Siestes Electroniques[2]
Pierre Vanni

Poster designed for 'Les Siestes Electroniques' (Toulouse, France).

Les Siestes électroniques

Concerts gratuits en plein air et soirées,
les musiques aventureuses s'installent
à Toulouse, du 25 au 29 juin.

1

 CL

The ETI laboratory[1]
Cécile Boche

An identity to promote ETI, a team of two specialising in interior decoration. Hand-making the props with ETI laboratory as the backdrop, Boche aimed to convey the freshness of their work and underline their artistic and illustration root.

 PO

Tate Pierre Huyghe[2]
Why Not Associates

Poster and exhibition design for French artist Pierre Huyghe's exhibition at Tate Modern.

070

MODERN

Pierre Huyghe
Celebration Park

5 JULY – 17 SEPTEMBER
Book now on 020 7887 8888
or at www.tate.org.uk

Supported by   Media partner
    THE TIMES

Part of Paris Calling, a season
of contemporary art from France

2

1

Things Are Not Quite What They Seem[1]
Jiggery Pokery

An editorial mini-set made, based on the themes of illusion, with fantasy and imagination. By combining the idea of the English potting shed and the feeling of a kid in a sweet shop, the summertime landscape reflected the daydreams of the design duo of Jiggery Pokery.

Photography: Satoshi Minakawa

Poster Magazine[2]
Studio Round

A unique look and feel developed for Poster, a seasonal fashion, design, arts and architecture magazine based in Melbourne. Themes for the issues Studio Round has designed for the client include space, customisation and personal.

Flying Clothes[1, 2]
Dan Tobin Smith Studio Ltd

An image to show a real energy of clothes and fashion accessories flying across a table, creating interesting shapes and compositions. The idea was drawn from films such as Zabrinsky Point, in which a house was detonated and filmed in slow motion. An air mortar was used to create the force behind the chaos.
Client: Another Man Magazine

Fridge[3]
Dan Tobin Smith Studio Ltd

Produced for the particular issue of Kilimanjaro Magazine, which was based on food, the waste of food and food as a force in its own right. Dan Tobin Smith liked the idea of a fridge being propelled when refrigerated food were expelled.
Client: Kilimanjaro Magazine

Cliché Tourist[1]
Jean Jullien

To impose an immediate impact to viewer, Jean Jullien created the cut-out letters and classic touristic sets that led viewers/tourists to ponder the letters' meanings, and put their heads in the hole of the cheesy-painted landscapes.

Cliché Nerds[2]
Jean Jullien

For the Cliché's launching party, 'A Night For Nerds,' Jullien developed the original idea of 'nerds' with 'school libraries.' The black book was an eye-catching point whilst the written text composed a ludic perception of the poster.

Cliché Future[4]
Jean Jullien

Jullien wanted to create a vintage poster and Cliché Future was a take on old sci-fic posters. Gigantic robots, heroic duo facing the danger in iconic poses and dramatic lighting. The result was this hand-made, querky pulp poster.

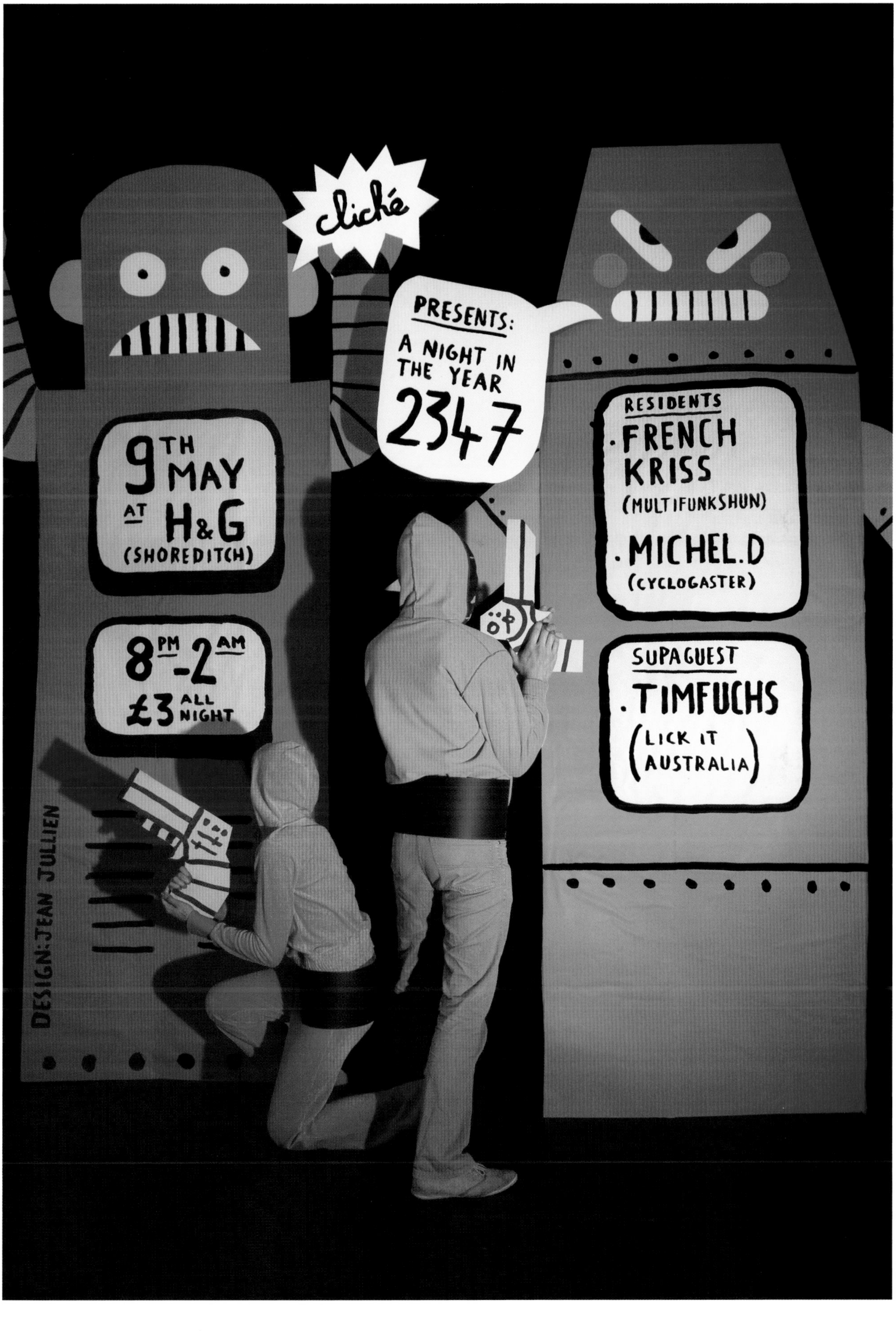
cliché
PRESENTS:
A NIGHT IN THE YEAR
2347
9TH MAY
AT H&G
(SHOREDITCH)
8PM-2AM
£3 ALL NIGHT
RESIDENTS
. FRENCH KRISS
(MULTIFUNKSHUN)
. MICHEL.D
(CYCLOGASTER)
SUPAGUEST
. TIMFUCHS
(LICK IT AUSTRALIA)
DESIGN:JEAN JULLIEN

CL

Manystuff REFLET[1]
Jean Jullien

Promotional materials for an exhibition show-casing a selection of young designers hosted by French online visual communication blog, Manystuff, Jullien visually translated his perce-pion of the blog's friendly style with a selection of eclectic icons/totems representing the young creatives collected by Manystuff.

PO

REFLET[2]
Jean Jullien

Promotional poster translating Manystuff's mis-sion, which is to collect designers and things they like. Jullien decided to use the icons he had designed for each designer featured in the show and mixed them in a paper maelstrom.

EX

The Desktop Wallpaper Project[3]
Jean Jullien

Made for Los Angeles-based Kitsune Noir, as part of the Desktop wallpaper project. With no specific guidelines and limitations, Jullien decided to make it a discreet and story-telling work companion, resulting in a little theatrical stage where the elements would be hung by black strings just like puppets.

PO

The Fables Of La Fontaine[4]
Jean Jullien

A poster for an exhibition at Central Saint Martins' Cyber Café on the theme of the Fables of French poet Jean de la Fontaine. Fable was an evocative subject for Jullien of his childhood memories and the incredible bestiaries, which were then rendered into the simple and naïve book of wonders.

Chris Lee - Worry No
Bleed

Chris Lee is a norwegian hip hop artist, who released his debut album in 2008. The idea was to create an album cover that was untypical for a hip hop artist, and reflected the playful style of Lee's music.

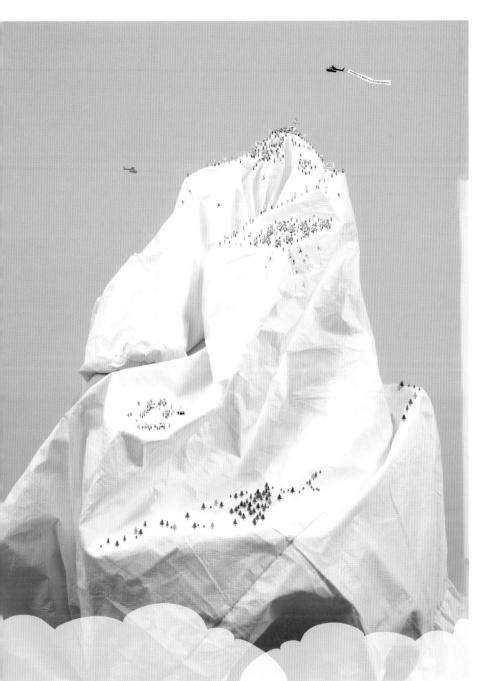

Höhenluft
Pixelgarten

'Höhenluft' means the air at high altitudes or mountain air in German. Combining digital and analogue techniques, the self-initiated work displayed a series of magical landscapes in large portraits. The mountain, being conquered by lively miniature people if look closer, was created by a person wearing a white jumpsuit.

1

2

ED

Musical[1]
Antoine+Manuel
Front and back cover design
for CNDCJOURNAL 10th issue,
choreographic center quarterly
publication.

ED

Orchestra
In The Dark[2, 3]
Antoine+Manuel
Front and back cover design
for CNDCJOURNAL 11th issue.

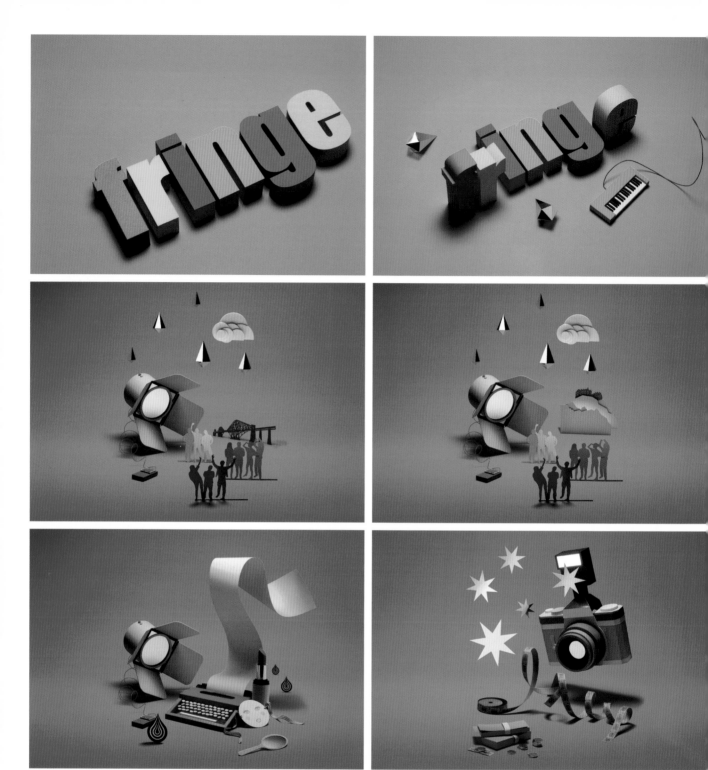

 AD

Edinburgh Festival Fringe 2008[1]
Marque Creative Ltd

A series of iconic sets created for The Edinburgh Festival Fringe 2008 campaign to communicate the essence of the festival. The scaled and simplified theatrical sets included stage lights, snapping cameras and Edinburgh landmarks.

Set design: Chrissie MacDonald
Photography: John Short

 EX

The Magic Machine[2]
Jiggery Pokery

A collaborative project inspired by kids' play and programmes, such as Bertha and Itsa Bitsa, what Anna Lomax and Lauren Davies from Jiggery Pokery used to watch when they were young. Built and documented over a period of three days, the Magic Machine capitalised on the idea of fun in the workplace.

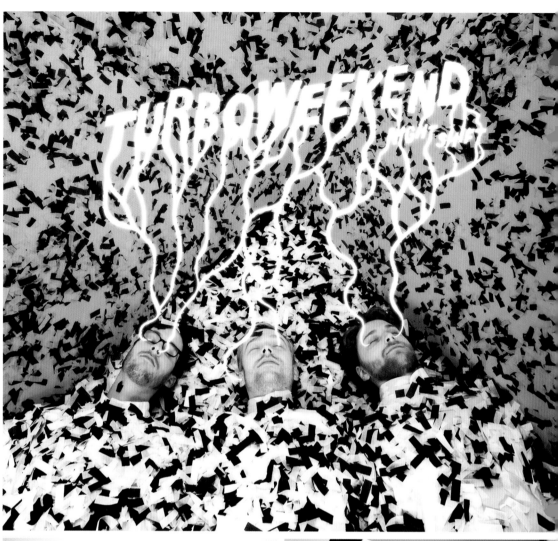

 Turboweekend

Hvass&Hannibal

Press photos and cover artwork for
Danish band, Turboweekend.

Photography: Brian Buchard
Client: Turboweekend, Copenhagen Records

D O K
T O R
K O S
M O S

PK

Doktor Kosmos 'Hallå?'
Sweden Graphics

Artwork created for the release of Doktor Kosmos CD 'Hallå?' The members of the band dressed up in a kind of mask costumes created out of cardboard and black sticky tape. They then were photographed. The resulting images were used for the album cover, fold-out booklet, tour poster, press images and animated stop-motion video. A series of fine art prints were also produced with the figures blown up to life-sized format.

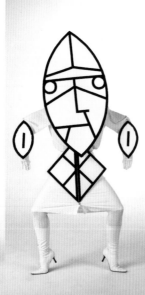
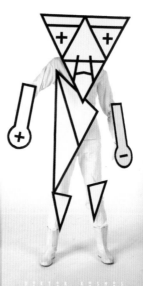

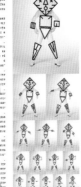

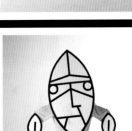

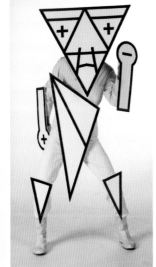
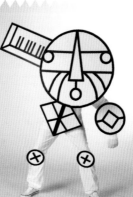
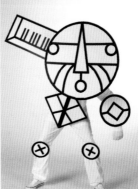

 PO

Vega Nightclub - April[1]
Mejdej

A poster for Vega Nightclub in Copenhagen, Denmark.
Different artists were responsible for a different month's
poster, and Mejdej designed the April's one. The grid
was part of Vega's logotype, depicting the atmosphere at
Vega: music, dance, surrealism, chaos and magic party.

 PO

Arvikafestival[2]
Mejdej

A proposal for a new visual concept for Arvikafestivalen, a Swedish music festival performing primarily
synth, electronica and heavy metal music. To visualise
the festival's music and surroundings, Mejdej created
an abstract universe containing forms, patterns and
surreal creatures.

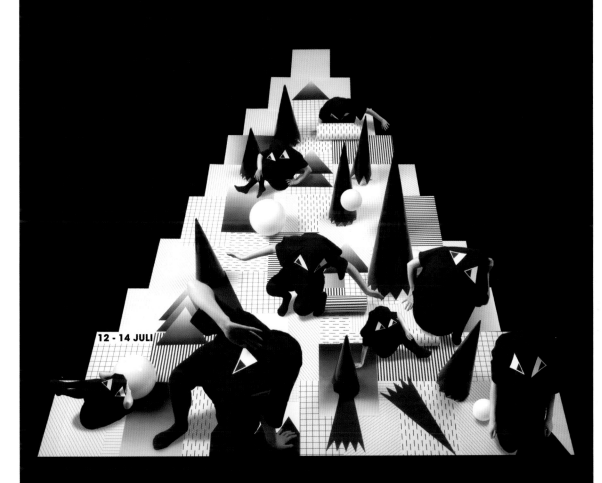

12 - 14 JULI

ARVIKAFESTIVALEN 08

LIVE THE MUSIC! SCISSOR SISTERS (US) BLOC PARTY (UK) INFECTED MUSHROOM (ISR) IN FLAMES (SE) THE MAGIC NUMBERS (UK) FRONT LINE ASSEMBLY (CAN) HOCICO (MEX) THE ARK (SE) TIMBUKTU (SE) WITHIN TEMPTATION (NL) VNV NATION (UK) HOT CHIP (UK) SLAGSMÅLSKLUBBEN (SE) PAIN (SE) MARIT BERGMAN (SE) MATES OF STATE (US) APOPTYGMA BERZERK (NO) MANDO DIAO (SE) ZEIGEIST (SE) PATRICK WOLF (UK) MELODY CLUB (SE) PORTION CONTROL (UK) SHOUT OUT LOUDS (SE) I AM X (UK) NOUVELLE VAGUE (FR) DARK TRANQUILLITY (SE) MUSTASCH (SE) VAPNET (SE) STRIP MUSIC (SE) SHINY TOY GUNS (US) KRISTIAN ANTTILA (SE) ASHA ALI (SE) MAIA HIRASAWA (SE) SVENSKA AKADEMIEN (SE) TINGSEK (SE) NECRO FACILITY (SE) JUVELEN (SE) WENDY MCNEILL (CAN) KEEP OF KALESSIN (NO) 120 DAYS (NO) HEY WILLPOWER (US) NINE (SE) CONSEQUENCES (SE) EMMON (SE) PLUXUS (SE) FROZEN PLASMA (UK) MISS LI (SE) HANS APPELQVIST (SE) IAMBIA (GR) SABATON (SE) FAMILJEN (SE) EMIL JENSEN (SE) HELLSONGS (SE) KLOQ (UK) DETEKTIVBYRÅN (SE) MIXTAPES & CELLMATES (SE) IDA MARIA (NO) LILLASYSTER (SE) BACKLASH (SE) PAPER FACES (SE) AERIAL (SE) MEMFIS (SE) ASHBURY HEIGHTS (SE) THE MELLOW BRIGHT BAND (SE)

BETALA 100 KR EXTRA OCH VI DONERAR 10st TRÄD TILL NAMIBIA. KÄRLEK TILL SKOGEN! WWW.ARVIKAFESTIVALEN.SE

2

The Lord

Jan Olof Nygren

The Lord examined the duality of perceived God's entity and human fear of the Divine. The work comprised illustrations and custom-made laser-cut 3D letters, fixed on a spray-painted and screenprinted MDF-board.

Objects Installed

From objects to assemblages which would eventually appear in a poster or on a desktop screen, the following are products of personality and constructions out of every imaginable material – cardboards, Perspex, metal tubes, balloons or simply some everyday objects. Whether they are sculptural or seemingly functional, they possess strong graphic qualities and a sense of materiality that pique the viewer's interests and sense of touch. With these manual realisations of abstract and playful thoughts, the creators' craft are tested and their mark made more evident reinforcing the bond between the artist, the work and the viewer.

Pg. 097 – 152

Round Identity
Studio Round

Studio Round developed two 3-dimensional typefaces to help communicating the range of attributes Round brings to different projects.

The unique characteristics of each typeface are medium specific. The paper typeface, based on Foundry Gridnik, was calculated and precisely crafted. In contrast, the cushion typeface is playful, whimsical and confident.

Eco Fashion
Byggstudio

This is an illustration made of plants, buttons and thread for a fashion magazine, Dansk Daily Magazine to arouse environmental awareness.

anadatone
iletto nyc

ndatone always picks poetic and elaborate titles for his records. Stiletto
c was asked to design the cover for the new album with the title: 'What
s nature done for me recently.' It was a great title and they started thinking
out a twist to the nature, exploring themes like fake nature, stylised nature,
a misunderstanding nature. The final creation was this abstraction of a
wer bouquet. All flowers and vase were hand-crafted by their fabulous
ern Saira Hussain.

Bonobo

Days to come

Bonobo – Days To Come

red design

Bonobo and his record label Ninja Tune operate in the crowded marketplace of independent leftfield dance music with target audiences aged from 20-35 spreading globally across Europe, USA and Asia. Clear distinction from competitors is needed while budgets and timescales are tight.

As a mature and increasingly recognised artist, red design initially wanted to show a portrait of Simon Green of Bonobo on the album cover. His reluctance led to the creation of alternative 'portrait' with Bonobo's possessions instead. After ransacking his home for objects, the team created a series of outdoor installations of these objects in forced perspective geometric shapes, creating an order and beauty from the ordinary and mundane ideas to an intriguing piece of work.

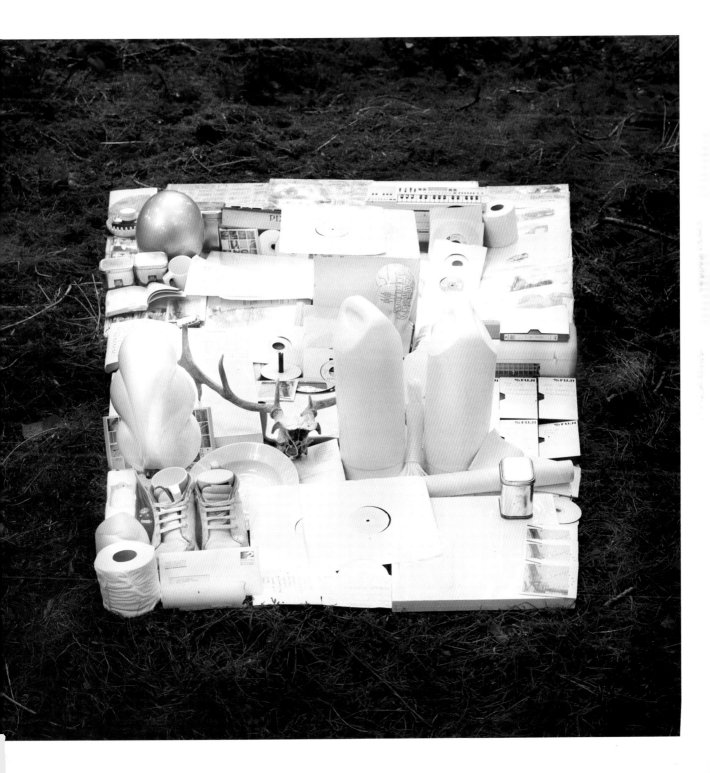

BN

Urban Forest Project
Stiletto nyc

A banner designed for the project by AIGA and Times Square Alliance in the summer of 2006. The theme was 'urban forest' and the goal was to beautify Times Square by inviting New York and international graphic designers to create a banner.

To do that, Stiletto nyc decided to bring a little green to Times Square and in the same vein, to play with the actual interest of the area, which is commerce.

The banners were later made into two tote bags by Jack Spade and sold for charity.

DESIGN TIMES SQUARE:
THE URBAN FOREST PROJECT

STILETTO NYC

Hopscotch
2005/06

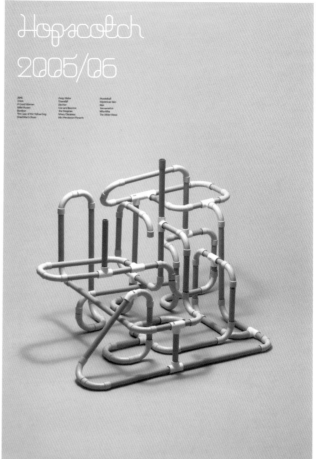

Hopscotch
2005/06

Hopscotch
2005/06

Hopscotch Compendium 2005/06
Mark Gowing Design

These posters were created to promote Hopscotch Films as a leader in an independent art-house cinema. Each sculpture was a typographic de-construction of the Hopscotch trademark made to be extruded into 3-dimensions. The intent was to provoke thoughts regarding the nature of art and culture, and in particular the role of film as the major art of the time.

Hopscotch
2005/06

2046
3-Iron
A Good Woman
Ballet Russes
Bombon
The Cave of the Yellow Dog
Dead Man's Shoes

Deep Water
Downfall
Election
Live and Become
The Magician
Merry Christmas
Mrs Henderson Presents

Murderball
Mysterious Skin
Rize
Transamerica
Wha-Wha
The White Masai

 PO

Relativity - 3 Posters
Son of Tam / Jason Tam

The idea of the triptych was to explore the conception of time, through a surreal and inexplicable realm. The dream-like setting and objects were meant to paint a sequence of imagery that seemingly had no relation to each other, just like the fragments of memory people carry in dreams and the reality.

YESTE RDAY

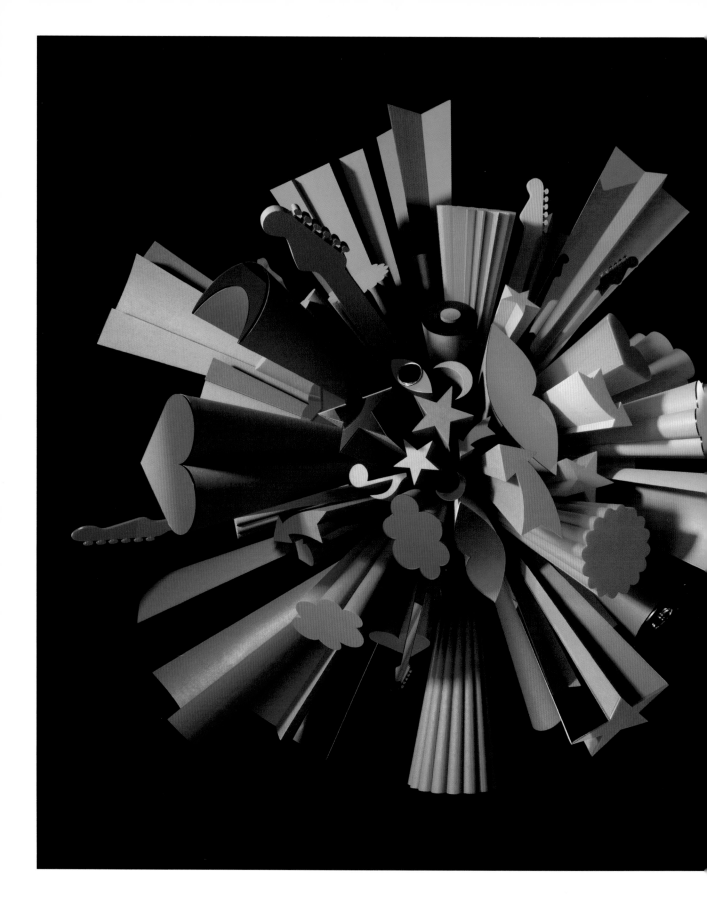

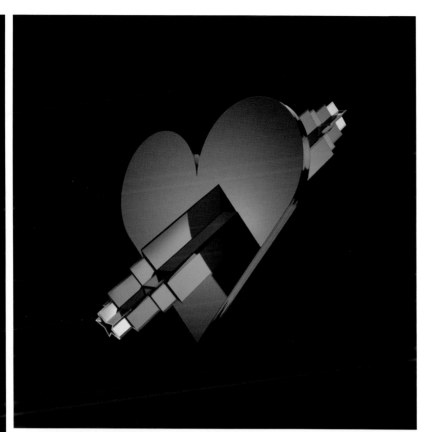

Unkle Jam
Dan Tobin Smith Studio Ltd

Commissioned by Virgin Records, this was an album cover and CD single for the new band Unkle Jam. Rachel Thomas designed the individual pieces out of a mixture of materials such as perspex and polystyrene. The idea of the hidden scale was essential to have made viewers unsure of the size and scale.

Set Design: Rachel Thomas
Photography: Dan Tobin Smith

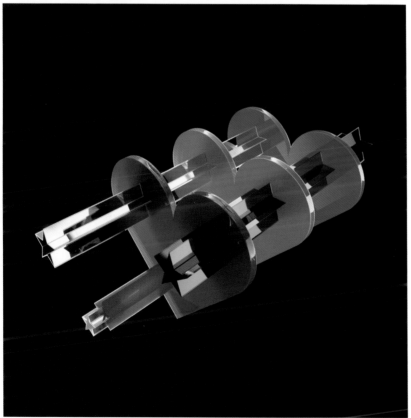

Quoi De Neuf
ELMO

project collaborated with Thomas Dimetto for Galeries Lafayette.
ey made three 'sculptures,' one for children, one for men and one
women, with real objects they liked. They then shot the work in a
picture and got it wired in terms of volume and depth.

otography: Studio ADCLIC

VI magazine[1]
Sweden Graphics

An image created for an outdoor advertising at bus stops. The client (a magazine) wanted a kind of image campaign that looked unlike real advertising. The image was a reflection of the magazine. Sweden Graphics cut up the client's old issues and took a lot of photos. They also made some other paper constructions as well as digital constructions and then retouched everything together. Some details were deliberately crudely '3D-rendered' while others were more realistic, all in the ambition to create an imge with a surrealistic feel.

The Cocktail Of A Thousand Hammers[2]
Jan Olof Nygren

A self-initiated experiment in fragmented narrative where viewers can create their own story. Nygren wanted to tell others the story about the power of fire, so he made a hommage with a poor man holding a Molotov cocktail as his weapon. The aim was to question if the use of violence is used as a political tool. To bring the graphics off the wall, Nygren used a laser cut, spray-painted and screen-printed MDF-board-3D-poster to create such effect.

Print Proof
Corriette Schoenaerts

The two senior designers from Designpolitie chose their favourite
pieces from their collection of printed documents accumulated
over the years. The 'living' image of a print proof was used as the
promotional poster for a major printing company. The theme for
this year is 'The love of printed matter.'
Client: Designpolitie

Form Christmas 08/ New Year 09 greetings campaign

Form

An email to existing/potential clients and friends to wish them a 'Happy Christmas' with the Christmas tree configuration by rearranging the studio's main shelving unit to represent a shape of christmas tree. Things were placed back to normal for the New year version. The whole process was filmed and sped up into a short movie which could be seen on Form's website.

Exhibition
Monday 25th – 27th June 2007
(Monday private view)

BA (Hons) Visual Communications
Leeds College of Art & Design
Blenheim Walk – *Vis Comm Studio*
Leeds
LS2 9AQ

The Nous Vous Collective Present:
'Good to GO!'
including projects completed between
November '06' & May '07'

POCKET-SIZED

DO IT YOURSELF

VINYL / CD

1. **7" / Sky Larkin** – Single **'One of Two'**
Design by - Nicolas Burrows

2. **7" / Mother Vulpine** – Single **'Keep Your Wits Sharp Her Words Are Quick'**
Each Ltd edition green 7" vinyl comes with a fold-out screen print.
Hand printed by Jay Cover & Mother vulpine.
Design by - Jay Cover

3. **CD / Disco Drive** – Album **'Things To Do Today'**
Design by - Tom Hudson, Jay Cover, William Edmonds

4. **10"/CD Tiger Force** – Album **'A wasp in a jar'**
Design by - Tom Hudson & Jay Cover

5. **7" / Tiger Force** – Single **'Syntax Error'**
500 individual hand crafted 7" vinyl sleeves
Design by - Jay Cover, Tom Hudson, Matt Bigland, William Edmonds,
Nicolas Burrows

NOUS VOUS PRESS

6. **POCKET-SIZED - ISSUE 1: SPACE** is the first project to
be published by NOUS VOUS PRESS. Asking contributors from
various countries and disciplines, the project aims to create a
diverse and interesting response to the vast subject of 'space',
condensed into a 128mm x 110mm hand-bound book.

T-SHIRTS

7. **BACK - FRONT**
• **Kill Robots** 'self initiated' - Jay Cover
• **Sky Larkin** - Jay Cover
• **Opposite cafe promotional t-shirt** 'Eat cake not war'
- Tom Hudson & Matt Bigland
• **Opposite cafe promotional t-shirt** 'Nice coffee not tigers'
- Jay Cover
• **Mother Vulpine** - Matt Bigland, Jay Cover, Tom Hudson
• **Sky Larkin 'One of Two'** - Nicolas Burrows
• **Wintermute** - Tom Hudson & Jay Cover

MACHO TALK

8. **"MACHO TALK"** is a series of creative investigations by the
nous vous collective. It's an opportunity to explore creative process
without any foreseeable outcome. It's exploring creative process and
letting the results inform your next creative project. *"It's writing
bullshit on an otherwise lovely print"*. Macho Talk encourages others
to do the same, its a creative resource, in which the nous vous
collective document their inspirations as well as encourage others
to submit investigative work.
visit: www.myspace.com/machotalk
www.machotalk.blogspot.com

WWW.NOUSVOUS.EU

9. **May 25th 2007** saw the launch of the nous vous collective's
website, a special virtual place, where the bearded chaps of the
nous vous intend to document their ongoing projects and
investigations. The website has provided a portal for the nous vous
to display their work on an international scale as well as giving
them the opportunity to visually collate their work together.

fig. 1: Orientation

WWW.NOUSVOUS.EU

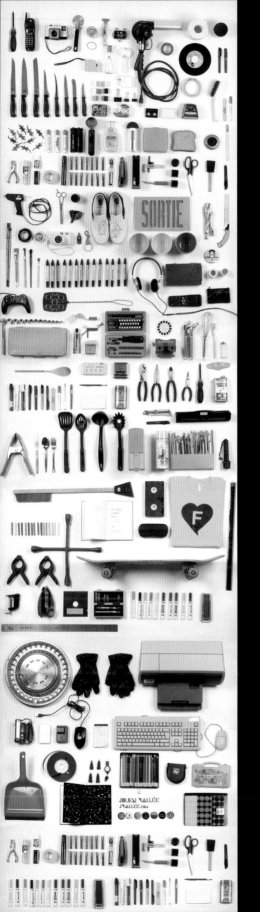

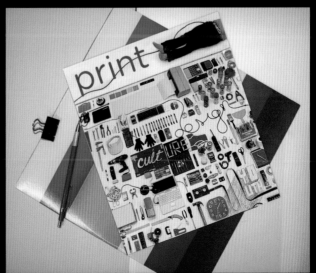

Comme des Garçons' new summer scent, Play, calls to mind imaginary endings and metaphysical scripts. From the packaging to the perfume proper, the legendary scents of Comme des Garçons stand at the forefront of amazing design and otherworldly odor. Here are some of HE's favorites from the past ten years.

AIRCENIUS

PHOTOGRAPHY
2A

1

LEFT TO RIGHT, FROM TOP ROW:
ANN DEMEULEMEESTER A/W, NUMBER (N)INE A/W, BURBERRY PRORSUM A/W, LANVIN A/W, JIL SANDER A/W, JUNYA WATANABE A/W, MARC BY MARC JACOBS A/W, CALVIN KLEIN A/W, GUCCI A/W, ACNE JEANS A/W, DIOR HOMME A/W

ACCESSORIES

2

 ED

HE Magazine issue 04:
Comme Des Garçons Parfums[1] /
HE Magazine issue 05: BOOTS[2]
Homework / Jack Dahl

HE Magazine brings men's fashion into a new and international level with features of the latest men's style. Visually attuned and obsessively original, each issue of HE features contributions from both the rising stars and pioneering legends of men's fashion, art, design and entertainment.
Photography: 2A[1], Dan Forbes[2]
Editor in chief: Daniel Magnussen

ED

Cover Magazine[3]
Homework / Jack Dahl

Cover Magazine is Denmark's leading publication in fashion, beauty and lifestyle. Avantgarde meets mainstream in Cover, it developed from the lifestyle guru Tyler Brûlé's recommendation in the Financial Times to the front page of style.com; from H&M's declaration that Cover is the only Danish source of inspiration for their catalogue to Grace Jones' exclusive perfomance at Cover's first birthday party; and from old Cover issues being sold for more than 140 euro a piece at eBay auctions to the demand for distribution all over the world.
Creative Director: Rasmus Skousen
Client: Cover magazine © Malling Publications 2005

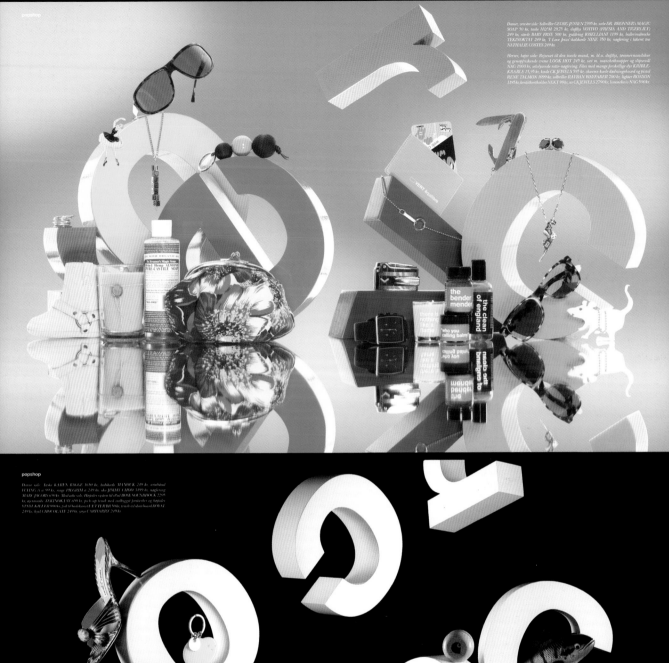

Damer, venstre side: Sølvriller GEORG JENSEN 2395 kr., serie DR. BRONNER'S MAGIC SOAP 30 kr., taske HGM 2925 kr., duftlys VOHYO (FRESIA AND TIGERLILY) 249 kr., smole BABY FRYE 300 kr. guldring ROSELLIANI 1399 kr., hallerinabroche TEKINOKTAY 249 kr., T Lace Jeans-halskæde XINE 350 kr., nøglering i lakret mc NATHALIE COSTES 249 kr.

Herren, højre side: Rejsesæt til den travle mand, m. bl.a. duftlys, trommemandskur og grundfriskende creme LOOK HOT 245 kr., set w. manchetknapper og slipsenål NAG 1060 kr., selvlysende ratte-nøglering Film med mange forskellige dyr KRIBLE-KRABLE 15,95 kr., kæde CK JEWELS 595 kr., charms-kæde dukkinghoved og pistol RENE TALMON 1099 kr., solbriller RAYBAN WAYFARER 700 kr., lighter ROSNON 1195 kr., kreditkortholder NEKT 99 kr., ur CK JEWELS 2790 kr., lommeknis NAG 500 kr.

 ED

Intro Fashion[1]
Pixelgarten

Cover design and fashion photography for the 'Mode Spezial' issue of German Magazine 'Intro.'
Production: Amelie Schneider at Intro

 PO

Celebrating Originality[2]
Co-op

The original brief from adidas was to develop a hero brand image for print and motion applications to support its sponsorship of Rooftop Cinema. The poster was extendedly used for the opening of the new adidas concept store on Chapel Street.

adidas Originals is intrinsically linked with the concept of time. Their product concept is taken from the past and reinterpreted for the future. The brand is timeless and always evolving.

The creative interprets the idea of bending space and time. An inter-galactic spinning product showcase was suspended entirely and photographed.

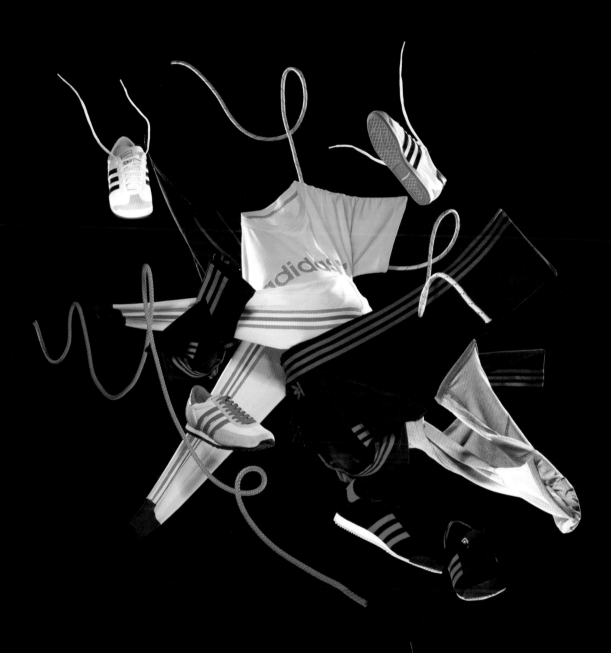

CELEBRATE ORIGINALITY

FROM TOP LEFT: THE SNEEKER RRP $140, LINEAR TREFOIL TEE RRP $60
KNIT PRESENTATION TRACK TOP RRP $150, BECKENBAUER TRACK PANT RRP $100
ZODIAK NYLON RRP $120, LEADER SUEDE RRP $120, PREMIUM BASIC TEE RRP $60

adidas®

ORIGINALS

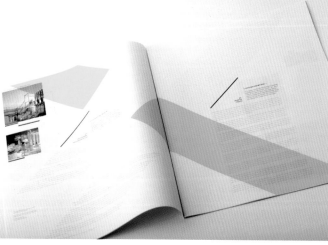

ID

Rooftop
Co-Op

Full identity system created for Rooftop Cinema based on the theme of 'New Context.' A selection of popular films were explored and re-imagined within Rooftop parameters. Iconic props from the films were constructed into unexpected forms culminating in a series of 'Rooftop-esque' posters that encourage viewers to embrace new perspectives.

Cinematic themes of drama and tension were reinforced by a diagonal grid system allowing for dynamic typography and brand patterning.

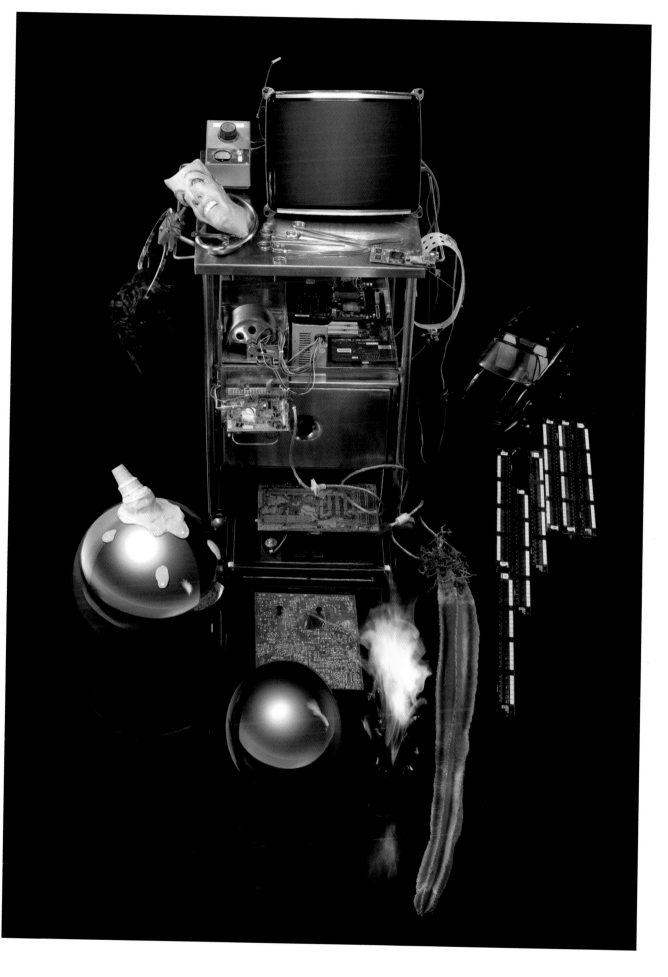

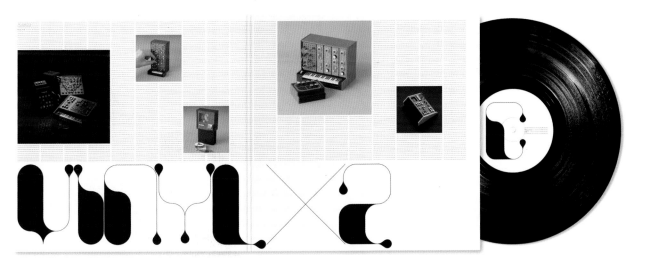

Moog Acid

Non-Format, Dan McPharlin

Album cover design with miniature models handmade and photographed by Dan McPharlin. The concept was based on the kind of Moog synthesisers that were used by the 1960s Moog synth composer, Jean-Jacques Perrey. The album was released as a CD jewel case with slipcase, and a double vinyl gatefold LP, featuring a typeface that was custom-made for the project by Non-Format.

Artists: Jean-Jacques Perrey, Luke Vibert
Client: Lo Recordings

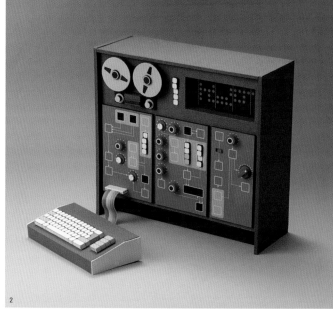

ED

Untitled¹
Dan McPharlin

This model was commissioned for a magazine story on men's watches. McPharlin had the panel finished about a year previously. As he had to ship these models to London for the final shoot, he found himself stressing over small parts that are prone to breakage. The solution to this was to have the machine's 'casing' protrude out from the control panel thereby helping to protect the delicate controls and patchcords from knocks and falls.

Art Direction: Joe Lacey

ED

Untitled²
Dan McPharlin

Another commission for a magazine story on men's watches, the model was built at a larger scale compared to McPharlin's usual work and subsequently packed with more details. Made to correlate with the digital watches on display through the use of a computer system with a digital sequencer, McPharlin decided to make some of these details a bit ambiguous without labelling the controls on any of these models so viewers can work it out themselves. His models could be good prototypes for real machines.

Art Direction: Joe Lacey

PK

Untitled³
Dan McPharlin

As a child of the 70s and 80s, McPharlin always thought of the 12" record sleeve as the ultimate expressive medium. However CDs and later downloads became ubiquitous in the 90s. Fortunately there has been a resurgence of interest in releasing music on vinyl accompanied by elaborate artwork in the last few years. These models were originally used on the back of the Mr. Chop - Sound From The Cave EP, but later the record label decided to use this photo for the disc centre. He was proud of himself being able to capture a nice reflection in the yellow machine's plastic window!

PK

Required Listening⁴
Dan McPharlin

This piece was produced for a compilation CD. McPharlin made models of three main music equipment needed in the composition. After finishing the models and photographing them, he realised that he had missed out the number '2' in title, which was actually 'Required Listening 2!' He then constructed the '2' in rush and shot it under natural light. Though he was not completely satisfied with the new composition, the CD was a great piece with the help of designer Matt Bilewicz who pulled the whole package together.

Collecting Flowers
- Fall

Grandpeople

This is commissioned for Oslo Architects Association's Fall programme 2006. The brief was to make an eye catching, colourful poster to promote the series of lectures, and to include some kinds of architecture reference. Grandpeople made a photographic poster with a composition of physical objects, subtly referring to the theme and to the world of architecure.

COLLE
CCTIERS FLOW
CTIERS
NG

COLLECTING FLOWERS

OSLO ARKITEKTFORENING 100 ÅR
Høst 2006

**21.09. ET UTVALG
DIPLOMPROSJEKTER FRA AHO**
Kristin Braut og Wenche Andreassen.
Siri Brudvik, Vegard Ramstad og Kristian
Ribe. Siri Liset, Børge Opheim
kl 20.00. OAF

**5.-22.10. MARKERING AV
OAF'S 100 ÅRS JUBILEUM**
Se eget program

11.10. BIG-BJARKE INGELS (DK)
kl 18.00. DogA Norsk Design- og
Arkitektursenter. Hausmanns gate 16
(NB: Merk sted) OAF i samarbeid med
Norsk Form.
www.big.dk

19.10. ZAHA HADID (GB)
kl 18.00. Arkitektur- og designhøgskolen
i Oslo. Maridalsveien 29
I forbindelse med OAF's 100 års
markering. OAF i samarbeid med Norsk
Form og AHO.
www.zaha-hadid.com

09.11. GENERALFORSAM
kl 18.30. OAF

VALERIO OLGIATI (CH)
kl 20.00. OAF

23.11. ATELIER BOW-WO
kl 20.00. OAF
www.bow-wow.jp

30.11. HELENA NJIRIC (H
kl 20.00. OAF

15.12. JULENACHSPIEL, O
Følg med på

OAF 100
OSLO ARKITEKTFORENING

Takk til våre samarbeidspartnere

vestre   4-PROG

Statoil   vitra.   minera

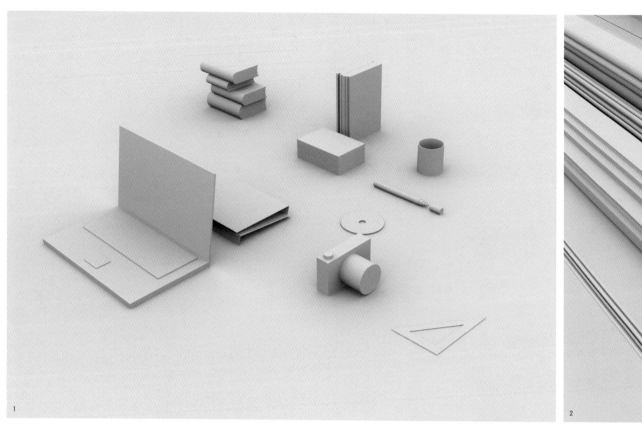

1

2

Meta Decktop[1, 2]
Extrud Desktop[3, 4]
Camille Baudelaire & Jérémie Harper

How can the aesthetic of softwares give birth to new principles
in design? Software codes, their organisation and interfaces
are the raw material of this work. Those tools led Baudelaire
and Harper to new principles of manipulation, composition
and association.

3

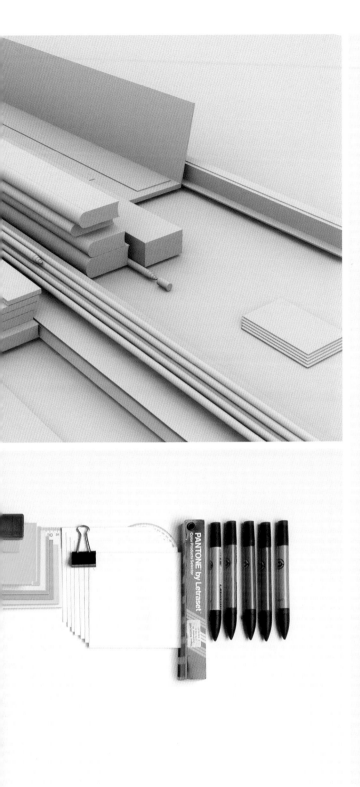

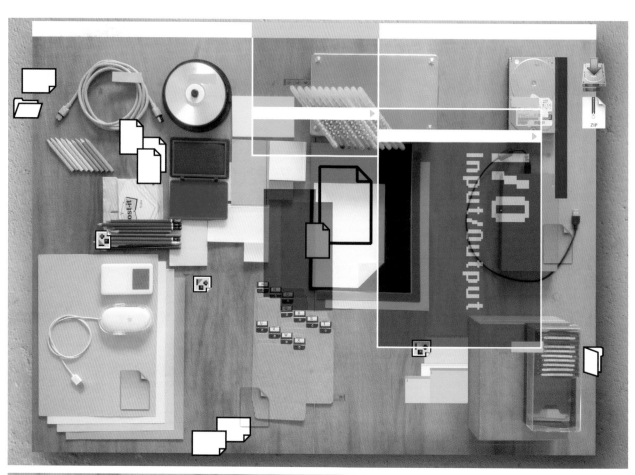

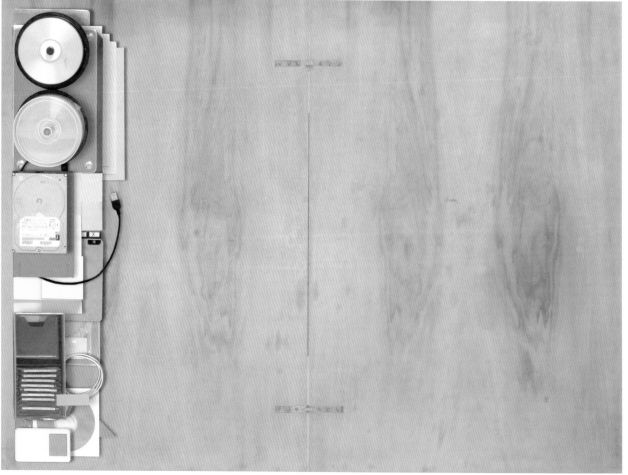

My_Virtual_Desktop

Jérémie Harper

In order to bring closer the organisation and the use of a graphic interface to real gestures, My_Virtual_Desktop is an interactive software displaying real objects in the perpendicular grid of a computer desktop.

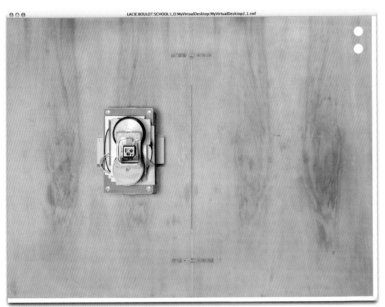

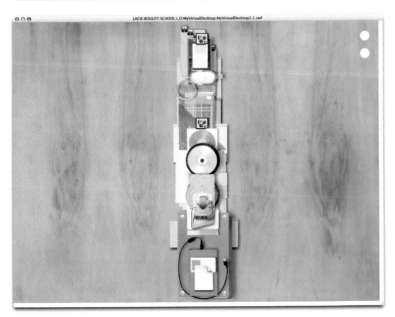

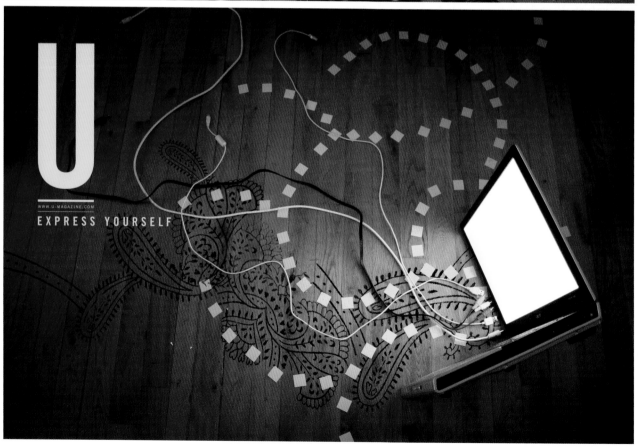

ED

U-Magazine
– Express Yourself
Julien Vallée

U-magazine was a fictitious project that took form through artistic expression. Artists were invited to express themselves through objects or materials at their disposition. The main idea was to create something from existing objects, in other words, to give a new life to these objects.

U

WWW.U-MAGAZINE.COM

EXPRESS YOURSELF

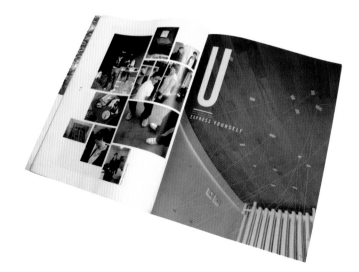

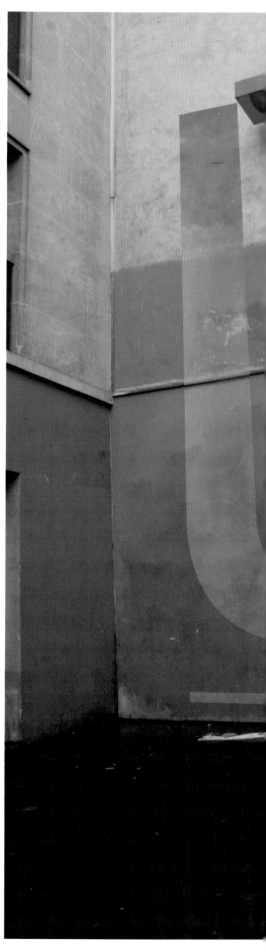

University of Brighton

Open Days

07.02.07
14.02.07

Undergraduate Open Days in the Faculty of Arts and Architecture

Introductory Talks and Guided Tours

Introductory talks include a welcome by the Head of the School of Arts & Communication and the Head of the School of Architecture & Design, followed by a presentation providing useful information about the University, admissions to art and design courses, and finance.

Guided tours of course areas are on offer after each of the introductory talks. There will be an opportunity to meet staff and students, to visit studios and workshops and to view students' work.

10.00 am & 1.30 pm
Sallis Benney Theatre, Grand Parade
• Fine Art Painting
• Critical Fine Art Practice
• Fine Art Sculpture
• Fine Art Printmaking
• Digital Music
• Performance and Visual Art – pathways
– Music, Theatre, Dance

10.45 am & 2.15 pm
Sallis Benney Theatre, Grand Parade
• Three Dimensional Design
• Wood Metal Ceramics and Plastics
• Fashion Textiles Design with Business Studies
• Fashion Design with Business Studies
• Interior Architecture/Architecture
(introductory talk morning only)

11.30 am & 3.00 pm
Sallis Benney Theatre, Grand Parade
• Editorial Photography
• Graphic Design
• Illustration

It would be helpful if visitors could arrive at least 10 minutes before the talks are due to start.

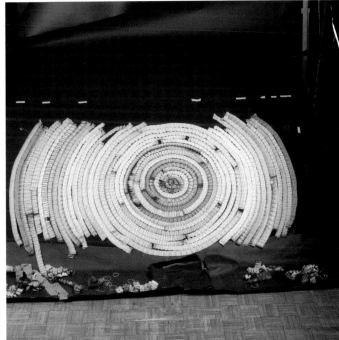

University Of Brighton
Open Day Poster

Vaughan Ward & Sally Hancox

An open day poster entry for the duo's university aiming to attract a new generation of student talent. Farbics of various lengths were folded, tied and then dipped into 2 or 3 types of food colouring. The strips were fixed onto an elevated background to create an unusual but intriguing perspective.

Northwest Film and Video Festival[1]
PLAZM

This work was designed to promote an annual film festival event focusing on the Northwest region of North America.
Art Direction & Design: Joshua Berger, Pe...
McCracken
Writer: Ginger Robinson
Photography: Jim Appleton
Macrame: Joelle McGonagle
Client: Northwest Film Center

Adobe Achievement Award
Sagmeister Inc.

Student-award poster depicting a designer creating an award-winning wo... out of paper coffee cups - running on pure caffeine as many design students do. Working with a modest budget, Sagmeister called in many favours of friends. They finished the work in a studi... with 30ft ceilings and a wooden floor constructed and arranged 2,500 filled coffee cups with many helpers.

1

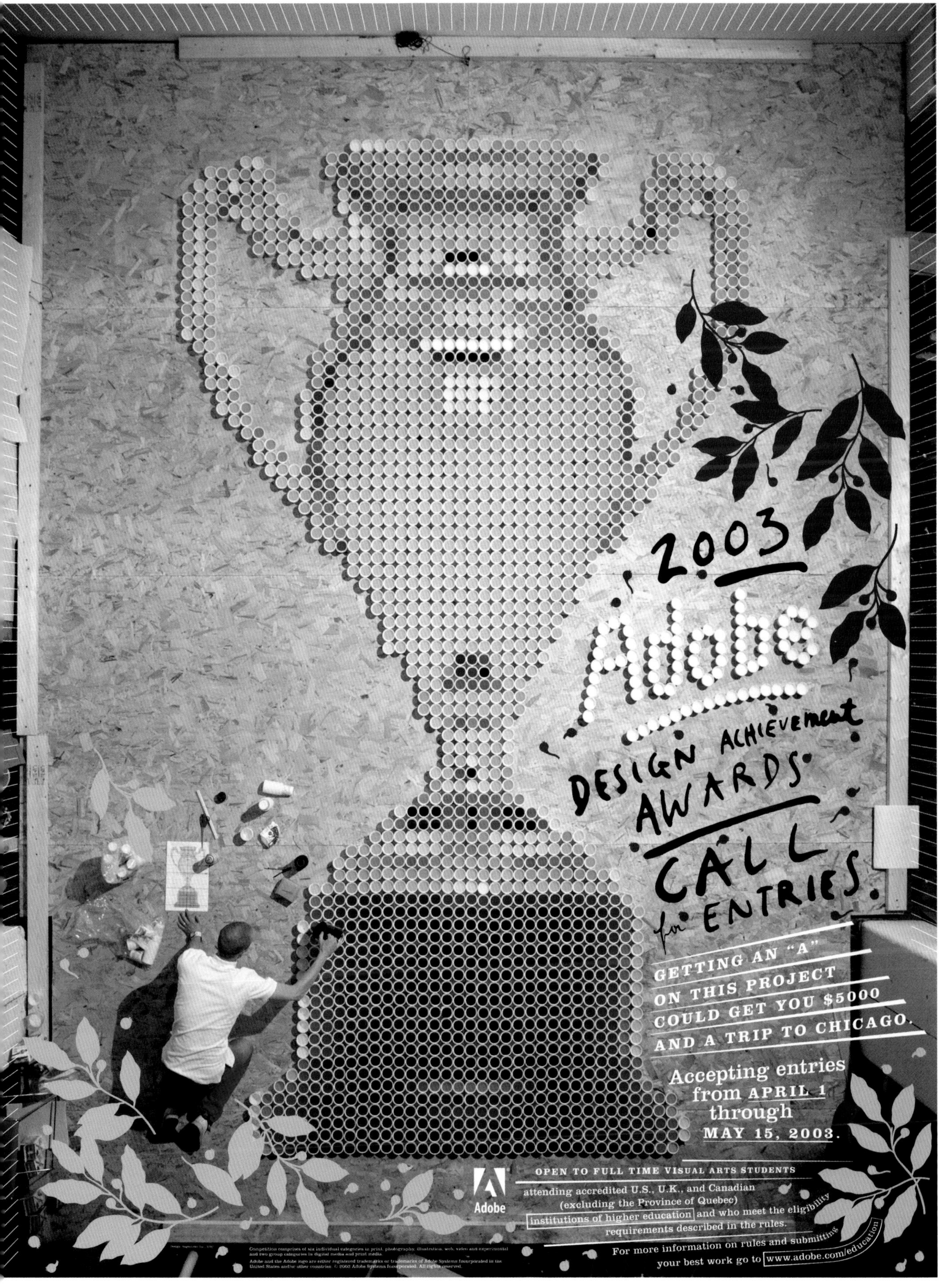

2003
Adobe
DESIGN ACHIEVEMENT AWARDS
CALL for ENTRIES.
GETTING AN "A" ON THIS PROJECT COULD GET YOU $5000 AND A TRIP TO CHICAGO.
Accepting entries from APRIL 1 through MAY 15, 2003.
Adobe
OPEN TO FULL TIME VISUAL ARTS STUDENTS
attending accredited U.S., U.K., and Canadian (excluding the Province of Quebec) institutions of higher education and who meet the eligibility requirements described in the rules.
For more information on rules and submitting your best work go to www.adobe.com/education
Competition comprises of six individual categories in print, photography, illustration, web, video and experimental and two group categories in digital media and print media.
Adobe and the Adobe logo are either registered trademarks or trademarks of Adobe Systems Incorporated in the United States and/or other countries. © 2003 Adobe Systems Incorporated. All rights reserved.

 ED

The Birds And The Bees[1]
Byggstudio

This is a set of illustration for an article on the birds and bees in the Sirene Magazine.

 ED

Where2go-travel Articles[2]
Byggstudio

A series of editorial illustrations for the magazine Where2go, featuring different destinations around the world.

AD

Coral outcrop

Jethro Haynes

This is a creation of a coral outcrop to be used for a print advertisement for a footwear company Pointer based in the UK.

ID

CENERE II

Stiletto nyc

Stiletto nyc was asked to design a carpet for a high-end clothing store, G.B. Cenere in Bassano, near Vernice in Italy. This is the second carpet design for the store. The architect's idea was to change the store feeling every year by changing the carpet design which would also be updated on the website. The store architecture is very polished and high-end so Stiletto nyc looked for a contrast to this while the elegance of the store could still be kept. The team thought of taking place in a section of the store where shoe boxes, tissue paper and packaging are taken out and left behind. The idea was to turn these paper and packaging material into what the team called 'beautiful trash' and this idea was expanded into store wallpaper and website.

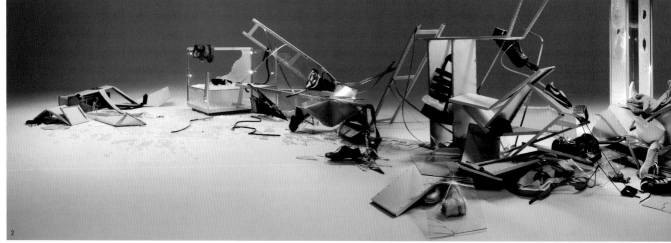

Evidence[1]
Dan Tobin Smith Studio Ltd

The studio wanted to create a similar lanscape to the
Sabotage image for Another Man Magazine. This time it was
to create a landscape of packaging that could bound the
fashion items and accessories together. Lyndsay Milne made
rough sketches so that they would work both as a panoramic
and as double page spreads in the magazines.

Set Stylist: Lyndsay Milne

Sabotage[2]
Dan Tobin Smith Studio Ltd

The idea for Sabotage was to create a landscape after a destructive force had passed through it. The panoramic image was made
up of four separate images then stitched together to make one
landscape. The aftermath showed all display cabinets and shelving
broken, smashed and bent out of shape.

Set Stylist: Lyndsay Milne

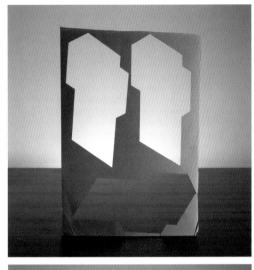

Sequence[1]
Chrissie Macdonald (Peepshow Collective Ltd)

This sequence explores the construction of a
3-dimensional form.
Photography: John Short

Oversized Ephemera[2]
Chrissie Macdonald (Peepshow Collective Ltd)

Giant pins, buttons and off cuts were made to
accompany Marie O'Connor's exhibit at 930 square
feet of Peepshow exhibition.
Photography: John Short

Celebrate the smoking ban
On the 1st of July we will be removing the 5000 ingredients found in a cigarette, from pubs, clubs and restaurants.
www.smokefreeengland.co.uk

Celebrate the smok
On the 1st of July we will b removing the 5000 ingred found in a cigarette from clubs and restaurants.
www.smokefreeengland.co.uk

 PO

National Smoking Ban
us design studio

These posters were produced for the smoking ban
that began in the summer of 2007. The posters raised
awareness of the smoking ban, where the balloons
not only showed the physical chemicals in public
places but also celebrated the ban.

Poster submissions
Studio Round

The posters are self-initiated projects. They responded to two propositions: Future? And Now is New.

Types Constructed

From delightful free-form objects to vast interiors for theatrical play, here comes the three-dimensional play with the established forms of type. Working with the basic geometry of type, designers seem to have fun conjuring diverse and imaginative physical manifestation of these letterforms using mylar balloons or wooden dowel sticks in the form of typographic sculpture or installation, freely apply on video and web format, or use as a physical signage. Set against the city skyline or displayed as a decorative item, the typeface takes on an identity and conveys messages influenced by its context and material used.

Pg. 153 – 219

6M1P

elgarten

doublespread for 6M1P Magazine. Pixelgarten built their name
1P out of real objects and set up a still-life setting which was
mbined with digital vector elements.

Zumtobel

Émilie Rigaud

A fictive report made for Austrian lighting company,
Zumtobel. Here text was considered as raw materials.
The typographic texture became lighter, and the number of words went down after page, until the pages
became totally white, left with the intrinsic luminosity of
the paper. The handmade volume letters composing
the name 'Zumtobel' give rhythm to the book in a
funny way.

Round Identity
Studio Round

Studio Round developed two 3-dimensional typefaces to help communicate the range of attributes Round brings to different projects. The unique characteristics of each typeface are medium specific. The paper typeface, based on Foundry Gridnik, is calculated and precisely crafted. In contrast, the cushion typeface is playful, whimsical and confident.

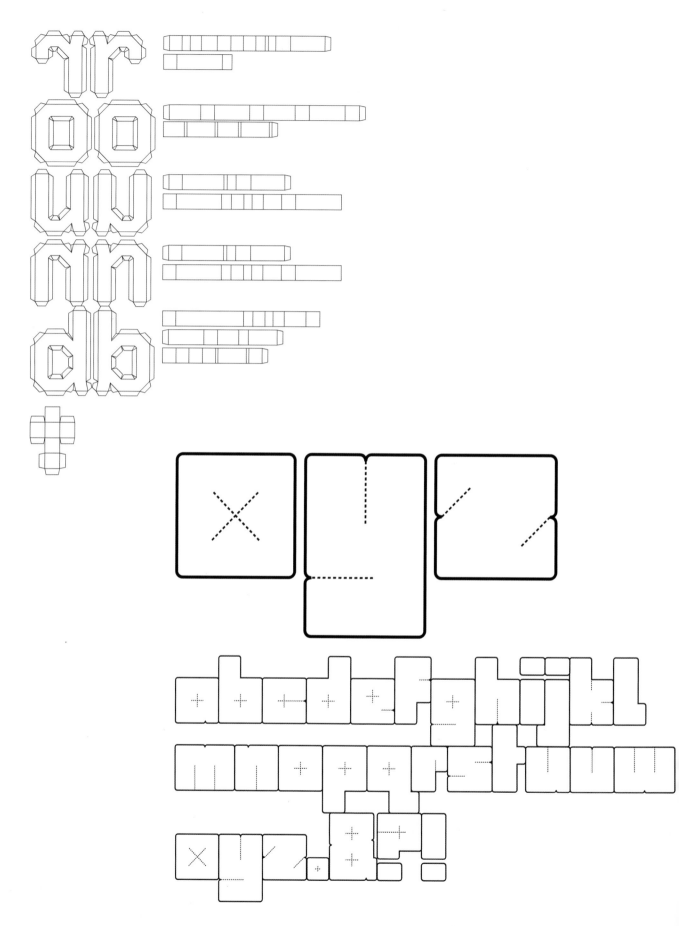

CN Alphabet
HudsonBec

ographic project run as part of YCN's annual
k. HudsonBec's task was to produce alpha-
s, which could be used as both a 2D typeface
3D title page photographs. The flat font was
ated by designer Michael Bojowski, with art
ctions from Alex Bec and photography by
ie Collinge.

Chaumont

Corriette Schoenaerts

Schoenaerts was asked to make a visual essay on the annual poster festival of Chaumont. Collaborated with Harmen Liemburg, the two came up with the idea of designing new posters for each of the 5 different exhibitions and rephotographing them. In the posters, they freely reflected upon the work of the exhibitors, the exhibition space and the medium of posters themselves.

Client: Items Magazine

www.stilettonyc.com, photo: chris jones

Stiletto Self Promotion - Poster, Reel Titles and Holiday Scarfs

Stiletto nyc

Stiletto nyc was looking for new visuals for their office. They wanted an image to promote themselves and present the studio's new work. That's how the word 'NEW' came into the game.

The team was also interested to find a way to have a suspended and very glossy and finished elements, in connection with natural light and nyc outdoor locations.

Disclosure Magazine
Jiggery Pokery
A celebratory front cover and centrefold for the
first issue of Disclosure Magazine, a monthly
Southampton-based magazine.
Photography: Jess Bonham

Play With Type
Jack Featherstone

A self-initated typographic project, that explores ideas
of process, form and context.

 AD

DIX30

Rita

A series of setups for an advertising campaign for a huge shopping center located in the south shore of Montreal, Canada. They were made to present its signature with objects varied with themes about holidays, seasons, etc.

ay with Shapes
yful

ography created based on the geometric
apes without any computer effects.

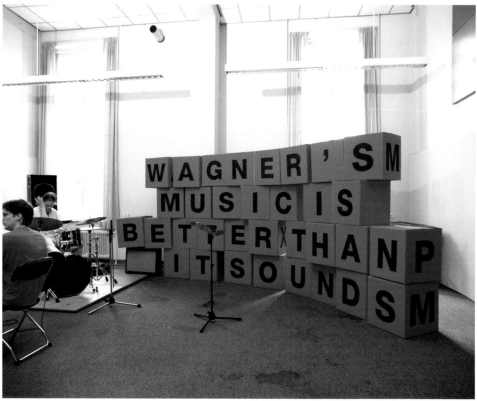

Quotes
Corriette Schoenaerts

Part of a marketing campaign for the Utrecht School of the Arts.
Quotations by world famous personalities painted on big cardboard
cubes, reflecting the ambitions of both the school itself and its prospective students, as well as the variety of the campus environment.
Client: Designpolitie

Department of Visual Arts

2005
Fall
Visiting
Artist
Lecture
Seri

Northeastern
University
Boston

From
Bremen/Amsterdam:
Florian Pfeffer
Jung & pfeffer   Design Communication Studio
Wednesday December 7, 6:00 PM
200 Richards Hall
Northeastern University

From
Los Angeles:
Shane Acker
Animator
Wednesday November 16, 6:00 PM
200 Richards Hall
Northeastern University

From
Chicago:
Marcia Lausen
Graphic Designer + founder of Studio Lab
Wednesday November 9, 6:00 PM
200 Richards Hall
Northeastern University

From
New York:
Elisabeth Subrin
Film and video maker
Thursday October 27, 6:00 PM
200 Richards Hall
Northeastern University

From
Princeton:
Photographer
Emmet Gowin
Monday October 17, 6:00 PM
Raytheon Amphitheater
Northeastern University

Interdisciplinary art & design studio
From
Amsterdam/New York:
COMA
Tuesday September 13, 6:00 PM
Raytheon Amphitheater
Northeastern University

From
Cambridge:
Annette Lemieux
Multi-media artist
Wednesday September 7, 6:00 PM
200 Richards Hall
Northeastern University

Please check:
www.art.neu.edu

For full lecturer's biographies

Northeastern
U N I V E R S I T Y
Higher Learning. Richer Experience.

EX

...all Lecture Series[1]
...rmen Liemburg

...oster made for Northeastern University (Boston)
...an announcement on lectures. Recycling a used
...oden 'Christmas tree,' and thinking of Boston and
...location at the Atlantic Ocean, Lienburg associated
... shape with a rock filled with seabirds.

Best Wishes 2008[2]
iLK

Personal work with paper-cut typography.

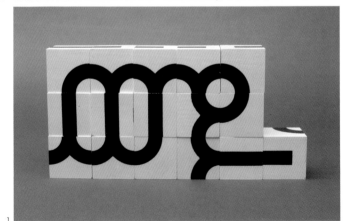

EX

From A to Z And Much More[1]
Courtine Alban

A 3-dimentional typographical game and drawing game. The game contains elements of the 'a quoi sers-je' font type and is composed of six identical cubes. All alphabetical letters are available for users to draw or write in 3D by combining the cubes together.

PK

Unkle Jam[2]
Dan Tobin Smith Studio Ltd

Album and CD single cover designed for the new band Unkle Jam. The individual pieces were made out of a mixture of materials such as perspex and polystyrene. The idea of hidden scale was important, the viewer should be unsure of the size and scale.
Set Design: Rachel Thomas

1

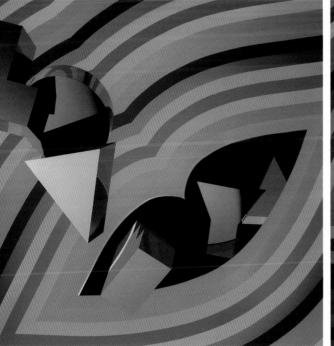

 EX

Berlin Backyards
MARIKI

An exploration of Berlin's architecture, in particular the courtyards and
the unusual spaces created by the structure of the buildings. A font
was developed from photographing the scene without resembling the
typographical forms. A series of wooden sculptures were produced
based on photographs of courtyards.

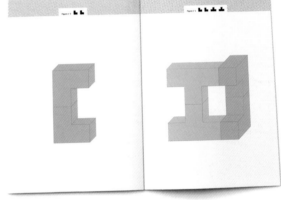

casse tête alphabétique

Alphabetical Puzzle[1]
Courtine Alban

A typographical game designed as a puzzle, made of eight cubes. Users can write in 3D by combining the cubes.

Aimer[2]
Akatre

This is a visual creation for the trismestrial program of Mains d'OEuvres.

Typeface 'Aimer'[3]
Akatre

Personal work. Typeface developed after the creation of 'Aimer' for Mains d'OEuvres.

1

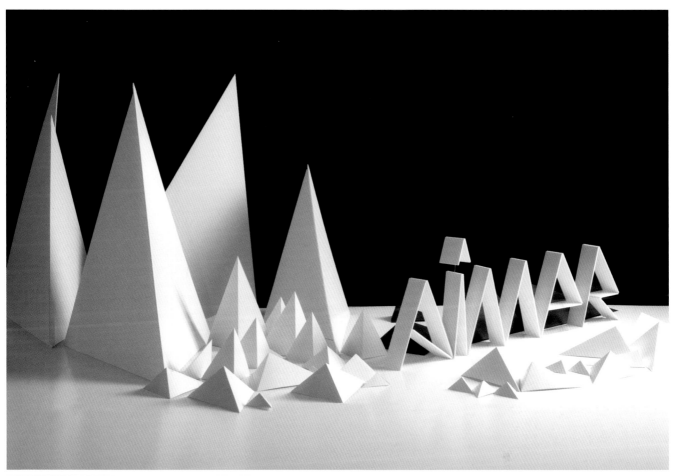
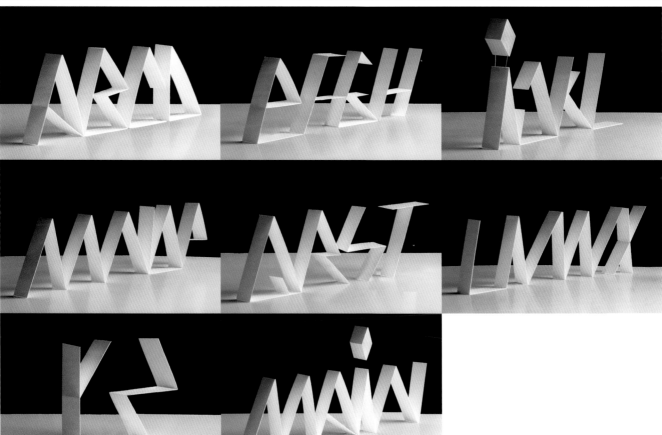

1 2 3

4 5

Mains d'Œuvres (MDO)
Akatre

For Mains d'Œuvres identity 2007-08, Akatre devised a hand-crafted, 3-dimensional typographic installation that was photographed and used on posters and flyers. These were based around 'ordinary and casual materials.'

1/ Danse Show Of Élèonore Didier Et Sofia Fitas (scotch tape); 2/ Danse Show Of Cindy Van Acker (paper); 3/ Danse Show Of Cindy Van Acker (scotch tape); 4/ Concert Of John Greaves (sugar pieces); 5/ Concerts of Great Lake Swimmers, Will Johnson, H-Burn, Jason Molina, et Stanley Brinks aka Herman Düne (sugar pieces); 6/ Danse show of Yves Musart (sugar pieces)

Boogie Playground

HORT

The idea was to photograph all information that had to be part of the vinyl as installations. Posters on the wall were the track names from the album. For the single releases, HORT just covered the other tracks with yellow surfaces.

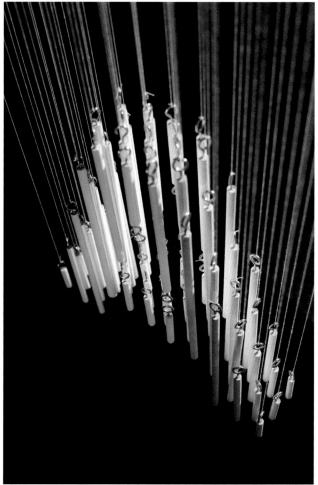

Agency
O&E agency

An organic and physical sign made from isolated
sticks. In which, the letter appearance would change
interestingly from different perspectives. Each letter
was made up of around 50 wooden dowle sticks and
hung individually with thread from a grid above.

Photography: Pelle Crepin

Double Death
Jan Olof Nygren

A contradictory typeface made to be 'ugly' yet beautiful,
legible yet hard to read. It was also designed to be
installed on a wall using fluorescent tubes.

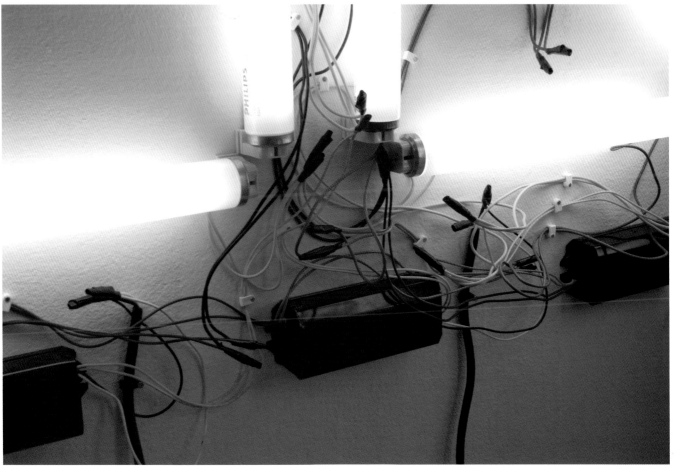

Creative Futures 2005
Dan Tobin Smith Studio Ltd

The Projects designed and created the set as the front
cover for Creative Review to celebrate the Creative Futures
prize, set for the upcoming talents from design schools.
The Projects took the logo from Creative Review and reinterpreted it with lamps and shot from exactly the same
distance from the front and the back of the set.

Set Design: The Projects
Client: Creative Review Magazine

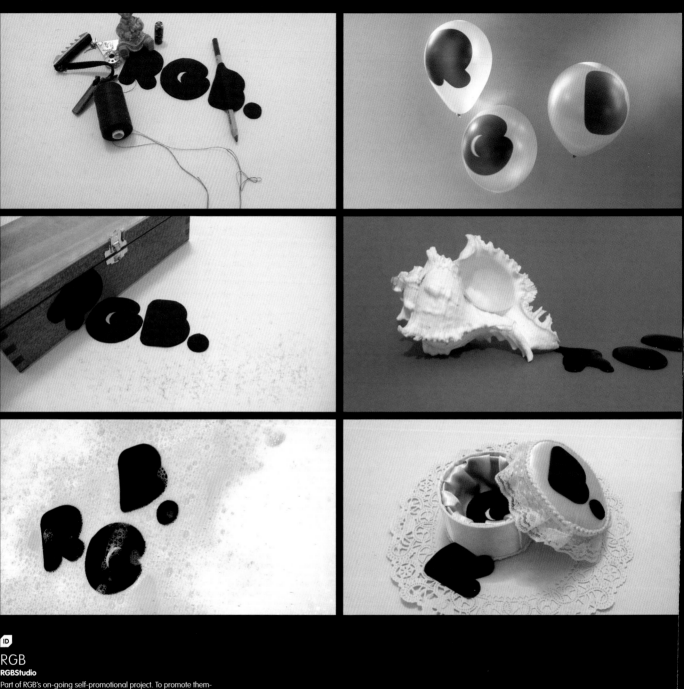

RGB

RGBStudio

Part of RGB's on-going self-promotional project. To promote themselves as a new studio with interesting and unconventional ideas for print and screen, RGBStudio prepared several hand-built scenarios which represent the playful nature of the studio, then introduced the 'RGB' lettering, not as a separate entity but as an integral part of the staged landscape. This has provided a platform for future personal

Oddjob 'Luma'

Sweden Graphics

Images created for the CD 'Luma' by a Swedish jazz group Oddjob. To make a difference with their previous album featuring their logo made out of plywood, Sweden Graphics sewed their logo in fabric and stuffed it into a 3D form. Since the whole shape was soft, it tended to fold and collapse and loose its distinct graphic shape, that was extremely complicated to arrange it hanging freely in the studio. The original idea was to try to suspend the logo with thin lines and retouch them from the final image, but the team soon gave it up and picked this kind of weird, happy bondage quality of all the lines holding the structure together.

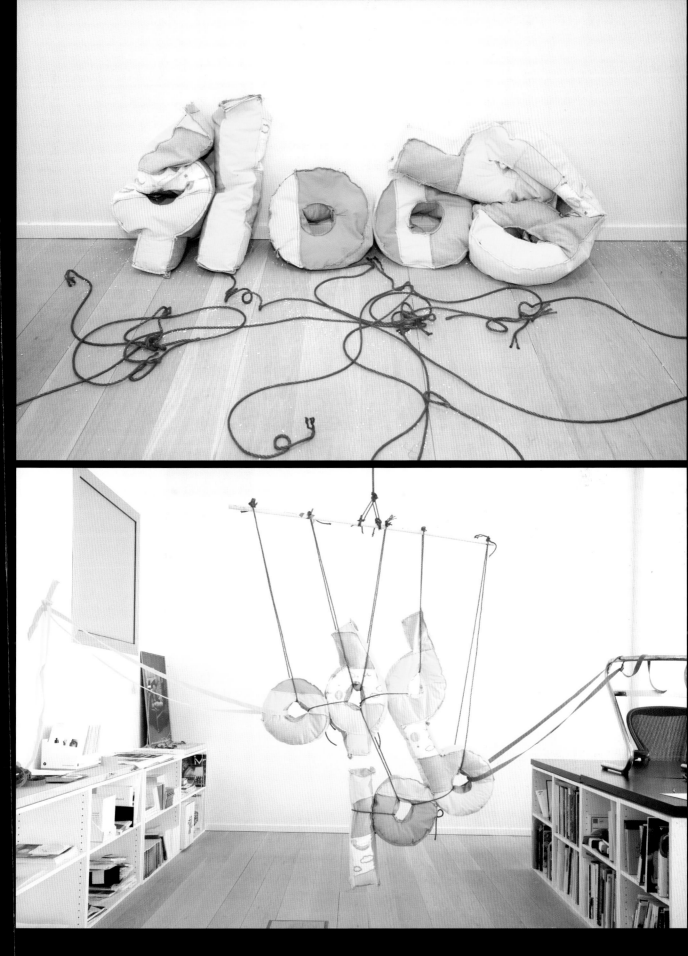

SIDEF
Synopsis inc.

Poster produced for the launch of Implant's new video – SIDEF. As Sidef has a very strong social awareness concept, Synopsis tried to put almost everything mentioned in the lyrics into the concept. Each letter was designed based on one of the 5 main topics - consumerism, religion, ecology, banking system, music industry. Distinct materials were used, including supermarket newsprints, crosses, Bible pages, Koran pages, Talmud pages, icons, rosenkrantz, used cigarettes, 2 years old dry roses, old/new money bills, cheap CDs, and many else they could put their hands on.

1

2

3

We are LAFORET[1, 3]
DRAFT Co., Ltd

An annual image visual of 2006 for LAFORET Harajuku. LAFORET means 'a forest' in French. 'Fashion in a forest' is the main concept of the image visual. LAFORET Harajuku was wrapped in this image of forest throughout the year.

DECORATION, LAFORET[2, 4, 5]
DRAFT Co., Ltd

An annual image visual of 2005 for the fashion-business built in Harajuku, Tokyo. Its concept is to decorate whole LAFORET and make LAFORET look like a cake. This image was displayed inside and outside LAFORET and signboards throughout the year.

4

5

Bounce Poster #2[1]
Aesthetically Loyal

The idea of this Bounce poster was simple; the logotype was developed using a composition of floating bouncy balls. Aesthetically Loyal shot it using an abacus style grid to build each letter individually, with the imperfections of the team's framing grid to create an interesting effect of misalignment.

Construction assistant: Jade Butler

Waterproof[2]
Antoine+Manuel

Poster designed for Waterproof show for Centre National de Danse Contemporaine, Angers (CNDC Angers) in 2006.

2

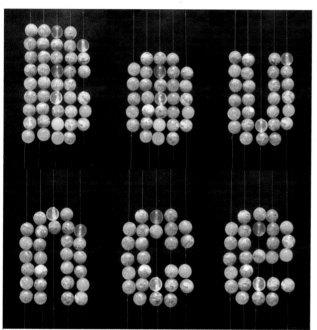

1

Videodanse[1]

Antoine+Manuel

Cover design for the CNDC publication CNDC-JOURNAL #12 in 2008.

Le Grand Dehors[2]

Antoine+Manuel

Cover design for a contemporary dance show brochure, done by mounting a printed paper on a foam cardboard, with plastic eyes and pins printed on it.

Good Look[3]

Antoine+Manuel

New dance season card.

2

3

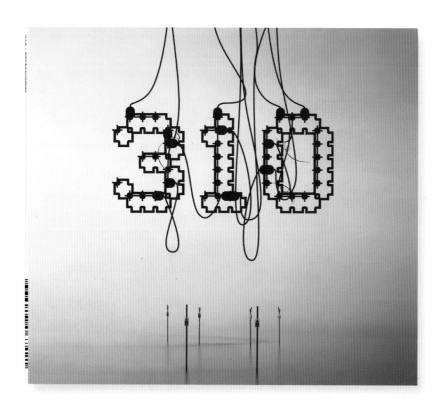

01: Opposite Corners
02: Shadow Traffic
03: A Fare To Remember
04: Night On The Ocean
05: EauMix
06: Swing Moderate White
07: Installation Linoleum
08: Bones Like Tikkas
09: Cloud Rooms
10: Moving Platform
11: 11:11
12: Study In Scarlet
13: Pacific Gravity (Vocal Version)
14: More North Than Portland
15: Come Back Again

310 is Joseph Danker, Tim Donovan and Andrew Sigler (aka Yes/No). Recorded and produced by 310. Music written by 310 except copyright control. Lyrics written by Andrew Sigler. All tracks arranged by Yes/No. Additional musicians courtesy of Idea & Amanda Records / Emma – Stephen Kruger (baritone guitar), Lou Ciccotelli (drum kit), Manning Platform – Mary Gross (violin), Pacific Gravity, Wendy New (additional vocals). Sonic Solutions by Chris Higginson. Special thanks to Yoruba Kawano. Art Direction and design by Non-Format. 310.org theleaflabel.com posteverything.com/leaf

RECESSIONAL

Recessional[1]
Non-Format

Six-panel digipak featuring photographs taken from the same spot on the coast of England, at various times of the day. The typographic illustration was created by Non-Format.
Photography: Tony Ellwood
Client: The Leaf Label

Misspeaking Too Soon[2]
Owen Gildersleeve

New York Times Magazine approached and invited Gildersleeve to create a typographic piece for the phrase 'misspeaking too soon' for William Safire's On Language column.

Customize Your Music[3]
Owen Gildersleeve

This is part of a series of experiments, for Graphic Magazine, in the customisation of different musical formats. The idea behind the series came from Gildersleeve's love for collecting music, and the interest he finds in exploring other people's musical collections.

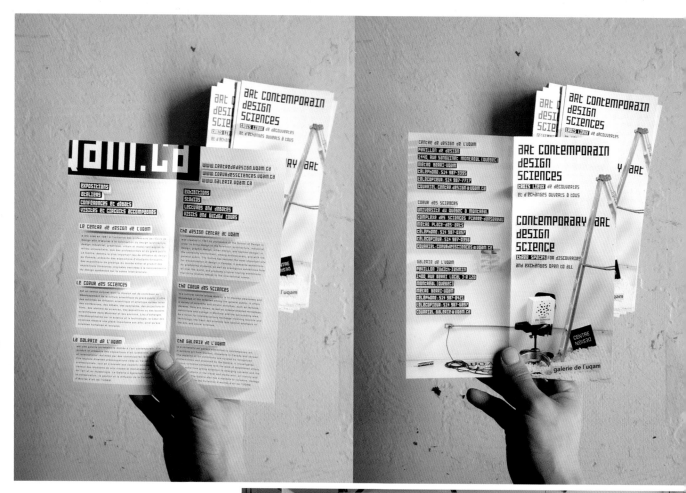

 ED

Three spaces[1]
Rita

A brochure to unite the three exhibition centers of the Quebec University in Montreal. The setup was to represent a common exhibition working space with everything that compose it: ladder, packing foam, electric extensions, etc.
Construction assistant: Jade Butler

 PO

Fashion Show After Party[2]
Owen Gildersleeve

Poster designed for the University of Brighton's fashion show after-party.

1

FASHION SHOW
AFTER PARTY

2ND JUNE
10PM - 3AM

/£4 WITH FASHION SHOW TICKET
/£6 WITHOUT

KABUKI (FORMERLY SUMO)
MIDDLE STREET

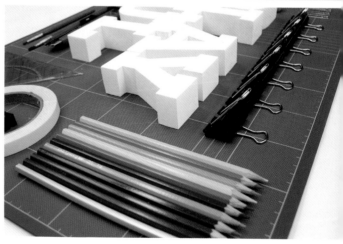

Play At Night
Playful

Pablo Alfieri completed the work in the dark using papers and fluorescent tubes to create an outer space environment for his new site.

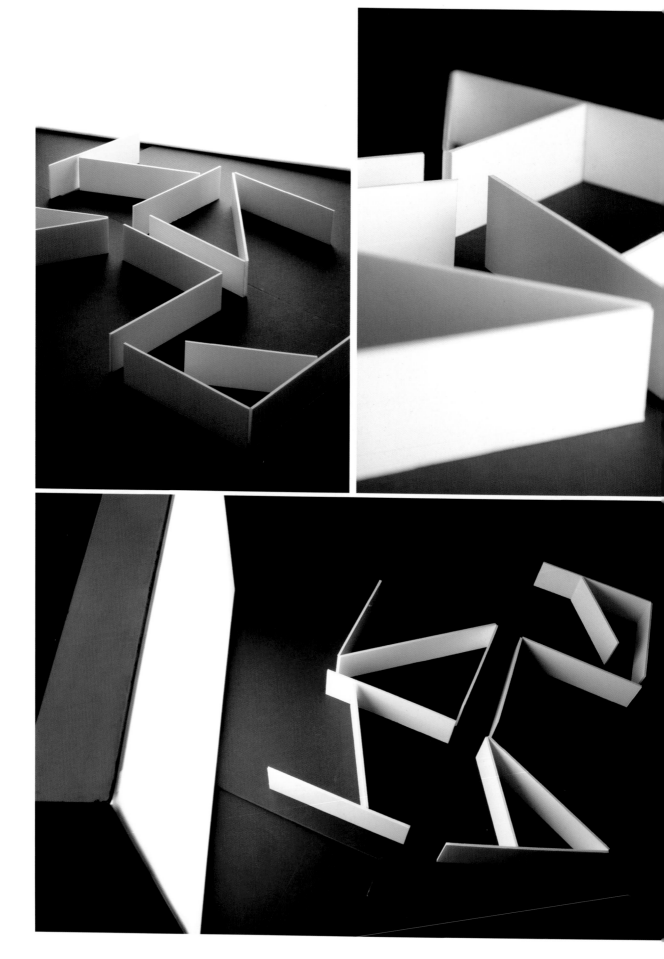

ASH

tre

illustration for grafik magazine's cover featuring a special report
photography. Akatre created a dramatic set of 3-dimensional
e, illuminated by a lightbox, referencing that intangible element
photography – light – as well as the tools of the trade and the
ctical application photography via the lightbox itself.

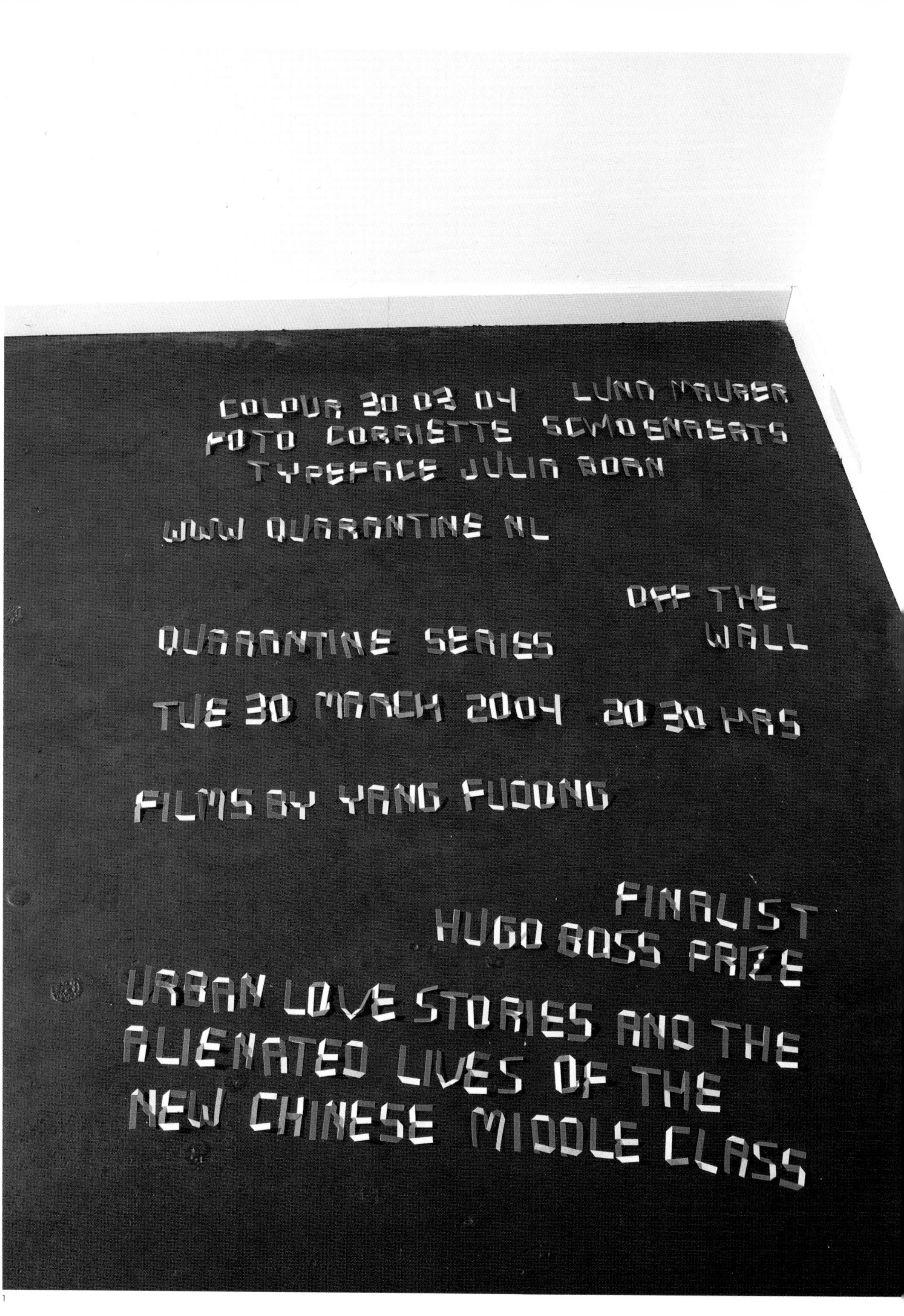

COLOUR 30 03 04   LUNA MAUBER
FOTO CORRISTTE SCHOENAERTS
TYPEFACE JULIA BORN

WWW QUARANTINE NL

                                OFF THE
QUARANTINE SERIES   WALL

TUE 30 MARCH 2004 20 30 HRS

FILMS BY YANG FUDONG

                        FINALIST
                HUGO BOSS PRIZE
URBAN LOVE STORIES AND THE
ALIENATED LIVES OF THE
NEW CHINESE MIDDLE CLASS

o

Quarantine[1]
Harriette Schoenaerts

n invitation announcing 'Off the Wall,' an exhibition
y Yang Fudong, done in collaboration with Julia Born
nd Luna Maurer.

o

What Is A Computer?[2]
kelgarten

is pixelfont created with paper boxes was for the
ok 'Eigenes und Fremdes im Schuettelbad digitalen
signs' (unpublished), illustrating the question 'Was
ein Computer? - What is a Computer?.'

Sing for Gough
Eric Chan Design Co. Ltd.

Poster series for the Gough Festival Hong Kong held in April 2007.
Gough Street, being one of the oldest streets in Hong Kong, was surrounded by buildings of several storeys high, built in the 50s and 60s.
People back then were used to hang and dry their clothes on bamboo
sticks outside their windows. The scene resembled an interesting
picture of a number of national flags flying in the sky. Riding on this
interesting scene, Chan made the Chinese name of Gough Street to
recap a collective memory of the old scenes. The red and blue cloth
flying in the sky echoes the joyful mood of the Gough Festival.
Photography: Lau Kwok Tim
Client: Gough Street Festival

Tai Tak Takeo Paper Sampler

Eric Chan Design Co. Ltd.

A set of 6 paper sample guides. Paper folds of Chinese numerals instead of commonly-seen roman numbers are placed against various backgrounds to show how paper materials can be integrated into our natural environment.

Letter-Box-Kite
Andrew Byrom

A series of 26 experimental typographic kites made from thin nylon fabric and fiberglass poles. The main objective was to find out if letters can fly, and the answer is ... yes.

...ualities Needed

...riette Schoenaerts

...ampaign for the Utrecht School of the Arts, showing the
...ecessary qualities required to be a good artist. These
...lities are character, dedication, boldness, imagination,
...ssion, ambition, ideas, fun and talent.

...ent: 178 Aardige Ontwerpers

Bio

Aesthetically Loyal

Anthony Kolber is a graphic designer from Melbourne, Australia. Graduated from Swinburne University in 2006, with a degree with honours in design, Kolber's design approach is greatly influenced by the ideologies of Bob Gill, Alan Fletcher and conceptual artists such as Joseph Kosuth and Hans Haacke.

Page 045, 200

Akatre

Based in Paris, Akatre is a graphic design studio founded by Valentin Abad, Julien Dhivert and Sébastien Riveron. Their works cover graphic design, typography, editorial, photography and artistic installation. They create and use their own typefaces as an answer for each of their projects.

Page 181-183, 210-211

Alice Guillier

Graduated from École Supérieure des Arts Décoratifs, Strasbourg, freelance graphic designer Alice Guillier has been working with La Bonne Merveille studio since 2007. She lives and works in Paris, and is specialised in book design, graphic design and photography.

Page 042

Andrew Byrom

UK-born Andrew Byrom opened his own design studio in London in 1997, with clients including Penguin Books and The Guardian Newspaper. His typeface designs have been featured in publications such as Print, Creative Review and Dwell. His works have been exhibited in design shows across the US and have been recognised with awards from the AIGA and the Type Directors Club.

Page 216

Antoine+Manuel

Antoine Audiau and Manuel Warosz met each other in art school, and shortly decided to work together under the name Antoine+Manuel. Working for various fields ranging from dance to fashion via contemporary art and design, the duo has defined a singular graphic style by combining hand-drawing and computer illustration with their own typography and photography. Their clients include Christian Lacroix, Habitat, Galeries Lafayette, Domestic and Larousse.

Page 086-087, 200-201

Bela Borsodi

Austrian Bela Borsodi is recognised for her award-winning editorial and advertising photography, combining unexpected still-life elements with fashion, styling and set design. Objects come to life in his playful fashion stories. He does still life photography in a very special way. Instead of just showing products for fashion magazines, he plays with perceptions, giving each one a personality. He glues together art and fashion photography, being part of the commercial entertainment and questioning it at the same time.

Page 066-067

Bleed

Working to blur the borders between graphic design, art, technology and commercial brand identity, Oslo-based Bleed has become a visible force in the world of creativity since its inception in 2000. Bleed's work spans from art projects and exhibitions, identity work for several international brands.

Page 080-081

Byggstudio

Byggstudio is a design studio founded in 2006 in Copenhagen by Markus Bergström, Hanna Nilsson and Sofia Østerhus. The variety of their works including illustration, set design and interiors favours from the group's mixed backgrounds in graphic and product design. An overall approach to design as a medium of communication beyond the products unites Byggstudio's work in strong contemporary, often playful expressions. The storytelling is always the focus of their projects.

Page 098, 142-143

Camille Baudelaire & Jérémie Harper

Camille Baudelaire and Jérémie Harper get to know each other at L'école Duperré in Paris. They have developed an experimental workshop since, and work on images inspired by the particular aesthetic of softwares, going back and forth between excessive minimalism and a required realism.

Page 130-133

Cécile Boche

Born in 1984 and grew up in France, Cécile Boche is a prospective MA graduate of Koninklijke Academie van Beeldende Kunsten, Holland. She sometimes collaborates with Brussels-based Benoit Lemoine.

Page 070

Chrissie Macdonald (Peepshow Collective Ltd)

Set designer, model maker and art director Chrissie Macdonald creates models and sculptural sets with card and acrylic, and photography for clients like Polydor Records, New York Times magazine, Dazed & Confused and Wonderland magazine.

Macdonald is the co-founder and member of the Peepshow Collective, where she works collaboratively with other members on illustration, animation, design, installation projects as well as individually on her own commissions, working closely with photographers to produce atmospheric images that often play with reality and scale.

Page 038-039, 148-149

Ciara Phelan

Ciara Phelan has recently finished studies in graphic design at the University of Brighton, UK. She enjoys creating innovative graphic design, illustrating and making things.

Page 033

CoDesign Ltd

CoDesign Ltd was co-founded by Eddy Yu and Hung Lam in 2003. The company specialises in branding and corporate identity, environmental graphics, literature and packaging design. Characterised by simple and effective design backed by bold and innovative concepts, CoDesign is trusted among major corporations and institutions in Hong Kong.

Page 018-025

Co-Op

Co-Op consists of graphic designers proficient in brand identity, art direction, printed collateral, environmental and publication design. For them, design is practised, refined and carefully applied. They strive to develop harmonious outcomes that marry both form and meaning through careful consideration, and approach projects with openness and imagination resulting in a lasting aesthetic for clients.

Page 121-125

Corriette Schoenaerts

Corriette Schoenaerts's works are concept-based, rather than style-based. She operates within the grey zone of art, fashion and commission, and refuses to persist with a particular style or theme since her interests lead her further than one little trick.

Schoenaerts has a big list of clients including Monocle Magazine, Jalouse, Dutch Elle, Frame Magazine and Surface 2 Air Paris (Rendez Vous Paris).

www.corrietteschoenaerts.com

Page 114, 162-163, 172-173, 212, 217-219

Courtine Alban

Born in 1981, Alban Courtine graduated from École Supérieure des Arts Décoratifs de Strasbourg in 2006. He has been working since as freelance graphic designer for several studios as well as for a book publisher. Courtine is devoted to typographics. The composition and construction of letter forms is a never-ending game for him.

Page 176, 180

Damien Poulain

Having lived and worked in Spain, Germany and Italy, Damien Poulain chose UK London as the perfect environment to develop his ideas and work. He works as graphic designer and art director in a wide range of fields but particularly on art, fashion and music projects for clients such as Dazed & Confused, adidas and various art galleries. His work is regularly featured in magazines internationally.

Page 046-047

Dan McPharlin

Born in Adelaide, Australia in 1977, Dan McPharlin works as an independent artist and designer after studying visual arts in university. His parallel work in sound and electronic music often influences his visual output. McPharlin has produced work for record sleeves, magazines, books and websites, and has exhibited his work in Australia and overseas.

Page 126, 128

Dan Tobin Smith Studio Ltd

British photographer Dan Tobin Smith, who received education at Central St. Martin, UK and London College of Printing, UK, gains inspirations from Seiju Toda, Lenn art Nilsson, Josef Sudek, etc.

He has been commissioned for Acne Paper, Another, China Vogue, Creative Review, Grafik, i-D, New York Times Magazine, Wallpaper, etc. and serving a contrasting client base including Absolut, Bacardi, British Airways, Coca-Cola, Honda, Orange, Shell, Sony, Volkswagen, etc. He is now based on the gritty eastern tip of City of London.

Page 026-032, 043, 074-075, 108-109, 146-147, 177, 190-191, 193

DRAFT Co., Ltd

Draft Co., Ltd was derived from Satory Miyata Design Office, founded by Satoru Miyata in 1978 upon his departure from Nippon Design Center. Draft's clients include Jack Daniel's, The Yokohama Rubber co ltd (PRGR), Mos Food Services Inc., Lacoste, Japan Energy Corporation, Wacoal Corp, etc.

The award-winning company is also known for its D-BROS product line launched in 1995.

Page 198-199

Émilie Rigaud

Émilie Rigaud, final-year student at the Ecole Natio-nale Supèrieure des Arts Dècoratifs, Paris, works as a freelancer on cultural associative projects such as the identity of a new social concert hall or the carrying out of an exhibition about earthquakes in Le Palais de la Découverte. Her approach is based on typographical experiment.

Page 154-155

Eric Chan Design Co. Ltd.

Eric Chan is a veteran graphic designer and corporate identity consultant. After graduating from The Hong Kong Polytechnic and The First Institute of Art & Design in 1981, he started his career at Hill & Knowlton (Asia) Ltd/Grapho, Leo Burnett and Bates Hong Kong.

Chan founded Eric Chan Design Co. Ltd, a design consul-tancy specialising in corporate and brand identity devel-opment, visual identity, company brochure, marketing collaterals, etc. He has won more than 250 awards locally and internationally in recent years, including the HKDA Gold Award and RIVER/GILBERT Paper Outstand-ing Design Awards Gold Award.

Page 214-215

Form

Founded by Paul West and Paula Benson, Form are driven by a passion for design and the power they have to make a difference to their clients and their products and services. Their expertise is in design and visual branding with a particular understanding of contem-porary culture. Their experience is grounded in years of successful art direction and design collaborations within the worlds of music, media, TV/film, sport, advertising, architecture, events and for design-led brands such as furniture and fashion.

Page 115

Grandpeople

Grandpeople is a Norwegian design studio established in 2005, by Christian Bergheim, Magnus Voll Mathiassen and Magnus Helgesen. They provide different and dis-tinctive solutions in graphic design, art direction and illus-tration to clients from around the world, and from indus-tries such as fashion, music, art, advertising, culture.

Page 065, 129

Gwen Yip

Born and raised in Hong Kong, Gwen Yip began her career as an art director at an advertising agency after her tertiary studies in Economics and Finance. She tells stories in writings and illustrations, and has published two books between 2002-03 to share her travelling experiences in Europe by the Trans-Siberian Railway. She became art director at Wieden + Kennedy Amster-dam in 2007.

Page 060-063

Harmen Liemburg

After graduating from Utrecht University in 1992 and Gerrit Rietveld Academie in 1998, Harmen Liemburg worked in collaboration with Richard Niessen awarded as the 'Golden Masters' and has been back on his own since 2002. His projects frequently involve collabora-tions with other (graphic) artists, resulted in elaborate and layered images that are usually screenprinted by himself. His designs and illustrations are utilized in print and architecture, and have been exhibited in group exhibitions all over the world.

Page 174

HELMO

HELMO is the graphic design duo Thomas Couderc and Clement Vauchez, who create posters, books, museog-raphy, pictures and even designs for architecture. They established 'la bonne merveille' with Thomas Dimetto in 2002, which remains today the name of the work space they share in Montreuil, Paris. They decided to change the composition in 2007. While the design do established the graphic design studio 'HELMO,' Dimetto started to work with Marcel, a French advertising agency.

Page 110-111

Homework / Jack Dahl

Establised in 2002 by Jack Dahl, Homework is an inde-pendent graphic design studio and consultancy that focuses on art direction, visual identity and communica-tion for lifestyle, fashion and cultural clients. Dahl was responsible for kickstarting a visual presence and direc-tion for international mens fashion publication HE maga-zine and Cover magazine (Copenhagen). Among others, he has worked with Self Service magazine and Work in Progress advertising design studio (Paris) on some of todays leading fashion references including Jil Sander, Prada, Pucci, Chloé, Celine, Colette and Virgin Records.

Page 118-119

HORT

HORT came into existence since 1994 under the pre-vious stage name of Eike Grafischer Hort. HORT is a direct translation of the studio's mission representing a creative playground with an unconventional working environment.

It is not just a studio space, but also an institution devoted to making ideas come to life. The multi-disciplinary cre-ative hub has been involving themselves in various other activities like teaching, creative workshops and advising companies on strategy and brand management. They are known to draw inspiration from things other than design and has also won lots of awards.

Page 049, 052-056, 184-185

HudsonBec

HudsonBec is an independent design studio based in London set up by Will Hudson and Alex Bec, who is also the co-founder of design studio 'If You Could.' Working on all projects from classic graphic design, typography, book publishing to exhibition curation and event management, Bec's real passion is for hands-on, tangible design with distinct personality. Believing in the philosophy 'The Eye is Blind if the Mind is Absent,' he always looks to add an extra, unexpected dimension to his work.

Page 160-161

Hvass&Hannibal

Hvass&Hannibal is a design and art studio based in Copenhagen, established in 2006 by childhood friends Sofie Hannibal and Nan Na Hvass. They work with art and design - basically everything from album covers to music videos, graphic art, silkscreening, art direction, illustration, installation and many more.

Page 090-091

iLK

Ludovic Prigent is a freelance graphic designer, illustrator and art director based in Paris. He works with another Paris-based freelancer Sébastien Moulène, who spe-cialises in Internet developement and integration.

Page 175

Jack Featherstone

Featherstone is a graphic designer and illustrator based in London, UK.

Jan Olof Nygren

Jan Olof Nygren has always desired to challenge rules and conventions, and come up with new ways to work with or fight against different situations and systems he encounters. He is fascinated with patterns, modu-lar graphics, the beauty of making these things, as well as the beauty of the items themselves. While studying 2D design on a Fulbright grant at Cranbrook Academy of Art, he started experimenting with 3D-poster-instal-lations. He started working as a graphic designer in Iceland in 2008.

Page 096, 113, 188-189

Jean Jullien

Jean Jullien is a French graphic designer based in London. He has worked for Cliché London, Amon Ray, Niwouinwouin, Kitsune noir, Threadless, Manystuff, Kromland Farm, Ronnie & Darin, The Walrus, AAAAAH!, Abana and Korean magazine Fantastique.

www.jeanjullien.com

Book cover, Page 076-079

Jethro Haynes

Jethro Haynes is a freelance illustrator, designer and model maker living and working in London. He is a fan of hand drawing and hands-on making.

Page 144

Jiggery Pokery

Jiggery Pokery is the umbrella for the collaborative work of Anna Lomax and Lauren Davies. Although their main focus has recently been set design and prop-making, the duo pay great attention to concepts and process, and are always trying to push the boundaries to main-tain diversity within their work.

Page 072, 089, 166-167

Julien Vallée

After three years of studies in multimedia, Julien Vallée decided to move on to graphic design in L'Université du Québec à Montréal and Penninghen superior high school of Paris. Through his oversea trips, he has developed a diversified creative spirit. The graphic and motion artist is now a freelance art director in Montreal, Paris and Los Angeles.

Page 034-036, 117, 134-137

MARIKI

MARIKI is an interdisciplinary design collective working in the fields of graphic design, moving image, illustra-tion and other media. The members of MARIKI met at the London College of Communication, UK. Each of them specialises in their own medium and they work as a group as well as individually. MARIKI is a group consists of Russian Maria Joudina, British Matt Robinson and Japanese Miki Tsuganuma.

Page 178-179

Mark Gowing Design

Mark Gowing Design in Sydney is a communications studio with clients in both the corporate and cultural fields, set up by Gowling in 1997. His works explore the potential of pure geometric form and custom typogra-phy and have won him numerous local and interna-tional awards. Mark's approach to visual communica-tion is driven by the belief that good design is simple honesty demanding cultural responsibility, which would bring good business as a result.

Page 104-105

Bio

Marque Creative Ltd

Marque is a branding consultancy with a contemporary view. They work collectively across three studios in London, New York and Glasgow. Their specialisations are to bring energy, dedication and sensitivity to position, identity and communication.

Page 088

Mejdej

Mejdej is a Norwegian and Swedish design duo based in Copenhagen, Denmark. Trine Natskår and Sara Andersson met at the Danish School of Design. They have been working together on different projects exploring a broad range within visual communication for the last couple of years.

Page 094-095

Merci Bernard

French graphic designer Merci Bernard is young and adaptive, passionate and openminded, who studied in a French art scool, École Supérieure d'Arts Appliqués de Bourgogne (ESAAB) for 5 years. He is a member of the French graphic collective Think Experimental and he explores all visual fields with the view of creating astonishing pictures.

Page 048

Non-Format

Based in London, UK and Minneapolis, USA, Non-Format is a creative team comprising Norwegian Kjell Ekhorn and British Jon Forss. They work on a range of projects including art direction, design and illustration for music industry, arts & culture, fashion and advertising clients. They also art direct Varoom, journal of illustration and made images.

Page 127, 202

Nous Vous

Established in 2006, Nous Vous is a UK based visual art collective interested in developing methods of communication and initiating concept based design/illustrative work. The team consists of Jay Cover, Thom Hudson, Nicolas Burrows, William Edmonds and Matt Bigland, who all studied Graphic Design and Visual Communications in Leeds, UK. They work across a variety of media, selecting an appropriate method of communication relating to the message, unless otherwise specified. They also publish work under the name 'Nous Vous Press.'

Page 037, 044, 116

O&E agency

Oscar is from Stockholm, Sweden while Ewan comes from the Aberdeen, Scotland. They met each other in a graphic design course at Central Saint Martins, London. They enjoy cross-pollinating different areas of design and trying out things outside their expertise. They began their collaboration since college years, and continued.

Page 186-187

Owen Gildersleeve

Recently graduated from the University of Brighton, UK, Owen Gildersleeve is one quarter of the Evening Tweed design collective. He enjoys making things by hand in his work, believing that it is important to work away from the screen as much as possible.

Page 203, 205

Pierre Vanni Studio

Pierre Vanni is a student at the Université de Toulouse-Le Mirail and has set up his studio in 2006. His education is a mix of art and design. He is more interested in renaissance art than traditionnal graphic design.

Page 069

Pixelgarten

Based in Frankfurt am Main Germany, Pixelgarten is a multidisciplinary studio run by Adrian Nießler and Catrin Altenbrandt, who get to know each other at the University of Applied Arts Offenbach, Germany. Crossing the border between fine art and design is how they generate new ideas and ways of visual communication. They also do installations, animation and fashion.

Page 040-041, 050-051, 082-085, 120, 153, 213

Playful

Pablo Alfieri is a graphic designer and illustrator born in Buenos Aires, Argentina. He started his career in graphic design in the University of Buenos Aires in 2002. He created 'Playful' six years later to showcase his personal works, and as where he could play and have fun with colours, typography and geometry, the bases of his creative work.

Page 171, 206-209

PLAZM

Founded in 1991 by artists as a creative resource, PLAZM publishes an eclectic design and culture magazine with worldwide distribution and operates an innovative type foundry. PLAZM is also a design firm that builds identities, advertising, interactive and retail experiences using custom typography.

Page 068, 140

pleaseletmedesign

pleaseletmedesign is a duo of young graphic designers comprising Pierre Smeets and Damien Aresta. Both graduated from Saint-Luc Higher School of Arts in Liège, Belgium, and took almost a full year in ERG (Graphic Research School) in Brussels, Belgium. They set up their own graphic design studio in 2004, and work on a wide range of projects including graphic design, books, posters, identities and stationnery to exhibition design, signage, titles sequences, and website in cultural sectors as diverse as music, architecture, cinema and advertising clients.

Page 064

red design

Established in 1996, red design has made its name by producing award-winning graphic design for the music industry. The team now delivers high quality, ideas-driven, still, moving and interactive design for the creative industries. Last year, the team was granted two Roses Design Awards: Film/TV Title and Animation for Sony PSP's Stop Frame animation and the Design Grand Prix 2007.

Page 010-013, 100-101

repeatafterme

repeatafterme is co-founded by Jonathan Prêteux, Benoit Lemoine and Guillaume Ninove. Born in 1983, Prêteux firstly studied at the Beaux-arts of Saint-Brieuc and, later, the Saint-Luc Institute in Tournai, Belgium, where he met the two partners, and finished his studies at the Esad in Amiens. He is having his internship at Studio Uniform, Montrèal in 2008.

Page 057

RGBStudio

Based in Leeds, UK, Rob Brearley is a freelance graphic designer and art director, who continues to develop a diverse portfolio of work, for a contrasting client base including PlayStation®, Harvey Nichols, Creamfields, The Advanced Digital Institute as well as smaller freelance projects. Using texture, typography, image and composition, he aims to develop relevant and memorable graphic design for environmental graphics, crafted print matter and animation.

Page 192

Rita

Rita's world is both 2D and 3D. Rita believes that graphic, object and event design are naturally interconnected. Working together, these modes of design complement each other, inspiring new creative solutions in form, function and communication. Inherent to Rita's style, is the combination of different aspects of design. In each project, the graphic treatment is integral to the format, and vice versa. This interdisciplinary philosophy applies to all levels, in all circumstances.

Page 170, 204

Sagmeister Inc.

Stefan Sagmeister formed the New York-based Sagmeister Inc. in 1993 and has since designed for clients as diverse as the Rolling Stones, HBO, and the Guggenheim Museum. Having been nominated five times for the Grammies, Sagmeister finally won one for the Talking Heads boxed sets. He also earned practically every important international design award. A native of Austria, he received his MFA from the University of Applied Arts in Vienna and, as a Fulbright Scholar, a master's degree from Pratt Institute in New York.

Page 141

Son of Tam / Jason Tam

Jason Tam (also called Son of Tam) is a Hong Kong-born but New York-based designer. Growing up with Transformers, Power Rangers, and Flintstones vitamin chews, he aims to create work that brings out the part of him that cannot be defined with a particular medium, language, or style. He is working his way towards his own personal renaissance.

Page 106-107

Sopp Collective

Based in Sydney and London, design studio Sopp has produced plentiful new and innovative designs for the music scene in Australia and Europe over the last 8 years. Their multi-disciplinary skills have enabled them to produce not just album artwork for bands, but also music videos, visuals and interactive installations. They thrive on experimenting with various processes, production methods and design styles in order to explore new routes of visual communication.

Page 014-017

Stiletto nyc

Co-founded by Stefanie Barth and Julie Hirschfeld in 2000 and based in New York and Milan, Stiletto nyc specialises in art direction and design for print and video. The studio takes on projects spanning motion graphics, print and environmental and has lately been immersed in creating the identity and website for Not on Our Watch, a non-profit organisation focuses on Darfur and Burma, founded by George Clooney.

The studio has been featured in various international publications and has won two Art Director awards for their motion graphics. Their clients include New York Times, MTV, Condenast, Nike, RCA records, etc.

Page 099, 102-103, 145, 160-161

Studio Round

Studio Round is a design company that builds partnerships with people they work with. They engage in a process that both involves and challenges both clients and themselves. Round works across a variety of mediums including, but not limited to books, exhibition spaces, magazines, billboards, signage, branded 3-dimensional environments, collaterals, websites, packaging, visual merchandising and a wide range of products. They draw on local and international experience and work with large and small clients. They love what they do.

Page 073, 097, 152, 156-159